Culture and
Customs of
Nigeria

D0081948

Culture and Customs of Nigeria

～∾～

Toyin Falola

Culture and Customs of Africa
Toyin Falola, Series Editor

GREENWOOD PRESS
Westport, Connecticut • London

Library of Congress Cataloging-in-Publication Data

Falola, Toyin.
    Culture and customs of Nigeria / Toyin Falola.
        p.   cm.—(Culture and customs of Africa, ISSN 1530–8367)
    Includes bibliographical references and index.
    ISBN 0–313–31338–5 (alk. paper)
    1. Nigeria—Social life and customs. I. Title. II. Series.
DT515.4.F35   2001
306'.09669—dc21   00–057650

British Library Cataloguing in Publication Data is available.

Copyright © 2001 by Toyin Falola

All rights reserved. No portion of this book may be
reproduced, by any process or technique, without
the express written consent of the publisher.

Library of Congress Catalog Card Number: 00–057650
ISBN: 0–313–31338–5
ISSN: 1530–8367

First published in 2001

Greenwood Press, 88 Post Road West, Westport, CT 06881
An imprint of Greenwood Publishing Group, Inc.
www.greenwood.com

Printed in the United States of America

The paper used in this book complies with the
Permanent Paper Standard issued by the National
Information Standards Organization (Z39.48–1984).

10 9 8 7 6 5 4 3 2 1

Every reasonable effort has been made to trace the owners of copyright materials in this book, but in
some instances this has proven impossible. The author and publisher will be glad to receive information
leading to more complete acknowledgments in subsequent printings of the book and in the meantime
extend their apologies for any omissions.

For two great colleagues:
Tunde Lawuyi of Iresi
and
Michael G. Hall of Austin

Contents

A photo essay follows p. 96

Series Foreword

AFRICA is a vast continent, the second largest, after Asia. It is four times the size of the United States, excluding Alaska. It is the cradle of human civilization. A diverse continent, Africa has more than fifty countries with a population of over 700 million people who speak over 1,000 languages. Ecological and cultural differences vary from one region to another. As an old continent, Africa is one of the richest in culture and customs, and its contributions to world civilization are impressive indeed.

Africans regard culture as essential to their lives and future development. Culture embodies their philosophy, worldview, behavior patterns, arts, and institutions. The books in this series intend to capture the comprehensiveness of African culture and customs, dwelling on such important aspects as religion, worldview, literature, media, art, housing, architecture, cuisine, traditional dress, gender, marriage, family, lifestyles, social customs, music, and dance.

The uses and definitions of "culture" vary, reflecting its prestigious association with civilization and social status, its restriction to attitude and behavior, its globalization, and the debates surrounding issues of tradition, modernity, and postmodernity. The participating authors have chosen a comprehensive meaning of culture while not ignoring the alternative uses of the term.

Each volume in the series focuses on a single country, and the format is uniform. The first chapter presents a historical overview, in addition to information on geography, economy, and politics. Each volume then proceeds to examine the various aspects of culture and customs. The series highlights

the mechanisms for the transmission of tradition and culture across generations: the significance of orality, traditions, kinship rites, and family property
distribution; the rise of print culture; and the impact of educational institutions. The series also explores the intersections between local, regional,
national, and global bases for identity and social relations. While the volumes
are organized nationally, they pay attention to ethnicity and language groups
and the links between Africa and the wider world.

The books in the series capture the elements of continuity and change in
culture and customs. Custom is not represented as static or as a museum
artifact, but as a dynamic phenomenon. Furthermore, the authors recognize
the current challenges to traditional wisdom, which include gender relations;
the negotiation of local identities in relation to the state; the significance of
struggles for power at national and local levels and their impact on cultural
traditions and community-based forms of authority; and the tensions between agrarian and industrial/manufacturing/oil-based economic modes of
production.

Africa is a continent of great changes, instigated mainly by Africans but
also through influences from other continents. The rise of youth culture, the
penetration of the global media, and the challenges to generational stability
are some of the components of modern changes explored in the series. The
ways in which traditional (non-Western and nonimitative) African cultural
forms continue to survive and thrive, that is, how they have taken advantage
of the market system to enhance their influence and reproductions also receive attention.

Through the books in this series, readers can see their own cultures in a
different perspective, understand the habits of Africans, and educate themselves about the customs and cultures of other countries and people. The
hope is that the readers will come to respect the cultures of others and see
them not as inferior or superior to theirs, but merely as different. Africa has
always been important to Europe and the United States, essentially as a source
of labor, raw materials, and markets. Blacks are in Europe and the Americas
as part of the African diaspora, a migration that took place primarily due to
the slave trade. Recent African migrants increasingly swell their number and
visibility. It is important to understand the history of the diaspora and the
newer migrants, as well as the roots of the culture and customs of the places
from where they come. It is equally important to understand others in order
to be able to interact successfully in a world that keeps shrinking. The accessible nature of the books in this series will contribute to this understanding
and enhance the quality of human interaction in a new millennium.

Toyin Falola
The University of Texas at Austin

Preface

NIGERIA is one of the biggest and most important countries in Africa, as well as a regional power. It is rich in traditions and customs, both indigenous and modern. This book analyzes Nigeria's culture, focusing on aspects that have defined the country and its people, the uniqueness of the society and its institutions, and the lifestyle of a new generation of educated people.

Nigeria exhibits great diversity in its culture. Ethnic groups and languages are numerous and traditional practices differ in details and emphasis. The spread of Islam and Christianity has affected Nigerian society in various ways. Colonial and Western contact has brought great changes and modified many indigenous institutions. This book captures the diversity and comprehensiveness of Nigerian culture. Even if it were possible to do so, it would be unrealistic to try to present the customs and traditions of all the Nigerian groups, which number over 250. Such a project would require an encyclopedia. Rather, I have identified and analyzed the salient elements of Nigerian culture broadly. Every major aspect is then illustrated with examples taken from selected groups. To make the book accessible to those unfamiliar with Nigeria, I have limited my examples to a few ethnic groups while indicating the wide range of people and ideas. This approach is not intended to slight any group but to respond to the limitation of space and the need to reach an audience that is new to the country.

Acknowledgments

THE IDEA of this series and book is not actually mine. I was invited by Greenwood to serve as the series editor and to contribute the volume on Nigeria. I gladly accepted both invitations, and I thank the publishers for the opportunity. My editor, Ms. Wendi Schnaufer, has been easy to work with. We both agreed on the format, as well as the list of scholars to be invited to contribute to the series.

Next, I must thank those who discussed the project with me at the initial stage and read the drafts: Rebecca Gámez, Manuel Callahan, and Vik Bahl. Then came help from various scholars of Nigeria, all professors: Wilson Ogbomo, Oyekan Owomoyela, Felix Ekechi, Gloria Chuku, Bayo Oyebade, and Axel Harneit-Sievers. Ann O'Hear read the final draft before I submitted it to the publishers. If future readers fall in love with this book as these early readers did, I will be more than fulfilled.

The writing of this book was interrupted by a lower back problem, but I did not give up. Indeed, as I was pounded by severe pain, my therapy was not the physical exercises being administered, but the powerful mental decision to finish this book before my back gave way. I thank the various friends, far and wide, who called to sympathize about my health; my wife, Olabisi, for taking care of me and running many errands; my children for not disturbing me; Akin Olusola for sending some materials from Nigeria; and a host of friends for enriching my social life. Toyin Akindele and his wife Sarah have been very good to my family. The year opened with a generous gift and birthday wishes arranged by Femi Owoseni of Austin and Tim Madigan and Louise Goldberg of the University of Rochester Press. I cannot thank these three people enough.

I owe my biggest debt to Nigeria. A land of great culture and people, it is once again a great joy to write on an aspect that has fascinated me for over thirty years. I have observed or participated in most of what I present in this book, and the photographs are mine.

Chronology

12,000 B.C.	Stone Age evidence indicates the antiquity of various indigenous groups.
500 B.C.	An iron civilization emerged, with one major center at Nok. Technology was altered, with great consequences on farming, urbanization, and settlements.
A.D. 200	Evidence of a metal age became abundant, indicating the spread of cities and villages.
A.D. 1000–1500	Foundation of many kingdoms such as Benin, Oyo, Hausa states and Kanem Borno.
ca. 1530	Christianity introduced to Benin, but the religion failed to take root in the country until a much later period.
1450–1850	Contacts with Europe and the New World, dominated by the slave trade which had profound consequences on the people.
1804	An Islamic revolution took place in northern Nigeria. It created the huge Sokoto Caliphate and led to the spread of Islam.
1842	The beginning of success in the spread of Christianity. A new elite emerged and Christianity and Islam became the two dominant religions in the country.
1861	The British establish a consulate in Lagos, beginning a process that led to the conquest of Nigeria.

1886	Formation of the Royal Niger Company with a charter to trade and enter into treaties in the Niger basin and its environs. In the same year, a peace treaty ended a prolonged war among the Yoruba-speaking people in the southwest.
1892	British attack on the Ijebu, a group of people among the Yoruba
1893	Establishment of a Protectorate over the Yoruba.
1897	Name "Nigeria" officially adopted.
1900	Establishment of a protectorate in northern Nigeria.
1902–1903	The Aro Expedition, part of the British conquest of Eastern Nigeria.
1914	Amalgamation of the Northern and Southern Protectorates.
1929	A major protest at Aba, eastern Nigeria, by women against colonial taxation and other forms of injustice.
1936	Establishment of the Nigerian Youth Movement, a leading political association that demanded major reforms.
1946	Richards Constitution enacted with a central legislature and three Regional Houses of Assembly. This marked the beginning of constitutional reforms that led to independence. Many nationalists were not satisfied with this constitution. A protest led to revision in subsequent years, and a federal constitution was eventually adopted in 1951.
1948	Establishment of the first university at Ibadan.
1954	Federal system of government introduced.
1957	Regional self-government proclaimed in the East and West, a major transfer of power from the British to Nigerians.
1959	Regional self-government in the North.
1960	Independence from Britain, October 1.
1963	Republic proclaimed. A Nigerian replaced the Queen as the symbolic head.

1966, January–July	The first military coup ended the First Republic, but created further political instability soon after.
1966–1975	Administration of General Yakubu Gowon presided over a war economy and later an economic boom.
1967	Beginning of the Nigerian civil war, July 3.
1967	Creation of twelve states to replace the existing four regions, but demands for more states continue as various groups see this as an opportunity to attain rapid development and benefit from federally distributed revenues.
1970	End of civil war, January 13. Nigeria embarked on a program of reconciliation and reconstruction, partly financed by oil revenues. While the East was reintegrated, secession demands by various groups have yet to end, while some outstanding issues of injustice during the war are yet to be resolved.
1973	Organization of Petroleum Exporting Countries (OPEC) oil-price increase led to an economic boom and prosperity for Nigeria. Development projects became grandiose.
1975–1979	Military regimes of Brigadiers Murtala Mohammed and Olusegun Obasanjo introduced far-reaching reforms in political institutions and became the first to transfer power to civilians.
1979–1983	The Second Republic, with Alhaji Shehu Shagari as president, was unable to create discipline among the ranks of the politicians and was ended by a military coup.
1983–1985	The military rule of General Muhammad Buhari was noted for firmness, investigations of political figures for corruption, and poor economic performance. A program of "austerity measures" introduced on April 1, 1982, did little to improve the economy.
1985–1993	Nigeria under General Ibrahim Babangida, with both failed economic and political programs. The regime introduced a Structural Adjustment Program, an economic policy that brought hardship to the majority of the population.

1991   A census put the country's population at 88.5 million,
                and this has since formed the basis of subsequent projec-
                tions of population increase.

1993   Presidential election, won by Chief M.K.O. Abiola, an-
                nulled June 12. The country was thrown into a pro-
                longed crisis thereafter. Short-lived Interim National
                Government, led by Chief E. Shonekan, characterized by
                chaos and public distrust.

1993–1998   Dictatorship of General Sanni Abacha, died June 8,
                1998. Nigeria's image was battered and opposition forces
                were repressed.

1998–1999   General Abdulsalami Abubakar in power, the eighth gen-
                eral to assume power in twenty-eight years of military
                rule. He presided over a successful transition to a de-
                mocracy in May 1999.

1999, May   A civilian regime with Olusegun Obasanjo as president.
                A slow program of economic and political recovery fol-
                lowed.

1

Introduction

The old mushroom rots, another springs up,
but the mushroom tribe lives on.

Akiga, a Nigerian chronicler

THE FEDERAL REPUBLIC OF NIGERIA is the most populated country in Africa
and one of the most well-known developing countries. It is the biggest country in West Africa, with an area of 356,669 square miles and a population
of over a hundred million which continues to grow at an annual rate of 2.96
percent, with a birth rate as high as its mortality rate. The capital is the
inland city of Abuja. Lagos, the former capital located on the coast in the
southwest, retains its preeminent position as the leading port and center of
finance and commerce. Cultural ideas and institutions are as varied as geographical conditions.

Nigeria is an agglomeration of hundreds of indigenous nations conquered
by the British in the second half of the nineteenth century and the first decade
of the twentieth century. In 1914, the Protectorates of Southern and
Northern Nigeria were amalgamated to form modern Nigeria. The British
governed until October 1, 1960, when the country obtained its independence. Three years later, it became a republic. Since then, an enduring democracy has eluded the country, as military regimes have been the most
pervasive phenomenon. The First Republic ended on January 15, 1966, followed by a military rule for thirteen years, then the Second Republic from
1979 to 1983, and thereafter a long period of military rule. In May 1999, a

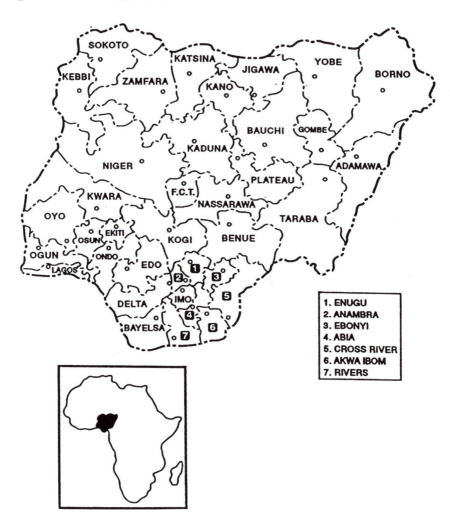

The thirty-six states of Nigeria, 1996.

democratic government replaced the military regime, with the hope of a new beginning after decades of political and economic crises.

LAND

Nigeria borders the Gulf of Guinea to the south; to the north is the Niger Republic, to the east are Chad and Cameroon, and to the west is Benin. The country's geography is diverse, marked by plains in the north, lowlands in the south, and plateaus and hills in the central belt, while the climate varies from arid to equatorial.

Generally, the climate is that of a tropical zone, with alternating dry and rainy seasons. The length of the rainy season increases from the north to south. In the south, the rainy season is from March to November with a dry interruption in August; in the north it rains from only May to September. Whereas the far north receives about 20 inches of rain in a year, the south can receive as much as 120 inches. The far north has a dry climate; the west and north have a wet and dry savanna climate, and the southeast has a wet climate, with heavy rainfall.

There are at least seven different relief zones: along the eastern frontier are hills; to the northeast is the Chad basin; inselberg landscapes dot several areas; three rivers, the Niger, Benue, and Gongola, form the major river basin troughs; the coastline is dominated by lagoons and inlets; to the southeast is the Niger Delta; and a coastal plain lies to the north of the delta, creeks, and lagoons. There are three basins that serve as drainage areas—the coastal, the Lake Chad, and the Niger-Benue.

The soil falls into four categories. The most fertile and most common is the ferruginous, known as the brown and red soil. Less common and in those areas with older sedimentary rocks are the ferralsols (red or reddish-yellow soil); and in places with young sedimentary rocks, mainly in the coastal area, is the hydromorphic soil (sandy soil, developed in areas of excessive moisture). In the dry north, with its loose soil and wind deposits, is the regosol or the brown soil. In the coastal areas, soils lose their fertility to erosion caused by heavy rainfall, in the north to desiccation.

The vegetation patterns fall into three categories determined mainly by the climate. In the Niger Delta and along the coast are freshwater swamps and mangroves. The country's oil resources are concentrated in the Niger Delta, where the swamps change to tropical rain forests just a few miles inland. In the forests, palm trees, cocoa, and rubber have been cultivated on a large scale since the nineteenth century. North of the forest belt is the tropical grassland or savanna, with its open land, short grass, and shrubs.

The type of vegetation found in different regions shapes the settlement patterns. The Ibibio and Igbo areas in the southeast are the most densely settled, followed by the Yoruba areas in the southwest. In the north, the major population concentrations are in the Sokoto, Katsina, and Kano regions. The least populated areas are in the eastern Cross River area, the Lake Chad Basin, and the middle belt. Some areas with high population density have witnessed problems of food shortage. In the case of the Katsina and Sokoto regions, infertile soil hampers efforts to produce adequate food. Among the Igbo in the east, erosion has reduced the quality of the soil, forcing many people to migrate to other parts of the country.

The south has many villages and cities, with populations that depend on farming, crafts, and fishing. Over the last hundred years, however, the economy has been and continues to be transformed to one based on modern mining and manufacturing. With the advantage of early Western education and the success of other industries and oil in the Niger Delta, many areas in the south have developed rapidly and have witnessed an expansion in their population.

The middle belt is not as densely populated as either the south or north, although it covers almost two-fifths of the land area. It is home to many small ethnic groups. The creation of states and the rapid development of state capitals have brought important changes to this area, in places such as Jos and the Federal Capital Territory at Abuja.

The north is home to the Hausa, Fulani, Kanuri, and a number of minority groups. In addition to farming, pastoralism is well developed here.

PEOPLES

Nigeria is a multiethnic nation with over 250 ethnic groups and languages, each having a number of distinguishing characteristics. Members of an ethnic group (for example, the Igala in the middle belt) speak the same language or dialects of the same language. They have a shared history, usually claiming to have descended from the same ancestor. For instance, the Nupe in the middle belt regard themselves as "children of Tsoede," while the Yoruba claim Oduduwa as their progenitor. Furthermore, an ethnic group develops an identity based on customs and traditions in a variety of ways including food habits, forms of address, and types of investiture. In the precolonial period (up until the late nineteenth century), most groups developed a political autonomy, except if they were vassals to larger kingdoms. Different branches of an ethnic group could live in villages or towns, and the most successful ones established kingdoms, such as the various Hausa states and the Kanuri empire in the north; Benin, established by the Edo in the south; and many Yoruba kingdoms in the southwest. An ethnic group occupies a territory and lays claim to land through historical antecedents of first habitation. Until the twentieth century, land belonged to the community and could not be sold. Strangers were accommodated through adoption by members of the community and land gifts. The commercialization of land began during the twentieth century, allowing people to purchase land in different cities.

Location of major ethnic groups.

The majority ethnic groups are the Hausa, Fulani, Yoruba, and Igbo, and the never-ending, bitter Nigerian politics involve all of them in the competition for federal power. The Hausa and Fulani live in the north, and it is hard for strangers to know the difference between the two groups as they have lived together for centuries. Since the Islamic revolution of the early nineteenth century, the Fulani have dominated local administration. They speak Fulfulde and their rural populations take to pastoralism. The Hausa speak Hausa, live in many cities, and move around as traders and itinerant workers.

The Yoruba in the southwest constitute the second largest group. The majority of them have always been city-dwellers. They speak many dialects of the Yoruba language, and they regard Oduduwa as their ancestor and Ile-Ife city as their ancestral homeland. They built many kingdoms, each headed by an *oba* (king) who ruled with a council of chiefs that represented different lineages within the city.

The majority of the Igbo live in the southeast, although a small proportion, the Western Igbo, live close to the Edo in the southwest. Traditional Igbo society lived in dispersed, mainly farming settlements, where the village was the highest level of political authority and power was diffused throughout its family heads and other adults. Like the Yoruba, the Igbo benefited from Western education during the twentieth century and can be found in almost all the modern occupations. In 1967, they seceded from the country, as Biafra, but after a civil war they were re-integrated into Nigeria.

Almost a third of the population belong to minority groups that are scattered throughout the country, such as the Tiv, Nupe, Jukun, and Igala in the middle belt; and the Ijo, Itsekiri, Urhobo, and Ibibio in the south. These groups have each developed their own customs, cultures, and political organization.

The majority of Nigerians (about 70 percent) live in villages of two types. In the first type, for example, among the Tiv in the middle belt and the Igbo, the village is a collection of dispersed compounds. Elsewhere, among the Kanuri, Yoruba, and Hausa, for instance, the village consists of a nucleated settlement including many compounds. Each compound comprises a man, the family head, and his wife/wives, children, and other relations. A village comprises people who share a common ancestry as well as assimilated strangers and tenants. An elder, in some cases the oldest male, serves as the village chief with authority to adjudicate cases and ensure community cohesion.

Different types of housing reflect regional differences and available local materials. In the savanna region to the north and in the middle belt, a typical village house is a round mud building with a grass roof or, where the weather is much drier, a flat mud roof. In the forest, the house is rectangular with mud walls and mat roofs. Along the coast, houses are made of bamboo with roofs of bamboo leaf or the raffia palm. In prosperous areas, roofs are made of corrugated iron sheets, which, over time, changes in color from gray to dust. In the cities, the architecture is modern, reflecting local innovations as well as influences from all parts of the world.

Culture and customs reflect the people's creativity, their adaptation to environments, and the impact the external world has had on them. In the pre-colonial era, groups in the north were drawn into the trans-Saharan trade via connections with North Africa and the Middle East. It was through this trade that Islam and the Arabic language and culture penetrated the region. Groups in the south were exposed to European influence from the fifteenth century onward and suffered the devastating impact of the trans-Atlantic slave trade.

Islam and Christianity are the two principal religions in the country. Muslims number close to 50 percent of the population and are concentrated in the north and southwest. The Christians number about 40 percent and are found mainly in the south and the middle belt. The missionaries and leaders of both Islam and Christianity compete for converts and attempt to insert religion into politics in ways that favor them. Since the 1980s, their competition has resulted in major conflicts in which places of worship have been burnt and hundreds of people have lost their lives.

Although now in the minority, traditional and indigenous religions persist as a small proportion of the population continue to worship the Supreme God and other gods, goddesses, and spirits, and also venerate their ancestors.

LANGUAGES

The official language of Nigeria is English, though the school system also encourages the learning of French to promote interactions with French-speaking neighbors and France. Both English and French are associated with the formal school system and economic sector. The electronic and print media have also contributed to the widespread use of English. Pidgin, a combination of English and indigenous languages, has also spread very widely, especially in cities, and, with the advantages of simplicity and linguistic innovations, has succeeded in promoting creativity in popular culture.

The majority of the population continue to use their mother tongues, numbering over 200. The most widely used languages are Yoruba, Igbo, Hausa, and Fulani. These are recognized for official business, especially in the states' legislative assemblies. Of all the indigenous languages, Hausa is the most widely spoken due in part to its success in the expanse of the north, the spread of the language by Hausa traders who travel widely, and its adoption by the northern political class as their language of choice in communicating with one another. In spite of these advantages, other groups, notably the Yoruba and Igbo, have refused the suggestion to adopt Hausa as the country's official language (either to replace or to compete with English) because of fear of northern domination.

EDUCATION

All tiers of government pay for the education system. Local governments administer many primary and secondary schools, while state and federal governments are responsible for university education. Private schools, both secular and religious, are allowed, especially at the elementary and secondary levels. The states control the majority of secondary schools, technical colleges, and trade centers. The demand for free education is great, over 15 million pupils attend primary schools, and there is at least one university in each state. Universities such as those of Ibadan, Ile-Ife, Nsukka, and Zaria, have

attained international fame, but the economic crisis of the 1990s has undermined their ability to teach and conduct research. Staff is reduced, facilities
are old and inadequate, and welfare services are poor. The first generation of
the modern elite were products of mission schools and those who wanted
higher education had to travel abroad to receive it. However, since independence, the country has produced its own educated class in numbers so high
that thousands have not found employment.

CITIES

Not all groups are village dwellers. Traditionally, the Bini, coastal peoples,
Yoruba, Kanuri, and Hausa have established city settlements. Coastal cities
such as Calabar, Creek Town, Brass, Buguma, Okrika, Bonny, and Opobo
Town developed as a result of trade, both internal and with Europeans. These
were once cosmopolitan towns that depended on the palm oil trade for survival. During this century, a few of them have also benefited in varying
degrees from oil exploration. Cities in the north are among the oldest, based
on wealth from agriculture and the trans-Saharan trade. They continue to
grow until the present. The Yoruba have more cities than any other group,
being the most urbanized group in Africa. Many Yoruba cities are very old,
like Ile-Ife and Ilesa founded many centuries ago; some were established
during the nineteenth century, such as Ibadan and Abeokuta.

New cities have emerged during the twentieth century, and older ones
have grown as well due to expanded economies, the creation of new administrative centers, and the development of new transport systems. Kaduna grew
as the new capital city of the north; Lagos expanded as an industrial and
commercial city; while Enugu in the east benefited from coal mining, its
railway station, and from being the regional administrative headquarters. The
biggest urban area is Lagos, although a number of industrial cities such as
Kano have also expanded.

Urbanization and an upgraded transport network have made possible extensive cultural intermingling in all cities, among Nigerians and between
Nigerians and foreigners, notably Europeans, Lebanese, and Indians. Migration remains a constant aspect of the country's demography, as more and
more people move from villages to cities. In the first half of the twentieth
century, when export crops such as cocoa and peanuts were very successful,
many people moved from the east and the middle belt to the southwest and
the north. A large number of Ibibio and Igbo have migrated to Lagos; many
southerners have relocated to the north to trade or work; while many north-

ern seasonal workers and small-scale entrepreneurs also go to the south. A buoyant economy in the 1970s also attracted other West Africans to Nigeria, although over a million were expelled in 1982 and 1983 when the economy witnessed a decline.

Cities have been difficult to manage, with problems of poor drainage and sewage disposal, water shortages, and overcrowding. Health services need improvement to cope with many cases of waterborne diseases and malaria. Whether in the cites or villages, good drinking water is scarce and most available sources are polluted. The government and private companies shoulder the responsibility of medical expenses, supplemented by individuals who go to private clinics. Before 1970, most medical facilities were owned by the missions, especially in the south. The Roman Catholics managed a large number of hospitals and clinics. Today, most hospitals are financed by the government, but the services are grossly inadequate.

RESOURCES, OCCUPATIONS, AND ECONOMY

Nigeria is rich in agricultural and mineral resources. Land is available for farming and pastoralism in most areas, but shortages exist in parts of the southeast and in some areas around Sokoto, Kano, and Katsina. Nature reserves include swamp forests (about 4 percent), tropical rain forests (20 percent), and savanna woodlands (75 percent). Dependence on firewood and charcoal for fuel, as well as the farming system of bush burning, has caused considerable damage to these areas.

Abundant natural gas and solar energy have not been fully tapped. The sources of power are based on three dams that produce abundant water power if used effectively. Available mineral resources include limestone, coal, lead, tin, columbite, iron, zinc, crude oil, and natural gas. Oil, mainly from the Niger Delta fields, is the leading revenue earner. Natural gas, the by-product of oil, is only now being exploited for sale, having long been flared.

The oil industry is the major economic sector. Oil production began in 1958 and it has increased to become the key component of the GDP (gross domestic product) and 96 percent of total exports. In addition there are several oil refineries and a host of oil-related occupations. Mining activities explore tin, columbite, and coal. Manufacturing is another important sector, including petrochemical industries in Port Harcourt and Kaduna, paper and pulp mills, an ambitious steel mills industry, various breweries, and factories producing other items, notably cement, textiles, soft drinks, and cigarettes. Manufacturing is concentrated in a few cities, contributing to urbanization.

As many factories depend on imported technologies and some imported materials, they tend to suffer whenever access to foreign currencies becomes difficult.

Traditional occupations have been influenced by environment and location. Groups who live close to major rivers and along the coast have developed fishing industries, and most of the others have taken to agriculture. Areas that can support agriculture have witnessed the growth of settlements and population. Most farmers cultivate small farms, using hand tools such as hoes and machetes to produce food crops, cash crops, and craft products for the market.

The major cash crops include cotton, peanuts, cocoa, rubber, and palm oil, all of which are sold to local industries and foreign markets. Food crops vary with location—in the north, they are mainly legumes and grains (corn, cowpeas, millet, and sorghum); in the south, they are root crops (cassava, yams, cocoyams, and taro). Farmers keep a small number of animals for food and social events. The nomadic Fulani groups are the most successful in livestock production (cattle). Communities around Lake Chad, along the major rivers such as the Niger and Benue, and on the coast take to fishing. Cattle and fish are two leading trade items that are sold all over the country.

Until the twentieth century, the production of food was adequate in spite of occasional famines in some places. Farming communities were well organized and their taxes or other contributions supported various political authorities. Many aspects of culture were originally intended to serve the needs of agrarian communities. Today, farming is no longer a prestigious occupation; the material rewards for small-scale farmers are small and discouraging, which has led to youth abandoning the villages.

Many Nigerians can be found as migrant workers in other countries. Before 1970, thousands migrated to Sierra Leone, Cameroon, Republic of Benin, Gabon, and Equatorial Guinea. Many were expelled from Cameroon in 1967 and Ghana in 1969. The oil boom of the 1970s reduced the number of migrants, but as the economy has declined since the 1980s, the number is now increasing again as Nigerians leave their country to find employment opportunities in other parts of the world. Thousands of Nigerians live in the United States and work in most sectors of the economy there. Nevertheless, citizens of other countries can also be found in Nigeria working in industries, mining, and import-export trade.

Traditional and modern economies continue to coexist in Nigeria. The majority of farmers rely on family labor and sell surpluses in the market after consuming and giving away part of the harvest. There is a host of traditional mining and manufacturing occupations producing tools, soap, textiles, ceramic, and items made of leather and wood.

Yet, the modern economy and market continue to grow stronger, with banking, currency, and a stock exchange in place. The naira, Nigeria's currency, was a strong regional currency until the mid-1980s when it began to suffer severe depreciation. The formal economy is dominated by the various governments (including the federal government and the state governments) who employ the majority of the wage labor. It is also the governments who initiate and implement development plans that allocate funds to various economic, social, and welfare sectors.[1] Public finance is based largely on oil revenues, royalties from companies, and taxes. The federal government collects most of the revenues, which are in turn allocated to states and federal ministries. The majority of the states cannot generate the revenues to run themselves and are therefore dependent on the federal government. Whenever oil revenues decline, the impact is immediate, especially on the state governments, which become unable to meet their recurrent expenditures.

The informal sector is diverse and strong. The majority of Nigerians are self-employed, organized into many small businesses that provide a variety of services, for example, hairdressing, singing, equipment repair, and the production of a wide range of household objects. So successful is this sector that it has created a foundation for rapid technological and industrial advancement.

Trade is integral to the economy. Domestic trade follows the traditional direction of south to north and vice versa, and from rural to urban areas. Goods are moved from one ecological zone to another: cattle, onions, and beans move from the north to the south; kolanuts, cassava, and plantain move from the south to the north; and yams move from the middle belt to many parts of the country. Most of these commodities sell in open traditional markets and there are also thousands of small department stores that carry imported items. International trade brings imports from Europe, Japan, India, China, and the United States, notably cars, tools, raw materials, and luxury items, valued at about U.S.$8 billion a year. Exports, worth almost $15 billion each year, include crude oil, tin, rubber, cotton, peanuts, and cocoa.

The transport system meets the requirements of the movement of trade and the migration of population. The transport pattern of goods is north to south and east to west, to reach the various ports and cities. The federal government maintains the trunk A roads that link all cities to the main port in Lagos. Areas with cash crops are better served with roads than other areas are. Railways were built very early in the colonial administration essentially to move goods to the ports, but they became one of the greatest vehicles in the movement of people, ideas, and cultures. The system has not changed much since it was completed: two single-track lines, one from Lagos to Kano (with limited branch lines) and the other from Port Harcourt to Maiduguri. Plans are under way to extend the lines. Since the 1960s, the railways have lost their importance to roads because of their slowness, inefficiency, and discomfort. When navigable during the rainy season, rivers, especially the Niger and Benue, are used to move goods and people. The two major seaports are located in Port Harcourt and Lagos and smaller ones in Calabar and Warri, and all are administered by the Nigerian Ports Authority. Major airports exist to service international and domestic flights.

On the whole, economic development has not been as rapid as Nigerians want, and the standards of living remain low. The modernization of the economy began rather slowly during the colonial period. Benefits to the people were then minimal as profits were invested abroad. The years of decolonization from 1945 to 1960 were the most optimistic for Nigerians as they expected great and rapid changes. Disappointments followed. Hope resumed again in the 1970s, when the country was awash in oil money. Rapid changes followed in construction projects, transportation, urbanization, welfare, and in the expansion of the labor force. To transfer economic power to Nigerians, the government enacted indigenization decrees in 1972 and 1977 to give greater participation in business enterprises to Nigerians. While a few Nigerians became wealthy from the exercise, indigenization did not initiate a process of greater industrialization as anticipated. The boom era was short-lived, giving way to the economic disasters of the 1980s and 1990s.

Current economic indicators reveal a society in trouble. Agriculture, the mainstay of the economy for centuries, has suffered major setbacks. By the mid-1970s, Nigeria became unable to feed itself and was even importing commodities that it could not grow in abundance. The currency of Nigeria, the naira, has suffered great devaluation; the inflation rate runs at 15 percent; the per capita income/gross domestic product (GDP) ratio is at $1,300/ $132.7 billion; GDP growth rate is 3.3 percent; external reserves and revenues have declined; and domestic and external debts are on the rise.

Nigeria's economy has come to rely on one major source: oil revenues. For the first half of the twentieth century reliance was on agriculture. This changed in the 1970s as increasingly enormous revenues came from oil. The consequences have been both negative and positive: Nigeria became a rentier state, one that relies on revenues collected from oil companies; public expenditure expanded; the scale of corruption increased; a class of millionaires emerged; the political class, bent on obtaining easy access to oil money, competed vigorously for power; and poor people suffered great hardship and injustice. A tiny class with large amounts of money lives with great privileges; it constitutes both an economic and cultural class in terms of consumption habits and lifestyles.

The country welcomes foreign investors, providing them with generous tax breaks and profit-repatriation opportunities. In addition, many public enterprises are being privatized to make them more efficient. In spite of all its problems, Nigeria's economy is the second largest in Africa, following that of South Africa.

GOVERNMENT

Nigeria is currently under a democratic government headed by a president. There is a federal system, similar to the United States. The federal government has its powers defined, as well as those of the states and local governments, in a federal, republican constitution. Since 1988, local governments have existed independently of the states with grants provided by the federal government. The states are headed by governors and there are legislative and executive branches in the states as well.

Much power and revenues reside in the federal government. The constitution gives the president power as head of state and chief executive. The president is elected by the people and can serve for two terms of four years each. The National Assembly consists of the Senate and House of Representatives. The constitution also establishes the Nigerian Police Force whose head, the inspector general, is appointed by the president.

The legal system recognizes the multiple heritage of the country—indigenous, colonial, and Islamic. Customary laws are applicable in a number of local communities, administered by chiefs. In the case of Islamic laws in Muslim areas, trained *alkalai* judges preside in the courts. Statute law derived from the British colonial system is now embedded in the constitution, and is used in the various courts with trained judges and lawyers who appear before them.

Government has been largely unstable. The military capitalizes on the lapses of civilian governments to stage coups. Once in power, military officers maintain their positions of authority. The main reason for instability is that the government has been a source of wealth to many who serve in it. Power is abused to steal money, to distribute favor to associates, friends, relations, and ethnic members, and to gain easy popularity in certain constituencies.

Kanem-Borno probably affected the political development of the neighboring Hausa states in positive ways. The Hausa live to the west of Borno, in an intermediary region that links them to the Western Sudan, the forest region to the south, and the trade routes to the Maghreb across the Sahara Desert. These advantages led to the emergence of several powerful states, each with a king, a major market, a walled capital city, and an impressive bureaucracy. Like those of Kanem-Borno, the Hausa rulers adopted Islam, but much later, in the fourteenth century. The Hausa states engaged in wars with each other that weakened their relations with such powerful neighbors as Kanem-Borno, Songhai, and the Jukun during the seventeenth and eighteenth centuries.

Both the Hausa states and Kanem-Borno were transformed during the nineteenth century by the successful jihad (holy war) of Uthman dan Fodio, a Fulani scholar and reformer. Although Islam was already accepted by Borno and Hausa rulers and chiefs, dan Fodio began to seek reforms in the religion in the late eighteenth century. He accused the kings of ignoring the Shari'a (Islamic law), of condoning "pagan" practices, and of showing little commitment to the spread of Islam. His twenty years of missionary enterprise eventually led to serious clashes with the Hausa king of Gobir, and a jihad ensued in 1804. The response to dan Fodio was not only spontaneous, it was widespread. A successful caliphate based in Sokoto emerged, becoming the largest territorial political unit in Nigerian history. The caliphate was divided into several emirates, each headed by an emir with enormous power. Islam spread as a religion, together with its education and legal system. The political consequences of the jihad have continued to the present day, providing the north with the opportunity to unite as a single political bloc.

British Rule

British contacts with Nigeria were strengthened during the nineteenth century. Initially, British traders joined other Europeans as traders between the sixteenth and eighteenth centuries to buy palm oil in exchange for guns and luxury items, and as missionaries to convert Nigerians to Christianity. To protect their commercial interests, the British attacked Lagos in 1851 and involved themselves in complicated politics in order to install a king favorable to them. Ten years later, they annexed Lagos, which became a separate colony in 1886. A British consul, based in Fernando Po, supervised the trade in palm oil, while various missionary organizations continued to be active in the area of southern Nigeria. In the east, George Taubman Goldie obtained a British charter in 1886 for his company, the Royal Niger Company, which enabled it to control trade as well as move to the north to administer a large area of the Sokoto Caliphate. The British later declared protectorates over the Lagos hinterland and the Oil Rivers area. Force was used where necessary, but many areas were acquired by treaties, the meanings of which were unclear to local chiefs and kings. In 1895, the two southern protectorates were merged into the Niger Coast Protectorate. In 1900, the charter granted to the Royal Niger Company was revoked, paving the way for the creation of the Protectorate of Northern Nigeria. Britain now had protectorates in both south and north, which were merged in 1914 to create modern Nigeria, under the control of a governor based in Lagos.

A system of indirect rule, of divide and rule, was introduced to govern local communities and to ensure that various ethnic units were differently managed. The architect of indirect rule in Nigeria was Lord Lugard, the first high commissioner of Northern Nigeria and the first governor-general of Nigeria. Starting with Northern Nigeria in 1903, the principles of indirect rule were that power at the local level would be left in the hands of kings and chiefs as before; European officers would supervise the kings and chiefs; and local customs would be maintained, unless they contained elements defined by the British as either "uncivilized" or inappropriate. In practice, indirect rule became known as "Native Administration," with the king or chief at the top, a core of local officials below him, a revenue system based on taxation, and an annual list of recurrent and capital expenditures. This system was later extended to the south, where it was accompanied by riots in 1918 at Abeokuta and in 1929 at Aba, primarily because of its requirement that people must pay tax and because it conferred additional power on chiefs and kings. The goal of indirect rule was to minimize administrative costs in terms of money and personnel: there was no need to bring many British officers from abroad to manage the huge country.

Changes were not limited to a new system of government. The primary interest of Britain was to exploit Nigeria's economy by developing a cash-crop economy and tapping mineral resources. Cocoa, peanuts, rubber, and cotton became the basis of the agricultural economy. All of them were shipped to European industries. Similarly, foreign firms mined tin and coal, which was used to power the railways. Lebanese and Indian traders came to the country to participate in retail trade. Domestic markets expanded and were integrated into an international market system.

To reorient the economy, the British had to build railways and roads to move goods to the port. New currencies were introduced to replace indigenous ones and to serve the demands of a new economy that relied on taxation to generate public revenues, to provide wages to pay the workers in the modern sector, and to encourage transactions in the marketplace. A new society, defined by the impact of the West, was born.

Colonialism and Culture

British rule created conditions that changed or modified old customs. It also brought many new cultures as well. In general, colonialism travels with cultural imposition as the colonizing power promotes its own civilization as superior, and as the colonized imitate the representatives of the colonizing agents. The colonized may assimilate or reject the imposed culture, but they must always face the reality of change.

Let us start with the changes in the indigenous culture. Preexisting nations lost their sovereignty as they became subordinated to modern Nigeria. Chiefs and kings suffered a loss of the power that is necessary to shape culture. As the country entered a subordinate phase of its history, it lost some of the power to determine the culture it wanted. With political domination, the British also brought aspects of cultural domination. The British believed that their culture was superior and attempted to undermine aspects of Nigerian culture with which they did not agree, abolishing elements that they found objectionable. Thus, they were relentless in attacking polygamy, trial by ordeal, and certain types of sacrifices. When it was convenient for the colonial administration, aspects of the past were retained. One example was the use of chiefs and kings in the system of indirect rule. Now known as "traditional rulers," they were used to implement new policies and collect taxes. These new powers alienated many of them from their people and reoriented the culture of power from that of serving communal interest to that of acting as an agency of alien domination.

New ideas, institutions, and values spread with British rule. For example, Christianity spread in the south and the middle belt where the missionaries had the best opportunity to work. Conversion to Christianity created a new individual who accepted an alternative worldview and rejected certain aspects of inherited culture. Some converts regarded Nigerian indigenous songs and rituals as "pagan practices."

Western formal education was adopted. The missionaries pioneered the establishment of schools in order to facilitate evangelization. They were aided by the colonial administration, which required educated workers in different sectors of the administration and economy. Nigerians were quick to accept Western education as it conferred opportunities and power in the colonial system. The education system favored boys more than girls and withdrew many young men from farming communities. Through the school system, the English language was able to spread.

New consumption and production patterns were introduced. Wage labor began to replace household labor in a number of economic activities. Where imported items were available, local industries that produced similar goods declined in importance. Cash-crop production reduced food cultivation and shifted the labor of women away from certain spheres to others.

To a number of Nigerian intellectuals of the period, the changes brought by the British were too great. They were afraid that indigenous cultures would soon be forgotten. Attempts were made to document indigenous culture and history, for example by the Rev. Samuel Johnson, who wrote a massive book on the Yoruba.[2] He and others appealed to people of their generation to seek the means to preserve local cultures. One author, Akiga Sai, lamented the loss of culture in the following words:

> It has been my constant prayer that God will help me to write this book in order that the new generation of Tiv, which is beginning to learn this New Knowledge, should know the things of the fathers as well as those of the present generation. For everything that belongs to the Tiv is passing away, and the old people, who should tell us about these things will soon be dead. It makes me sad to think that our heritage is being lost, and that there will be none to remember it. . . .
>
> You, then, my Tiv brothers of the new generation that can read, read and tell others, who cannot, of the things of our ancestors; so that, whether we have learnt to read or not, we all may still know something of our fathers who have gone before us. And do you, however great your knowledge may be, remember that you are a Tiv, remain a Tiv, and know the things of Tiv; for therein lies your pride. Let us take heart. The old mushroom rots, another springs up, but the mushroom tribe lives on.[3]

A few others went beyond this appeal, developing ideas of cultural nationalism, which argued that Africans should reject many aspects of Western culture and seek self-government.

Independence Movements

The effort to reject the political and cultural domination of British rule gave birth to nationalism. Nationalism was originally expressed in anticolonial resistance as various groups and rulers struggled to prevent the British conquest. When this failed, nationalism took the form of demands for reform and for progress to favor Nigerians, especially those with Western education. From the second decade of the twentieth century to 1939, nationalism demanded changes and the intellectuals of the period wrote books, essays, and pamphlets to assert the relevance of indigenous traditions. The elite wanted the system to promote their own mobility and to provide opportunities for their children and others. They desired modernity and wanted their country to look like Britain in infrastructure, governance, and order.

The radical moment came in the 1940s when World War II instigated far-reaching changes that triggered demands for self-government. The British responded by granting concessions that included provisions for more educational and social amenities and constitutional reforms. These ensured that the path to Nigerian independence was not paved with violence.

The Richards Constitution was enacted in 1946. It made the government quasi-federal with regional houses of assembly and houses of chiefs, and a central legislative council in Lagos. Leading nationalists like Chiefs Obafemi Awolowo and Nnamdi Azikiwe denounced the Richards Constitution as ignoring the wishes of Nigerians. To address their fears and involve them, a new constitutional conference gave birth to the Macpherson Constitution of 1951, which created a central house of representatives in a federal system.

Regional conflicts and competition among the politicians created the need for another revision, the Lyttleton Constitution of 1954, which established a federal system and a tri-regional structure of the North, South, and West in addition to the Federal Territory of Lagos. A weakened federal government in Lagos was composed of an executive branch, as well as a senate and a house of representatives. When the regions were given wide power, with their own governors, premiers, cabinets, civil services, and legislatures, the politics of regionalism began in full force.

The Western and Eastern Regions obtained internal self-government in 1957 and the North two years later. The North feared the domination of federal power by the southern elite; the south feared that the North would use its vast size to advantage; the minorities in all the regions were afraid of domination by the Hausa, Igbo, and Yoruba. Thus, on the one hand, there was joy at the impending end of British rule. Yet, on the other hand, there was fear that regionalism and ethnic differences would tear the country apart. The country became independent on October 1, 1960, with a federal constitution and a parliamentary system based on that of the United Kingdom.

From a Republic to a Military Government, 1960–1979

Nigeria did not enjoy any prolonged moment of peace during its first ten years. Struggling from one crisis to another, the First Republic collapsed early in January 1966, and a three-year civil war began in 1967.

The First Republic was defined by the politics of regionalism. The North was dominated by the Hausa/Fulani, the West by the Yoruba, and the East by the Igbo. The three regions were bitter rivals and they all wanted to control the federal government. They could not agree on how to divide the national revenues, how to distribute federal cabinet positions, or how to even conduct a head count. In 1962–1963, the government of the West collapsed when conflicts over the census figures almost tore the nation apart; the 1964 federal elections were tainted; and public order broke down a year later following another election. The first military coup occurred on January 15, 1966, leading to the death of Prime Minister Tafawa Balewa and the powerful premier of the north, Ahmadu Bello, the *Sardauna* (traditional chief) of Sokoto. Things fell apart. Ever since, enduring political stability has eluded the nation.

Major General Johnson Aguiyi-Ironsi was the first military leader. He came to power under a cloud of suspicion that the Igbo wanted to dominate the federation. The army that he represented became divided. Fearing a loss of control, northern officers wanted to use the army to restore the balance of power. Ironsi saw regionalism as a threat to the country; his attempts to abolish the regions and impose a unitary system ended in anti-Igbo riots and ultimately a coup by northern officers on July 29, 1966. Lt. Colonel (later General) Yakubu Gowon was installed in power.

If the northern army got what it wanted, it came at a high price. The Igbo embarked upon a plan to secede; anti-Igbo feelings led to the massacre of hundreds of innocent people in northern cities; and peace conferences to settle the conflicts among the leading politicians and military officers ended in failure. On May 30, 1967, Colonel Ojukwu, the Igbo leader, declared the birth of the Republic of Biafra. War broke out on July 6, 1967. Biafra resisted strongly, but it lost the war due to a lack of military resources, the federal side's greater firepower, and a failure to procure food for its population, the majority of whom were killed by hunger rather than bullets. An official surrender was pronounced on January 15, 1970. One outcome of the political crisis was the creation of states in 1967, the disbandment of the big regions into twelve states, and the centralization of power in the federal government.

Although still governed by the military, Nigeria entered its most prosperous phase in the 1970s. The early 1970s were marked by an oil boom, which brought substantial revenues. Not only was the money used to rapidly repair some of the trauma of the war, it enabled the federal government to consolidate its power, to expand public expenditures on many programs, and to create a comfortable middle class.

In the realm of politics, Gowon was overthrown on July 29, 1975, following a careless decision not to vacate power and disengage the military, thereby losing a golden opportunity to become the country's first modern hero. Brigadier Murtala Mohammed succeeded but he was killed in a failed coup on February 13, 1976, paving the way for his second in command, Lieutenant General Olusegun Obasanjo, to come to power. Under Mohammed and Obasanjo, plans were made for a transition to civilian rule, and the Second Republic came into being in 1979.

The Second Republic, 1979–1983

Nigeria discarded its British-type constitution in preference for the American-style presidential model. To be elected by popular mandate would ensure that the president would become a symbol and agent of unity. He would choose his cabinet, with the approval of the legislature, although he alone had the power to remove cabinet members.

Five political parties dominated the scene, each able to win elections at the state level and to send representatives to the central legislature. The strongest party was the National Party of Nigeria (NPN), which produced Alhaji Shehu Shagari, the president, in 1979. The NPN was motivated by power sharing so that its members could control access to federal resources. The NPN federal government failed to pay attention to declining oil revenues, poverty, and falling living standards. Instead, it took to massive food importation and the building of the new capital city of Abuja in order to divert money to party members. Violence and public protests accompanied economic decline.

Elections to transfer power always generate problems in Nigeria. In 1983, the NPN wanted to remain in power, to control the federal government and as many states as possible. Against the background of widespread discontent, the NPN knew that it could not just rely on free and fair elections to retain power. Predictably, the party engaged in massive electoral fraud to determine the outcome of the elections. Shagari and his party claimed landslide victories in the August–September 1983 elections. Not only did this undermine the democratic process, it provided the opportunity for the army to abort the

Second Republic. A successful coup occurred on December 31, 1983, and the military was back in power for another fifteen years.

The Period of Military Rule, 1984–1999

Nigeria entered the worst years in its modern history under the three successive regimes of Muhammad Buhari, Ibrahim Babangida, and Sanni Abacha, each worse than his predecessor. The styles were different: Buhari was stern but organized; Babangida was urbane but ruthless; and Abacha was crude and callous. By the time the three regimes were ended, the military had been discredited, its officers had lost credibility, professionalism was destroyed, and the entire military force was deeply resented by the public. Nigerians had lost hope in their future.

The Buhari regime (1983–1985) focused on fighting corruption and reducing excessive public expenditures. He was able to bring some order into public life, but his "War Against Indiscipline" included the persecution of a number of innocent people, and his style was abrasive and high-handed, which alienated him from the public. An ambitious general, Babangida, capitalized on these lapses. He was less dictatorial in the beginning, but he later revealed his dark side: a love for power and its excesses, a passion to stay in power for as long as possible, and a belief in the use of corruption as a management device. Babangida's era witnessed social decadence, economic decline, the fall of the middle class, and the most prolonged political crisis since the civil war.

The Babangida years (1985–1993) were marked by both economic and political failures. In 1986, a structural adjustment program (SAP) was introduced. Rather than improve the economy, SAP brought further currency devaluation, the destruction of the middle class, inflation, unemployment, and massive retrenchment of workers. As fuel prices rose, so did transportation and food costs. The post-1986 era witnessed countless protests and riots, and the country became a dangerous place.

Babangida's political program also ended in catastrophe. He promised to disengage but had to be forced out of power by crises. He micromanaged the transition program, including the creation of two political parties, and prohibited the participation of leading political parties and possible rivals. The straw that broke the camel's back was the presidential election of June 12, 1993. Thinking that chaos would follow and he would be able to capitalize on it, Babangida originally allowed Chief M.K.O. Abiola and Alhaji Bashir Tofa to contest the elections. When it was clear that Abiola had won,

Babangida and a handful of military officers annulled the elections. The nation and the international community were united in their opposition to this decision and their pressure to resolve the crisis ended in his exit from power and the establishment in August 1993 of an interim national government headed by Chief Earnest Shonekan. Shonekan was a weak pawn in the hands of the powerful military who overthrew him in November of the same year. General Sanni Abacha came to power.

From November 1993 to June 8, 1998, Nigeria became a pariah state, foreign investments declined, and domestic opposition to Abacha's regime was relentless. Abacha was the most authoritarian ruler that the country has had to date. He used maximum force to deal with the opposition, killing and incarcerating as many as he could lay his hands upon. He was also very corrupt, crudely taking money from the Central Bank and privatizing public property. He did not disguise his ambition for even more power, as he turned the existing five political parties created during his regime into a propaganda machine to install him as a civilian president. Throughout his regime, various political forces emerged to demand not just an end to military rule but a renegotiation of the federal and territorial structure of the country. The popular options were either to divide the country or to create a confederacy with the weakest center possible.

The sudden death of Abacha in 1998 created a fresh beginning for the country. Abacha's successor, General Abdulsalami Abubakar, initiated a successful transition program. Nigeria improved its international image, and new political parties competed for power. Three political parties have thus far been successful in controlling power: the All People's Party (APP), the Alliance for Democracy (AD), and the People's Democratic Party (PDP). The PDP is the strongest, having won the most governorships as well as the presidential elections of May 29, 1999, that brought Obasanjo to power.

Events since Obasanjo has come to power reflect the fragility of the country's democratic institutions and the various problems still left to resolve. Obasanjo has launched an anticorruption crusade, but fellow politicians and civil servants have not been enthusiastic about it. At both state and federal levels, many politicians continue to demonstrate that their purpose in politics is not to improve the country but to secure generous contracts for themselves. There is no new political orientation, which may mean that the military will come back if there is prolonged instability, or that the most corrupt set of people will capture power. A damaged economy must travel a long road to recovery, although many are willing to wait for change to come. Religious tensions have surfaced with church burnings in Kano and Ilorin, two cities with an Islamic majority. Zamfara State has introduced the Shari'a law and other states have threatened to follow suit, a decision that will damage interreligious relations. The most serious communal conflicts are in the oil-producing minority areas of the Niger Delta where many communities and youth organizations protest against both the government and the oil companies for damaging their environments and marginalizing them.

Nigeria has all the advantages necessary to become a great nation and regional power. Its natural and human resources are enormous; its intellectuals are enterprising; its population is large, vibrant, and growing; its size commands respect; revenues from oil continue to flow; and the market for domestic and international products is huge. It has been successful in the creation of new cultures and the preservation of some old ones.

CULTURAL ISSUES

As the subsequent chapters show, customs and culture are rich, varied, and changing. Elements of Islam, the West, and indigenous traditions are embedded in many cultural practices. Ancient indigenous practices like masquerades and secret societies coexist with Islamic and Christian traditions. In spite of colonial contacts and the introduction of Islam and Christianity, many aspects of the past have survived. The spread of new culture has always been uneven, affecting the cities more than the villages, the coastal areas more than the hinterland. Age-grade societies, secret societies, chieftaincy systems, and the indigenous religious priesthood have all survived the onslaught of external impact. Farming is still the most common occupation, just as in the past.

The scope of Nigerian culture is broad, reflecting the country's past and present, while intellectuals speculate about the future. Among elements of the past that have influenced contemporary culture are the indigenous worldview, Islam, Christianity, the slave trade, and British colonialism. The strong emphasis on kinship dates back to a time when individuals needed to protect one another against insecurity from attacks by powerful neighbors; and the practice of polygamy reflected the need of an agrarian society for household labor.

Individuals continue to be drawn into these primordial customs to define their obligations to society and the values that guide their lives. These traditions have also been used to separate one ethnic group from another, to differentiate Nigerian groups from foreign ones, and to criticize those who want to accept Western culture wholesale. All groups have preserved their customs in their languages. Astute politicians have used the need to preserve languages as a political tool to consolidate ethnicities—by teaching a standard form of a language in schools and popularizing its usage, they are strengthening group identity at the same time.

Many primordial customs survive in modern Nigeria, although some in modified forms that reflect historical changes or the reality of survival in a different world. They have successfully borrowed from foreign cultures to reinvent themselves. For instance, many local languages now have a written form, borrowing from the Roman alphabet and developing their own orthography. Songs, proverbs, and rituals are now preserved in media forms and can be replayed for leisure or performance. All aspects of primordial cultures that confer prestige (for example, chieftaincy institutions) have been retained as part of the definition of contemporary social status. The ability of the primordial to "modernize" has ensured its survival.

The degree to which individuals accept or reject primordial customs varies a great deal. Those who have been converted to Islam or Christianity may refuse to take part in certain traditional festivals that they regard as violating the tenets of their world religions. In cities, where modern culture coexists with the primordial, many are drawn more into the modern in such aspects as music, lifestyles, and the use of English. However, it is rare to find any Nigerian living in Nigeria who has rejected all aspects of primordial customs. At the very minimum, the individual is able to speak a Nigerian language.

There are, however, many communities, notably in the rural areas, where not only are primordial customs followed but their violation incurs severe sanctions. In such places, ethics and moral conduct in interpersonal relations are defined by the values of old. Thus, they continue to stress the importance of respect for elders, the authority of husbands over their wives, the need to work hard, and the habit of generosity to members of the kin group and the larger community.

Yet, culture is not static. Just as history and society change, so do various aspects of culture. Both Islamic and indigenous culture coexist with new cultural forms. The foundation of modern Nigerian culture, defined by the adoption of Western components, was laid in the second half of the nineteenth century. The use of English and the existence of various legal and political institutions reveal the impact of colonial rule. The major occupations are all modern: medicine, law, accountancy, teaching, and estate management; and entry into them is a mark of civilization or of defining the self as "modern." A taste for bread, milk, sausage, clothes, cars, and a variety of luxury items reflects the impact of globalization since the fifteenth century. Since the nineteenth century, as elite numbers have expanded, so, too, has travel to the West to receive education, to vacation, or to seek out "high culture."

There is a popular as well as an elite culture. The media spread contemporary cultures through different programs, while universities formalize the teaching of old and new traditions. The school system, mass media, and globalization are promoting a culture that people subscribe to throughout Nigeria, irrespective of their location or ethnic identification. The use of English and pidgin is one example, as these languages serve to popularize a national culture through music, art, education, medicine, Christianity, and Islam. Unlike primordial culture, the Nigerian-wide customs are not identified with one group but with many people. Violations carry no sanctions as the new customs are not at all defined in moral terms, and many aspects of this national culture are derived from the West.

The existence of primordial, modern, and Nigeria-wide cultures means that Nigerians have a variety to choose from; in other words, there are cultural choices to make or individuals can reflect eclecticism or ambiguity in what they choose. For instance, an educated man may speak English or a Nigerian language, depending on his preference or politics. He may have two wives and suffer no moral or legal consequences. He may attend a Christian service in the morning, enjoy a local festival in the evening, and later visit his Muslim friends to celebrate with them.

The existence of multiple cultures also means that participation is not always equal. The educated and successful middle class have better opportunities to participate in the modern sphere or the Nigeria-wide culture—they can speak better English, buy cars, televisions, and videos, and travel abroad. Economically marginalized people have limited opportunities for leisure. Location is also a factor, as aspects of modern culture flourish more in cities than villages. The ability to enjoy some aspects of modern culture has instigated a desire for change and progress in many local communities where demands are made for better roads, radio and television sets, and department stores.

Culture and customs travel beyond their frontiers. Various aspects of Nigerian cultures have reached other lands, as in the jazz music of Anikulapo Kuti and the *juju* music of King Sunny Ade (see Chapter 8). Nigerians can also be found in Western cities wearing their beautiful attire and communicating in their impressive accents.

Nigerian governments and intellectuals have always realized that culture is relevant to development. In seeking an identity for the country and its institutions, the emphasis has been on using various components of culture, especially of the past. Nigeria wants to develop its technology and infrastructure and modernize various aspects of its life, but it does not want to give up aspects of its older culture such as dress, food, music, and indigenous languages. Religious organizations and public leaders continue to call on Nigerians to promote the communal ethos of traditional societies, instead of the individualistic ethos of capitalism. These organizations and leaders want to link communal culture to the individual by insisting that Nigerians must be socialized to local, not foreign, cultures, and asking the individual to subordinate his or her desire to the collective aspirations of society.

Nigerian governments have promoted culture in a variety of ways, formulated a cultural policy, and established official agencies to promote culture. The belief is that successful economic and political programs must pay attention to the people's customs and beliefs and recognize the plurality of values, ideas, and institutions. The federal government and the various state governments fund museums, agencies to collect and preserve cultural objects, research institutes and seminars. Culture is also part of foreign policy as African countries have come together under the banner of cultural promotion. In 1977, Nigeria hosted the Second World Black and African Festival of Arts and Culture, which brought thousands of representatives from African countries and the diaspora. The core components of the cultural policy of Nigeria are to preserve, promote, and present culture, and to use various aspects of Nigerian culture to ensure development into a strong nation.

NOTES

1. Toyin Falola, *Decolonization and Development Planning in Nigeria* (Gainesville: University Press of Florida, 1996).

2. Samuel Johnson, *The History of the Yorubas* (London: C.M.S, 1921).

3. Akiga Sai, *Akiga's Story*, translated and annotated by Rupert East (Oxford: Oxford University Press, 1939), 2–4.

2

Religion and Worldview

RELIGIOUS IDEAS and worldview affect the ways millions of Nigerians explain reality, understand how the country works, relate to other members of society, react to events and changes, and reflect on and even predict their future and that of their country. Religious ceremonies are the events that attract the largest number of people. In Nigeria, these ceremonies are frequent and far more important even than soccer, the most popular sport. There is no open opposition to organized religions either by the state or by private individuals. Indeed, the Nigerian university campuses are centers of vibrant religious activities as many academics include issues of faith in their scholarship. Nigeria, then, challenges all those theories positing that religion will decline in importance as society modernizes, since there remains strong evidence of religious conversion, devotion, and activism throughout the country.

In most societies, religion is very important to individuals who seek solutions to their emotional problems, answers to the meaning of life, and an understanding of their complex reality and existence. A person may seek religious counsel if s/he is worried about relationships with others in the community; another may be troubled by a relationship in his/her work place; and many may want to satisfy God without understanding the means to do so. Nigerians also turn to religion to deal with the problems of suffering, sickness, death, and insecurity. They try to forestall these problems or seek solutions to life's challenges in their faith and religious rituals.

As in other countries, religious ideas and worldview in Nigeria are inherited as part of the socialization process. But as individuals relate to historical phenomena and face the reality of their own existence, they impose fresh meanings on inherited ideas. They may even abandon those ideas to which they have been socialized, as in the case of those who have converted from indigenous religion to Islam or Christianity.

WORLDVIEW

Religion occupies a preeminent place in Nigerians' worldview as it provides ideas to explain the origins of their country, their personal conditions, and their future. Their worldview also reflects the changes taking place within organized religions, notably within Islam and Christianity. Religion in both traditional and modern forms prevails throughout the country, as religion is important to the way the society functions, develops its cohesion, and understands and explains events between people and in nature. To ensure good health, children, and prosperity, it is strongly believed that spiritual beings must be worshipped.

The universe continues to be regarded with awe and confusion. Lightning, thunder, and illness are events that people still struggle to explain because they are not necessarily explained by science. Thus a farmer in a rural area may say that plants grow because the god of fertility blesses them. A city-dweller can attribute an automobile accident to evil forces.

Those who subscribe to a traditional worldview believe very strongly in witchcraft and magic. In many societies, witches are blamed for almost all problems or calamities, from crop failure to mysterious death. Good fortunes and destiny can be altered by witches. Successful marriages can be terminated by them. In periods of economic decline and social unrest, the belief in witchcraft becomes stronger, as individuals and communities seek an exterior explanation for their misfortune. Witches can transform themselves into any object of their desire, for example, owls or bats, and work to destroy people by causing sickness, death, impotence, poverty, and other problems. The belief persists that religious actions must be taken to overcome witches' power; consequently, a specialized profession of "witch doctor" exists in many communities to deal with witches and minimize the problems that they create.

Similarly, knowledge of magic is very powerful as symbols can be manipulated to produce desired results. Whoever knows the symbol or "language" of the storm can calm it. Communication with animals or animal amulets or charms can be used to protect against evil or to cure diseases. Another assumption in the use of magic is that "like acts on like." A headache can be cured by applying a hot remedy to the head. The statue or likeness of one's enemy can be made and magic applied to it in order to damage the enemy.

Spiritual beings are invested with much power and with all the attributes that human beings fear or find attractive; they are moody, vindictive, and generous. They can solve personal and emotional problems, but humans must negotiate with them in order to live a meaningful life.

This is a rational, if impersonal, way of understanding reality. As in interpersonal relationships, the traditional worldview moves from what is known to what is unknown. Elements that are known are used to interpret the unknown. If the personal realm attributes incidents to chance, the impersonal may say that chance is exaggerated or nonexistent since human beings are under the control of gods. Thus, if a young person dies in mysterious circumstances, the death will be attributed to a hostile being. If it is to be discovered through divination or other means that the death was a result of illness, they can still say that a witch or an evil spirit caused the illness.

Traditional beliefs continue to change as Nigerians go to school, receive ideas from other places, and travel to other countries. Science and formal education have reduced the number of those who believe that gods and witches are responsible for every problem. Western science has spread with Western education and has introduced its rationality. Nevertheless, many Nigerians still believe that death can be caused by the "evil eye," witches, and all sorts of enemies; that luck and destiny account for success; and that God bestows power, wealth, and all forms of blessings. While a mechanic knows how a car works, the knowledge does not stop him from paying homage to the god of iron.

Several aspects of the modern worldview are influenced by Islam and Christianity, both universal religions with missionaries and organizations that seek to gain and retain followers. (About 50 percent of the population is Muslim and 40 percent is Christian.) Islam spread from the north and Christianity from the south, creating a "religious map" that continues to affect many aspects of Nigerian history and culture. If indigenous religions are localized in their spread and practices, Islam and Christianity are very aggressive in their conversion efforts and have taken advantage of indigenous religious beliefs. Conversion to both religions has been facilitated by the strong belief that they provide solutions to problems in interpersonal and community relations; and that if expectations are unfulfilled after many sessions of prayer to a particular god, one can change religion, sect, or allegiance to a religious leader, rather than abandon one's basic faith. Both universal religions have profited from the fact that indigenous religions are receptive to ideas from them and receptive to incorporating new knowledge and gods into the existing system. The worshipers of local gods take to other religions either to broaden what they already have or to transform their beliefs to better meet their expectations. In other words, both Islam and Christianity enable Nigerians to add to, or reject, what they already believe to meet the changing demands of society.

Islam and Christianity have capitalized on change to convert and shape the people's worldview. In Islamic belief, a degenerate society with moral degradation and corrupt leadership can be changed by force, if need be. Thus, the jihad (holy war) in the nineteenth century reformed the society and contributed to the expansion of Islam. Both Islam and Christianity have taken advantage of changes in trade, education, and politics by offering explanations for the changes. They offer the promise of social mobility by promoting literacy and schools. The networks established by coreligionists have been used for economic advancement (to secure contracts, participate in trade, obtain jobs), thus promoting the idea that membership in a religious organization brings prosperity.

Although cultural and religious forms and practices are varied, the worldview that underlies them is much more consistent. All cultural and religious forms stress that religions should remain the source of morality, that members should be devout, even intensely spiritual. In the view of most Nigerians, spiritual beings exist to transform them and their lives from bad to good, from poor to wealthy, from weak to powerful. Spiritual beings and priests should explain personal and collective tragedies, underdevelopment, and political decadence. A popular belief is that the forces of evil and darkness are overwhelming and they manifest themselves in sickness, poverty, disempowerment, and the failure of the country. Healing can come through religion by destroying all evil and negative forces. One way to know that evil has been conquered is to receive abundant blessings in wealth, property, advancement, and health.

Another area where Nigerian traditional beliefs and Islam and Christianity intersect is that of interpersonal relations and individual behavior. People are expected to be community oriented, that is, individuals must help members of the large kinship group and others. "It takes a whole village to raise a child," the Yoruba will say to underscore community responsibility. Respect for age and for religious and secular authorities is very important. Old age is celebrated: "where there is an old man, nothing goes wrong" is one popular adage. Within the household, the younger is supposed to respect the elder, and a wife is advised to obey her husband. Conflicts among family members are to be resolved through peaceful means. Individuals are expected to work hard, live modestly, train their children, and avoid troubles. However, the demands of modern occupations, the scarcity of resources, high unemploy-

ment rates, and state mismanagement have all contributed to the undermining of many of these age-old habits. Thus, as in most other countries, moral
lapses, corruption, theft, and violence challenge the accepted worldview.

INDIGENOUS RELIGIONS

Like all religions, indigenous religions encompass beliefs about the existence and role of God in the origins and welfare of the universe, society,
individuals, and the environment. In Nigeria, each religion is an intelligent
combination of the worship of many spiritual beings and the veneration of
ancestors and ancestresses. The religions also have systems of rituals that
commemorate the relationship between people, unseen forces, and historical
events. Religions help to overcome many failures and obstacles to self-
actualization by promoting social cohesion in the lineage and the larger community.

Indigenous religions are virtually innumerable in Nigeria where the
boundaries of the community, village, or language group are also those of
the religion. Even within the same society, households may alter the mode
of worship to suit their own preferences. Not only are practices different
from one place to another, but there is no attempt to strive for institutional
consistency or to create a single holy book that priests can read and interpret.
Indigenous religions are localized, confined to a specific ethnic group, place,
or aspect of natural phenomenon.

However, indigenous religions are based on a number of essential, common assumptions. They include beliefs in God, gods, and ancestors; cults
(that is, the worship of gods and goddesses); secret societies comprised mainly
of men from different wards and occupations that enforce law and order;
and powerful witches who can destroy individuals and communities.

Religion constitutes the most important body of ideas in the community.
Not all ideas are religious, as is to be expected, but a shared philosophy of
life and vision of society are part of what the community defines as its religious ideas. These beliefs explain the origins of human beings and groups
and of life's intangible features.

Indigenous religions also explain the relations between human beings, the
various gods, and the Supreme God. It can be argued that God and gods are
invented in the images of man and worldly institutions but invested with
power far beyond that of man and addressed as heavenly bodies superior to
the most powerful of kings. They have the ability, if properly worshiped, to
bestow all that human beings desire.

In addition to the abstract, indigenous religions also deal with the verifiable, the visible. Religion serves as the source of power of chiefs and kings, the explanation and foundation of secular political authority. Sources of traditional power are ultimately connected to religion and access to some kind of ritual superiority.

The most important activities in public life, festivals, celebrations, ritual performance, and the various ceremonies connected with rites of passage, all have religious undertones. People are brought together in large gatherings focused by religion, be it the Igbo yam festival or the annual masquerade of the Yoruba. The transition from one season or moment to another is also marked by ceremony.

The following examples indicate that religious forms, beliefs, and practices are many-fold, as they are shaped by different ethnic and social groups and power structures. The Yoruba in the southwest, a large group that believes in the power of kings and chiefs, highly urbanized and socially stratified, are looked at first. The Igbo, traditionally more democratic with village-oriented communities, are considered next, and the third example is drawn from the minority Kalabari group in the Niger Delta.

Yoruba Religion

Among the best known of African indigenous religions is that of the Yoruba, a group united by their language, a belief in Oduduwa as their ancestor, and Ile-Ife as their original homeland. Indeed, many legends make Ile-Ife the origin of humankind and civilization.

Yoruba religion explains that the world was created by Olodumare, the Supreme God, who used Oduduwa as an agent. In this creation myth, Oduduwa founded the world and the Yoruba people.

Oduduwa is a religious figure associated with power, used to legitimize the emergence of dynasties represented by kings and kingdoms and to describe the political constitution of the Yoruba. The sixteen early Yoruba kingdoms are treated in historical tradition as having been founded by his sixteen children, all princes who migrated out of Ile-Ife to establish political dominance in different parts of the Yoruba country. Princes must derive their legitimacy to govern and their claim to power through a connection with Oduduwa and Ile-Ife. This is a powerful political charter that excludes a majority of the populace from a position of royalty and links the acquisition of power to God.

The Yoruba have constructed a hierarchy of spiritual forces, similar to their political hierarchy which gives immense power to kings, then chiefs, then lineage heads, with ordinary people at the very bottom. In this hierarchy,

God is the supreme deity with the ultimate power, the creator of the universe, the final judge.

Below God is a plethora of gods and goddesses, the *orisa*. There is a god for most material items and nonmaterial ideas; for instance, Osun and Oya are river goddesses, Sango is the god of thunder, Ogun is the god of iron. There are major gods, such as Ogun, and there are many local ones below them, associated with lineages, towns, or geographical features like hills, rivers, or trees. Gods are also associated with occupations—for instance, blacksmiths worship Ogun, the god of iron; traders in some places worship Aje, the god of wealth.

A worshiper may be devoted to one but is obligated to worship a number of others as well. For example, a devotee of a local god, Okebadan in the city of Ibadan, could also have Sango as his principal god. Sango requires him to worship Esu, the god of energy and crossroads. The worshiper joins others in the celebration of their own gods and can be found playing a prominent role in the Ogun festival. Most people venerate their ancestors with sacrifices and prayer and participate in the masquerade festivals that bring the ancestors back to life. No worshiper can see the entire complex of the religion, as he or she deals only with a small part of a larger spectrum.

The religious calendar is congested, as each god demands its sacrifices, rituals, annual ceremonies, and other activities. The Yoruba pantheon is both large and complex, and personal success requires the ability to negotiate it. The gods and their demands appear too many for one person to satisfy, but in practice, the worshipers are clever. The individual has the opportunity to make choices, although he or she is expected to worship his or her lineage god, to worship *ori* (destiny, as symbolized by the head) and venerate ancestors. When the gods disappoint, the worshiper can pledge allegiance to another, or merely add a new god to already worshiped ones. A worshiper can even get angry with a god, and burn or throw away its idols in order to create new ones that may bring better fortune. Certain emergencies may call for more attention to one god instead of another. For instance, war and violent situations will privilege the worship of Ogun, the god of iron; prolonged rainfall, thunderstorms, and lightning will privilege Sango; if rivers overflow and floods are expected, this is the time for Oya, the river goddess.

The priests, worshipers, gods, spirits, ancestors, God, indeed, the entire cosmology is united by Ifa, the divination system based on the interpretation of the verses of *odu*, a large body of religious, social, and philosophical knowledge. Ifa prescribes the god to worship, the sacrifices to make, the rituals and ceremonies to perform. Ifa is a divination system. Ifa has an answer to most problems. The *babalawo*, the Ifa priest and diviner, is a skilled interpreter of *odu* who knows the verses needed to solve the problems posed by his clients. He can foretell the future and divine for an individual, a lineage, and indeed a whole town. The worldview of destiny, the need to satisfy the gods and ancestors, and the possibility of preventing future problems make divination the most popular and perhaps intense aspect of Yoruba religion.

The *babalawo* is a "master of secrets," a storehouse of knowledge, a psychologist and historian. Like the gods, he can resolve some emotional problems. He can seek the means to overcome the power of evil, witchcraft, and sickness. As many clients are worried by the practical problems of poverty, the *babalawo* can advise them about occupations that will bring future success or a trading project that will end in profit. To divine, the *babalawo* uses a set of objects that acquire meaning when an *odu* becomes associated with them. Ultimately, the *babalawo* worships Orunmila, the god of Ifa, for its wisdom and magical power.

Igbo Religion

The Igbo believe in Chukwu, the Supreme God, who has various messengers such as the sun, sky, and earth. Like other Nigerian groups, the Igbo believe in spirits of earth and fertility and in patron gods of some occupations such as metalworking. Land is venerated through a system of religious beliefs known as *ala*, which rewards and punishes people according to their behavior. Wishes for prosperity, long life, health, productive marriages, good harvests, and a peaceful afterlife form the core demands of worshipers.

The Igbo also believe in the power of ancestors, as do many other Nigerian groups. The ancestor behaves like a spirit, with a permanent presence among the living: he or she is an onlooker, giving rewards or punishment according to the behavior of the living. Ancestors can be reincarnated as new babies to further enhance their presence. Each person produces another generation through reincarnation. One may reincarnate to repeat an old behavior or to correct the lapses of an earlier life.

Priests perform a variety of religious functions. One is to administer oaths, sanctioned by ancestors. The *ofor*, the symbol of oath making, strikes fear in people who believe that evil may follow their misdeeds or transgressions. There is also a specialized group of diviners who interpret the oracles when they are consulted by individuals seeking help. A community, too, may need answers to environmental problems (for example, why there is not adequate rain), or social issues (why young people take to vices). Guidance from diviners may be sought to settle disputes or identify criminals when thefts are reported.

In spite of the fact that Igbo villages are scattered and spread over different areas, the Igbo have been successfully united by religion. In addition to their common beliefs, a major historical phenomenon in the southeast in the pre-colonial period was the emergence of the oracle system (the "long juju") based at Arochukwu that united traders and people. This is yet another example of how religion serves economic and political purposes and responds to change. Arochukwu is in eastern Igboland on the border between the Igbo and the Ibibio. During the seventeenth century, the Aro people established a flourishing trading network with their neighbors and among their many colonies in various areas. At the root of this success was the ability of the Aro to turn the oracle system into a source of power. Aro priests were consulted far and wide on a variety of issues, including the ways to overcome problems and resolve conflicts between individuals and communities.

Kalabari Religion

The Kalabari are part of the larger Ijo minority group in the Niger Delta. They live in many fishing villages and are united by subscribing to a similar culture, rather than claiming, as the Yoruba do, descent from one ancestor. A village is governed by an elder, in cooperation with the senior age-grades. An age-grade is an association of people born during the same period, dividing society along age and generational lines. The Niger Delta region was drawn into the trans-Atlantic trade and became famous for supplying palm products during the nineteenth century. The connection with international trade brought not just wealth but social changes and conflicts among entrepreneurs who wanted to use their money to acquire political power. Ijo villages and towns competed, some rising and others falling in significance.

For the Kalabari, there are two forms of existence. The first is *oje*, the material world, the physical reality that can be seen. The second and more important is the spiritual order, known as *teme*. *Teme* is divided into layers or hierarchies of spiritual forces. On the very top are the creation gods, followed by the lesser gods including ancestors ("water people") and local heroes. Gods and ancestors have their role to play in the existence of the living and they are contacted through specialized religious agencies. The spiritual beings that the people worship the most are not those at the top of the hierarchy, like the Supreme Being, but those below, the "water people" and village heroes. Because the majority of the population is connected with the fishing industry, many religious practices focus on the "water people."

Individuals worship and contact spiritual beings for a variety of reasons and through different agencies. The gods are not necessarily easy to reach, as they are remote from the world. To contact them, the worshiper has to make offerings and invocations and wait for the gods to respond, which may be immediately or much later. Individuals may seek contact with various village heroes or "water people" looking for the one that will answer their wishes.

Intermediary agents, known as masquerades and organized by a society of the dead, the Ekine, are used to reach the heroes and ancestors. The masquerades communicate with the gods and ancestors, relaying people's wishes to the gods and dramatizing for the worshipers the gods' assumed habits and behavior.

Kalabari religion also has its priests and priestesses who serve as intermediaries with the spiritual beings. They can reach the "water people" and village heroes through "possession." A possessed priest or priestess acquires the voice of a god and speaks to the people as that god.

Indigenous Religions and Change

Indigenous religions have survived for centuries and in the modern world they are often labeled as "traditional" to connote longevity or pertinence to the past, two assumptions that are misleading.

All religions respond to change, including indigenous ones. New prophets and religious leaders can appear on the scene; new movements can be born; new ideas can influence the interpretation of religious knowledge. Indigenous religions have responded to the historical changes of the twentieth century, to technology and to foreign influence. For example, the Yoruba Ifa has accommodated new verses that recognize the technical changes of the era. Some verses contain words such as gun, mirror, foreign liquor, and references to other religions. New elements from other religions can be added to the indigenous through a process of accretion that does not undermine the overall belief system. Ideas can expand and practices can be modified to suit specific situations.

Indigenous religions have had to respond to the growing influence of the two universalist religions of Islam and Christianity and to the subsequent loss of millions of worshipers. Nevertheless, indigenous religions have interacted with both Islam and Christianity in many creative ways. The intensity of the Christian mode of worship in Nigeria, with the use of songs and drums, has been attributed to the influence of traditional religion. The emphasis on preaching against evil forces, witches, and enemies, so common in many Pentecostal and Islamic organizations, is a carryover from traditional belief systems.

There are also cases where indigenous religions have modified their practices and modes of thought in response to Islam and Christianity. For instance, many now stress the role of the Supreme God, even when previously the emphasis was on the lesser gods and forces. In the north, where Islam has been so successful and so widespread, the ancient Bori spiritual cult has transformed itself in order to survive. In pre-Islamic days, members possessed by the spirit could bring good fortune or cast spells on people. As Islam consolidated itself, the Bori cult adopted some spirits that were given Islamic names and functions. It has become a cult dominated by women with power that men also respect. The ability of indigenous religions to incorporate new elements is due to their openness to other religious influences: gods and ancestors can be infused with new meanings and functions derived from other agencies and ideas; the divine representative of another religion or the new religion itself can be added to the pantheon of gods and given a status within it, as part of the established hierarchy.

Aspects of divination, charm making, and the consultation of priests to solve welfare and health problems have not only endured, they have been integrated into Islam and Christianity. A number of Muslim priests combine aspects of indigenous divination with that of Islam to prescribe and to foretell the future. Both Islam and Christianity combine many forms of religious beliefs, borrowing many aspects from indigenous religions in order to appeal to millions of Nigerians. Various elements of "primordial cultures" have survived, to the extent that both Islam and Christianity seek accommodation with them. For instance, Christianity has been forced to recognize that a man can have two or more wives as well as a strong Christian faith.

The present-day reality of indigenous religions in many communities is manifest in the continuing worship of gods, in kingship rituals and influence, secret societies, masquerades, diviners, healers, and witch doctors.

ISLAM

Islam began to penetrate different parts of northern Nigeria from the eleventh century onward. Between the fourteenth and the eighteenth centuries, it reached different cities in the north through the activities of long-distance traders and Islamic clerics from the Western Sudan and North Africa. As the traders moved from one location to another, they promoted Islam and used it to build trust with their clients, many of whom had been drawn to the religion. Communities of learned men, the *Ulama*, emerged in different parts of the north, and they persuaded chiefs and kings to adopt Islam. Until the seventeenth century, Islam was essentially a religion limited to merchants and the political class. It expanded in the eighteenth century, gaining ground in more cities and among other segments of the population such as the urban-based Fulani.

Islam became a religion of the masses during the nineteenth century with the successful jihad led by Uthman dan Fodio. This militant movement accomplished far more than traders and missionaries had done in the previous century. The jihad reformed the practice of Islam by abolishing a number of pre-Islamic habits; new emirs (kings) were devout Muslims; and populations conquered by the jihadists were compelled to accept the religion.

Islam began to spread to the southwest slowly from the eighteenth century onward, mainly through the activities of Hausa traders. In northern Yorubaland, Islam spread partly because of the dan Fodio jihad that established its southernmost emirate at Ilorin. Traders and preachers from Ilorin went to other parts of Yorubaland to spread Islam, but they had to compete with Christian evangelists. In the end, the Yoruba are divided by religion, but without many conflicts, as Muslims and Christians have to coexist not only in the same city, but in the same household as well. Although Ilorin, Iwo, Osogbo, and Ibadan have become cities with predominantly Islamic populations, they are not without large Christian communities. With the exception of Ilorin, Islam has not become the "communal religion" as it has in many cities in the north.

Islam gained a widespread following during the twentieth century in the southwest and added to its adherents in the north. Various Islamic organizations devote considerable resources to evangelization. Conversion to Islam has been incessant and, by and large, has occurred through peaceful means, with preachers and missionaries as agents. Small communities have had to accept Islam because it integrates them into a larger world of ideas and commerce. Islam can create both regional and global opportunities for communities that borrow the political ideas of others to reshape their own societies, participate in long-distance trade, or change their worldview.

Personal conversion is much more common, as Islamic preachers engage people on a one-on-one basis. New converts can calculate benefits, which may include the opportunity to adopt Arabic, or another important language like Hausa, and experiment with different or new lifestyles associated with the religion.

Devout Muslims hold to five important ideals: a belief in Allah (God), and the prophet Mohammad as His messenger; five daily prayers at specific times; almsgiving (*zakat*) to the poor and the needy; fasting; and pilgrimages to the holy city of Mecca.

Muslims belong to different strands and brotherhoods or *sufi* movements. There are two major brotherhoods, the Tijaniyya and the Qadiriyya orders (the *tariqa*). The Tijaniyya pray with their arms crossed while Qadiriyya hold their arms at their sides. The Qadiriyya brotherhood is much older and it has spread widely in northern Nigeria since the nineteenth century. Qadiriyya members are expected to read and engage in spiritual pursuits in order to understand Allah. There is no end to intellectual pursuits and clerics see Islam as a lifetime pursuit of religious dedication. The Tijaniyya was introduced during the nineteenth century and it places less attention on intellectual pursuits: salvation is possible through action, commitment to the faith, and devout practices. There are also organizations, known as anti-*sufi* movements, opposed to these two brotherhoods on the basis of doctrinal disagreements.

The Ahmadiyya movement, of Indian origin, is popular in the southwest where it has contributed to the development of secular education. A split in the organization in 1923 produced the Ansar-ud-Deen Society, which has been equally active in education. These and many other organizations always maintain that they should not be compared to Christian sects, because Islamic beliefs are more consistent and there is only one holy book, the Qur'an, written in its original Arabic language.

The Enduring Legacy of Islam

Almost half of the Nigerian population is Muslim, a testimony to the success of this religion in spreading over a long period and maintaining its hold on the people. Conversion is owed not just to the ability of traders, missionaries, and jihadists but also to the prestige of the religion. Conversion provides access to literacy, language, a new ideology, and contact with an agency of modernization. Many ideas existing in indigenous culture (especially in ethics, in a supreme deity, and in the power of dreams and charms) are similar to those of Islam, thus making the transition less painful than it might otherwise be.

Once Islam is accepted in any community, it brings great changes. Unlike indigenous religions, it has its holy book, the Qur'an, which promotes literacy and documentation. The very idea of literacy is in and of itself a revolution. Thousands who did not read and write previously now keep records and send and receive correspondence from near and far. In this way, Arabic has spread as a language to different parts of Nigeria.

Qur'anic education is an important aspect of life in all Muslim communities. Islamic education is broad, exposing students at several levels to the Qur'an, religious history, Islamic law, and Islamic social practices. At the lowest level, students memorize the first ten chapters of the Qur'an and are introduced to reading and writing. In the "tablet school" stage, parents send their children to a neighborhood teacher (the *malam*) who receives no salary but occasional gifts. In the next stage, the "law school," students are introduced to Arabic grammar, literature, law, and elementary sciences. Here the focus is on *fiqh* (Islamic knowledge), *seerah* (the history of the prophet Mohammad), and the *sunnah* (the practices of the prophet). Dedicated students can proceed to advanced schools to specialize in certain branches of Islamic education. The system banishes illiteracy and promotes Islamic education, but its repetitive nature limits its creativity and growth.

Traditional Qur'anic schools that consist of students studying under a teacher remain popular, although Islamic education is now part of secular education from primary to university levels. Nigerian Muslims attend Western-type schools and train in all the modern occupations. The established interaction between Nigerian Islamic teachers and their counterparts in other countries continues through meetings, letters, and seminars. Islam has many social dimensions. It is very much opposed to the consumption of alcohol, thus restricting the sale of alcohol in Islamic areas, and it discourages gambling as well. It is not opposed to polygyny, and married women can be kept isolated from public view in purdah (seclusion). The education of women in secular schools has become very common, although this does not mean that educated women reject Islam or its expectations of their role in society and households.

Islam is used to promote interactions among members of the same occupation. Long-distance traders take advantage of shared beliefs to create flourishing colonies in many places and to deny non-Muslims credit and the opportunity of bulk buying. In southern cities, Islam is one source of unity for northern migrants who live in separate neighborhoods known as Sabon Gari or "Hausa Quarters."

Since Nigeria is part of a larger Islamic world, both at informal and formal levels, Islam has an impact on its politics. It is a member of the Organization of Islamic Conference, an international organization that discusses matters affecting Islamic countries. The brotherhoods are transnational, with leaders in several countries. Imams, secular teachers, and other professionals have been recruited from Egypt, Saudi Arabia, Pakistan, Indonesia, and India to teach in northern Nigerian schools. Traditional Islamic schools continue to recruit teachers from other Islamic countries to give advanced instruction, while Nigerians also travel abroad for additional training.

Within the country, Islam is national and transethnic. Muslims are united in pan-Nigerian organizations (for example, the Jama'atu Nasril Islam[1] and

the Islamic Council for Nigeria) that protect their interests. They come together in the pilgrimage and religious festivals, notably the Eid el-fitr, which
comes at the end of the Ramadan fasting, and the celebration of the birth of
the Prophet Mohammad.[2]

The pilgrimage to Saudi Arabia is one of the ultimate ambitions of Nigerian Muslims. It enables them to renew their faith, demonstrate their importance and success to friends and relations, interact with Muslims from
other parts of the world, tour holy sites in Mecca and Medina, and pay respect
to the memory of the founder of their religion. The number of pilgrims is
high every year, and the government has struggled to keep the number to a
manageable size to avoid overburdening scarce transport facilities. Pilgrims
are recognized in public by their symbols, notably a "Mecca cap," and are
entitled to a special title (Alhaji for men, Alhaja for women), a much sought-
after privilege. The pilgrimage creates a lasting bond among Muslims in the
country—thousands proclaim their faith on their return, and sponsor projects of Islamic revival.

The best known aspect of the impact that Islam has had on Nigeria is the
spread of the Shari'a and the demand by a number of Islamic leaders for its
application in different states of the federation. Christians are very much
opposed to this demand, fearing that it will lead to the imposition of Islam
as a state religion. The Shari'a is an Islamic code of law administered by
trained clerics and derived from the Qur'an, the Hadith (containing some
of the accounts of the life and statements of the prophet Mohammad), and
the Ijma (the consensus of opinion among Islamic leaders).

Islam is a missionary religion whose preachers and teachers devote much
of their time to conversion. They travel from place to place seeking converts
and establishing mosques and schools. They put to effective use all the new
transport systems, notably the railways, throughout the country in an effort
to spread their religion.

At various moments, Islamic leaders and their followers are forced to discuss the need to purify Islam, either because non-Islamic practices have been
added to it or people are not as devout as they wish. The discussions often
become contentious and public. In the past, nomadic people and rural Muslims have criticized the corruption of Islam by city-dwellers. Purification
movements can emerge to fight city-dwellers and nominal Muslims by ini-
tiating a jihad. There are austere and puritanical groups among Muslims who
criticize the excesses of city life and the corruption of power.

There are also movements that simply desire progress for Muslims and
others. Social justice, fairness, political empowerment, and corruption-free

application of the law have driven purification movements to elaborate their criticisms of society. These movements, emerging at different times and with popular leaders, are part of the vibrant culture of Islam.

A major expectation in the purification movements is that a Mahdi—the last reformer—will appear one day to "clean" Nigeria of all its problems, reform the world, and unite all Muslims before the end of the world and the Day of Judgment. This idea of millennialism has persisted for a long while as part of the history of the growth of Islam in the country. During the nineteenth century, many Muslims believed that dan Fodio, the leader of the jihad, was the Mahdi. He denied this but said that he was a forerunner to the Mahdi. At various periods, an influential leader has been labeled as the expected Mahdi or one is said to be in the making. Anticolonial and/or anti-Western millennial prophets have emerged to condemn the impact of foreign influences, the acceptance of secularism and/or so-called infidels in government, and the corruption of Islam in Muslim communities.

Nigeria is undergoing an Islamic resurgence. More and more Muslims are demanding their rights and privileges in educational and public matters. Clerics and leading Muslims want the Shari'a and are even ready to fight for it. A growing movement of Shiites want a theocratic government or something similar to the Iranian system under Ayatollah Khomeini. Less radical organizations want the purification of Islam and the promotion of non-Western culture. Whether they are "fundamentalists" or "modernists," many Muslims turn to their religion to advocate an alternative path of development for the country, which they regard as moving in the wrong direction.

CHRISTIANITY

European relations with the Nigerian area began in the fifteenth century, dominated by commercial interests. Unlike Muslim traders, European traders had no interest in converting Nigerians to Christianity and dealt only with the groups that facilitated trade, notably the political and merchant classes. Early attempts by the few missionaries to make converts in places like Benin, Warri, and the Delta were not successful. The success story of Christianity began in the nineteenth century, after the abolition of the slave trade. Many liberated Africans were converted and many of the new converts became "native agents" who worked with foreign missions to spread Christianity among their own people. Conversion in the early years was motivated by a desire not just to preach the gospel but to redeem Africans from their so-called barbarism and economic deprivations; to create a so-called industrial class that would produce for the market; and to produce a new elite that would be the agents of change.

These ideals have not only shaped the outcome of the missions but have influenced many aspects of Nigerian Christianity. Christianity has always been accompanied by Western education. Indeed, the missionaries pioneered the formal Western educational system in Nigeria. Originally, the aims of the educational system were limited. The missionaries wanted Nigerians to be able to read the Bible and they trained them to do so. Next, they wanted them to be able to become "industrial workers" who could manufacture small items and craft products, and possess sufficient vocational skills to work as bricklayers, carpenters, painters, and so forth.

Education was a great attraction to the converts. Some among them became so dedicated that they became missionaries themselves. A few became distinguished church workers, and one became a famous bishop and one of the country's modern heroes (Ajayi Crowther). As knowledge of new occupations spread, the most common path to them was secular education, and those who could mobilize resources traveled abroad for advanced training in medicine, law, nursing, and other professions.

Cities close to the coast, notably Lagos, Badagri, Warri, and Abeokuta, were the first to take advantage of mission work, as a number of their people accepted Christianity and Western education. The Yoruba in the southwest took the lead, but others in the Niger Delta and the east soon followed. Christian missionaries were numerous and aggressive in their evangelization projects. The early missionaries included Anglicans and Methodists, followed by Catholics. They competed vigorously among one another, mainly for converts, as in the case of the Anglicans against the Catholics in the east.

Slowly, mission work spread to the hinterland. The greatest expansion came in the first half of the twentieth century, as Christianity expanded throughout the south and the greater part of the middle belt. The missionaries supported the British conquest, although there were cases of tension between them and the colonial officers, especially over the extension of Christianity to Islamic areas. Many missionary agencies wanted to convert the Muslims, but the colonial officers did not encourage them to penetrate the north as they would have wanted. British officers also held in contempt the educated Nigerians trained by the missionaries, accusing the educated Nigerians of demanding too many privileges in power and jobs, wanting to imitate European lifestyles in inappropriate ways, and taking an anticolonial stand.

Christianity recorded a phenomenal growth, spreading to many parts of

the role of prayer and the Holy Spirit, and to respond in various ways to indigenous customs. They promote a puritanical approach and insist that members must help one another in their various businesses. They believe in emotional worship, faith healing, spirit possession, and above all, prophecy. Some also borrow ideas from American evangelical and Pentecostal churches in fund-raising, open revivals, and television evangelism.

Like Islam, Christianity has become both radical and intense. New churches emerge each year; open revivals are now part of the cultural landscape; people place hope in prayer to bring change to themselves and the nation at a time of great economic difficulty; and many people devote considerable time and money to church activities.

Like Muslims, Christians have formed associations to defend their religion. The most important has been the Christian Association of Nigeria, which makes statements from time to time on the management of the country, organizes rallies and protests against Muslim actions, fights to prevent the use of the Shari'a, and raises funds to rebuild churches damaged in religious riots.

RELIGION AND POLITICS

Religion is connected with politics and social change in Nigeria. Islamic and Christian leaders condemn the country's political lapses, denounce corruption and negative social changes, and call on devout members to avoid moral excesses. In the face of political and economic decay, religious leaders have been creative in seeking the commitment of their members to their faith. Religion has been used to explain the Nigerian reality of poverty and political problems. The hand of God is seen in all events considered positive, such as the death of Abacha in June 1998 after all opposition forces had failed to dislodge him from power. Nigerians have turned to religious ideas to explain virtually all the country's problems.

The differential impact of both religions has created tension and conflicts. The south has used its early advantage in Western education to dominate the modern sectors of the economy and to keep expanding its school system. Some southern leaders express the view that the north has slowed down the progress of the country with its conservatism. The north, on the other hand, argues that the rush to modernize is at the expense of Islam and tradition.

There is also a growing culture of religious violence, either to put religious ideas and cosmologies to practical purpose or to extend them to the civic arena. Since the 1980s, there have been many incidents of violent clashes between Muslims and Christians, notably in such northern cities as Kaduna and Kano. The riots have led to the loss of thousands of lives and damages to religious buildings, commercial stores, and residential buildings.[3] Both Islam and Christianity have acquired political significance in a variety of ways. Politicians have manipulated religious constituencies to obtain and consolidate power.

Of all the divisive issues, the most important are secularism and Islamic law. In the 1976 draft of the presidential constitution the country is defined thus: "Nigeria is one and indivisible sovereign Republic, secular, democratic and social."[4] This appears simple enough, but the Muslims objected to the inclusion of the "secular" and fought successfully to remove it. While the Christians see nothing wrong in it, the Muslims argue that it gives the impression that the state will ignore religion and that morality will be based on nonreligious traditions. Muslims always contend that secularism is alien to Islam, which does not divorce politics from religion.

Many Muslim leaders want to establish Shari'a courts in most states of the federation. A few even go further to say that Islamic law should form the legal basis of the entire country. As far as Christians are concerned, secular laws are more important and they see Muslims as nursing a desire to transform the country into an Islamic state. While there is now a Federal Shari'a Court of Appeals, the extension of the Shari'a to all legal matters at the state level remains a point of contention and an issue that may create serious religious tension.

OTHER RELIGIOUS MOVEMENTS

New religious movements are numerous in Nigeria, similar to those in other countries. A few operate in the margins and are not well-known. Several are very eclectic in nature, combining many religions to create something new for a small congregation, such as the Sat Guru Marahaji (the "perfect master") that combines Hinduism with Islam and Christianity.

These movements have some major differences from Islam and Christianity. They have gurus that are regarded as prophets and role models. The gurus vary in what they say: some preach the acquisition of wealth, others moderate living. The gurus claim some divine attributes and are powerful within their communities. However, they do not deny their members the opportunity to grow spiritually and minimize the role of an intermediary in their relations with God. Islamic and Christian leaders describe members of many of the new religious movements as "pagans" who worship strange gods, and their gurus are considered confused. These movements and gurus certainly have a different orientation, but they do not regard themselves as paganistic, believing that their Christian and Muslim critics have corrupted their own religions and have limited access to God.

The movements that believe in magic and the occult connect very easily to indigenous views and gain the approval of those who are not deeply committed to Islam or Christianity and those who want to combine these world religions with something else.

Of the growing movements, those that can be described within the general category of "spiritual science" are probably the most important. They resemble cults in American society. However, in Nigeria, many of them reject the label of "cult," as members can become targeted by the state due to all sorts of unfounded allegations. In the context of indigenous religions, a cult describes the worship of and beliefs in god in a positive manner. It is better to use the various names that these organizations call themselves, and to see them not as cults with negative connotations, as they are often portrayed in Western media.

These movements are numerous, they are diverse in their practices, they follow various procedures in their membership, and they relate to the public in different ways. Nevertheless, many of them share several common features. For instance, they seek spiritual answers in pseudoscience and through very diverse scientific methods: the occult (the discovery of the secret and esoteric); metaphysics (knowledge through reason, not necessarily based on logic); mysticism (the use of intuition and illumination to reach or manipulate spiritual forces); and psychic activities (the ability to overcome physical forces).

Members of these groups claim that they are more spiritually fulfilled than practitioners of other religions who are unable to understand their practices, and that esotericism is an integral aspect of the religious experience. In some organizations, the members claim that they have ecstatic episodes. Their leaders claim that they have spiritual power and they rely on methods that manipulate hidden forces to reveal messages in worship and consultations with members. A combination of knowledge of physical and human experiences, knowledge of the cosmos, and spiritual insights define the procedures of some groups.

There are groups that claim to be Christian or semi-Christian, drawing ideas from the Bible, Buddhism, occultism, and yoga. One example is the Aetherius Society (AS), which was founded in Britain in 1955 by a medium. Members, mostly men, emphasize spiritualism and claim to possess the ability to communicate with beings in other universes. Other organizations with syncretic elements include the Superet Light Mission, the Institute of Religious Science, and the Church of New Jerusalem.

The movements reflect the impact of foreign ideas on Nigeria, as all of them have their origins outside the country. Some come from the United States and other Western countries; these include Rosicrucianism and the Church of the New Jerusalem. Others come from Asia or eastern Europe, including the Unification Church founded by Rev. Sun Myung Moon of Korea, the Eckankar, the International Society of Krishna Consciousness (Hare Krishna), the Subud Brotherhood from Indonesia, the Grail Movement from India, and the Tensho-kotai-jingu-Kyo from Japan. A few Nigerians are now indigenizing them, as in the case of the Holy Order of Science and the Esom Fraternity Company. One illustration should suffice to show their impact on Nigerian society, although these movements are very different from one another in their beliefs and practices.

The Rosicrucian movement has drawn from various traditions to define its beliefs: Egyptian occultism, Freemasonry, parapsychology, Theosophy, and Western magic. The most popular Rosicrucian group in Nigeria is the Ancient and Mystical Order of the Rosae Crucis (AMORC), with its symbols drawn from ancient Egypt. AMORC was founded in New York in 1915, as an esoteric fraternal organization. It spread to Nigeria and has continued to gain in membership there.

The headquarters is in Lagos with branches in different parts of the country. Members in areas without an AMORC office can receive literature and attend occasional meetings in other places. AMORC proclaims itself as an order of learners, a cultural fraternity of mystical philosophers whose purpose is to "master life," to control both the physical and spiritual realms. For AMORC, religion is not necessary for this, but a set of philosophical tenets can solve problems and guide one in attaining self-fulfillment and, ultimately, mastering psychic power and cosmic consciousness.

Spiritual activities include readings, meetings with fellow members, and public programs. The philosophical documents are sent from San Jose, California, as courses for study and reflection. Established members organize public lectures, broadcast the activities of AMORC on local television, and hold a weekly ceremony at the official lodge for all members.

The emphasis on reading raises an important point about the connection between literacy and spirituality. Other movements such as the Grail and Christian Science expect members to read. While the majority of Nigerians are thus excluded, those with the ability to engage the literature derive considerable benefits. They are able to rise within the spiritual hierarchies, reaching the highest and most sacred levels without a mediator. Spiritual knowledge can be acquired through self-discipline, an empowering individualist ethos. In Islam and Christianity, the priesthood does not yield this power to the congregation; these other movements offer more concrete means of self-empowerment.

AMORC in some ways resembles a secret society, and this has drawn serious opposition from Islamic and Christian quarters. The burial of members is carried out with secret rites that resemble magic. Discussions in weekly ceremonies are confidential. There are different grades in the spiritual hierarchy, and each is marked by the demonstration of esoteric knowledge.

The Masonic character of AMORC and similar organizations has not been a great disadvantage in recruiting and retaining members. Secret societies are not alien to Nigeria, and there are hundreds of indigenous societies and Freemasonries. AMORC provides an opportunity to build a network with members drawn from different occupations and different parts of the country.

In spite of the established nature of Islam and Christianity, other movements will continue to draw converts, although not in very large numbers. The movements also have their appeal for those fascinated by small congregations, the possession of secret knowledge, and alternative religious traditions. They meet the religious needs of people alienated by other religions or wanting to combine their inherited religions with new ones. Most are converted from other religions, mainly Christianity. Converts from indigenous religions are fascinated with the occult aspect, which is similar to their own practice of divination. As a member grows in spirituality, he can become his own occultist, in full control of his consciousness and free from the power of professional priests or religious leaders. The individualism embodied in these practices and the self-actualization they bring may be the magnet that draws young people and city-dwellers into these movements.

Various religious traditions thrive in Nigeria, but the dominant ones are Islam and Christianity. Indigenous religions have survived to some degree but are threatened by a host of factors: they are under attack by Muslims and Christians; they are not well suited to the new economic and political milieu; Western education and science are undermining some of their assumptions; and their priests do not have the money to compete with other religions. Nevertheless, they have been modified in creative ways, and some aspects (for example, healing, divination, belief in witchcraft) have influenced the ways Christian and Islamic organizations package their messages.

Spiritual science movements continue to grow but they remain marginal. Members can develop their spiritual and mystical power, meditate, and hope to attain the highest order in the movement.

Christianity continues to expand its frontiers and to adapt itself to the

Nigerian environment. Established, mission-oriented churches (for example, the Catholics and Anglicans) remain the largest. However, those who find their worship rather dull have the options of attending prayer meetings, fellowships, and revivalist movements and joining a host of independent churches that emphasize prophecy, the power of healing and prayer, and spirit possession.

Islam, too, continues to grow. Its members in power try to protect it or argue for the recognition of Islamic rights, such as the Shari'a, at the national level. The pilgrimage to Mecca remains popular, and Islamic countries such as Iran, Saudi Arabia, and Libya are interested in developing cultural and political relations with Islamic communities in Nigeria.

While all these religions compete, their members also interact with one another, and the political leaders hope for a peaceful plural society. An ecumenical union seems impossible, but tolerance and respect for different traditions will continue to sustain mutual coexistence. Religions also affect other aspects of the culture as will be discussed in the following chapters.

NOTES

1. "Society for the Victory of Islam."

2. See Chapter 7.

3. See Toyin Falola, *Violence in Nigeria: The Crisis of Religious Politics and Secular Ideologies* (Rochester, NY: University of Rochester Press, 1998).

4. *Reports of the Constitution Drafting Committee*, Vol. II, Federal Ministry of Information, Lagos (1976), 36.

3

Literature and Media

Let me play with the whiteman's ways
Let me work with the blackman's brains
Dennis Osadebey, 1951

I accept it [that is, the Nobel Prize] as a tribute to the heritage of
African literature, which is very little known in the West. I regard
it as a statement of respect and acknowledgment of the long years
and centuries of denigration and ignorance of the heritage which
all of us have been trying to build.
Wole Soyinka, South, 1986

NIGERIANS have successfully turned their acquisition of Western education
and the English language to great advantage. Osadebey's poem says it all:
they will use Western infrastructures and technologies to communicate African ideas. No sooner did they begin to read and write than they established
newspapers of their own to capture events and communicate nationalist feelings. The media expanded from the 1950s onward, first with the establishment of the first television station, then, after independence, the birth of
additional television stations, newspapers, and magazines. When Wole Soyinka received the Nobel Prize for Literature in 1986, the first African to do
so, it marked a victory for Nigerian (and African) creative genius, the end of
a long road in modern intellectual history that began in the nineteenth cen-

tury, and the beginning of a new journey leading to the transformation of the continent.

To capture an extensive cultural terrain, we can speak of literatures both in Nigerian languages and in English. Orthographies have been developed for many indigenous languages and they have become vehicles to express ideas, document changes, and produce creative work. Inherited traditions in oral literature have survived as new talents circulate their unpublished ideas and others publish in local languages. Older written traditions in the Arabic and Ajami languages are not abandoned.

The most famous authors are those who write in English, since their works are connected to an international market. The most popular television dramas are in indigenous languages or pidgin, which is a combination of English and indigenous languages. This contradiction has generated a prolonged debate on the role of language in popular culture, which literary figures and the media depend upon to sustain themselves. Should African authors write primarily in their indigenous languages or in European ones? Meanwhile, they do both, yet the most visible writers remain those who use English because they have both a national and an international audience.

ORAL LITERATURE

All Nigerian ethnic groups had developed creative literature before the emergence of written languages and the arrival of Islam, Christianity, and Western education, and many aspects have survived to the present day despite the destructive impact of those new traditions. Some have become integrated with written literature, while many are now preserved in ethnographic and creative writings, videos, and audiocassettes.

Oral artistic expressions include a variety of genres: proverbs, songs, festivals, oral narratives, and others that describe and analyze creativity, values, traditions, and histories. They document and explain changes in culture and life. Performers chant, recite poems, create fiction. While oral literature entertains, it also reinforces existing values, seeks to transform values, and rationalizes institutions. The language of communication is rich, meant to excite and inspire the audience, and tales are transmitted from one generation to another, thereby preserving the most important genres and works.

Poetry is an important form of oral literature. Kings, chiefs, the wealthy, and families are celebrated in panegyrics that praise them and their ancestors. The *ojebe* poems among the Igbo praise those holding noble titles. The *kirari* among the Hausa honor their kings and entertain guests at weddings and other important ceremonies. Among the Yoruba, the *oriki* comprise an extensive body of verses of praise and descriptive names to eulogize kings, chiefs, families, ancestors, towns, and great individuals. To cite one example, when the king of Nupe, Etsu Bello, bought a car in 1918, a drummer composed a lengthy poem of praise, part of which reads thus:

On the day when *Etsu* Bello bought the motor-car,
The bottles of the glass-makers turned into red beads.
And the kernels of the gombara grass became necklaces.
Etsu Bello, who has horses, and who now has a car.

If praises are lavish, satirical song-poetry can make devastating comments on leaders, warriors, and ordinary citizens. Where the practice is fully developed, as among the Tiv, Urhobo, Igbo, Ijo, and Ibibio, it shows democracy at work, the power of literature to impact politics. Groups as well as individuals are subjected to intense scrutiny. Where the politics does not allow the artist much liberty, he or she can disguise criticism in rich metaphors and idioms. Some societies, such as the Tiv, organize public contests using satire, instead of wrestling, as a feuding device.

Poems can be about any subject and include abstract ideas. Trees, mountains, rivers, roads, and important animals all have poems composed for them. To cite one example from part of Yoruba folklore, whose author is anonymous but translated by E. L. Lasebikan in 1956:

Why do we grumble because a tree is bent,
When, in our streets, there are even men who are bent?
Why must we complain that the new moon is slanting?
Can any one reach the skies to straighten it?
Can't we see that some cocks have combs on their heads, but
     no plumes in their tails?
And some have plumes in their tails, but no claws on their toes.
And others have claws on their toes, but no power to crow?
He who has a head has no cap to wear, and he who has a cap
     has no head to wear it on.
He who has good shoulders has no gown to wear on them, and
     he who has the gown has no good shoulders to wear it
     on . . .
Good eaters have no food to eat, and great drinkers no wine to
     drink:
Wealth has many colors!

Different occupations have songs that celebrate their impact on society. The *ijala* among the Yoruba is a developed form of song among hunters.

The labor force and the products of labor have their songs devised to encourage hard work, to ensure cooperation, and praise favorable harvests.
Drinking ballads, maiden's songs, and children's songs are other examples of
light-hearted poetry. Equally common are elegies that mourn and celebrate
death and the passage of time.

There is a category of esoteric poetry associated with rituals and divina-
tions, which is harder for the uninitiated to learn and understand. Ritual
poems have the power to manipulate spiritual beings, prepare charms, harm
enemies, and attract good luck. This form necessitates an outstanding understanding of the environment and allows for the possibility of enhancing
the use of medicine and science.

Prose narratives are common and diverse, including a rather large body of
different forms: legends, myths, epics, and tales. Some are narrated as history,
others as fiction. One good example is the Ijo *Ozidi* saga that celebrates
heroes. All societies have hundreds of tales that preach morality, like those
associated with the tortoise and hare. Some societies have professional story-
tellers who preserve and creatively reinvent old tales while composing new
ones.

Various aspects of oral literature have become part of written literature
and offer enormous cultural resources upon which modern Nigeria depends
in building an identity and motivating its citizens.

LITERATURE IN ARABIC AND NIGERIAN LANGUAGES

The spread of Islam and the Arabic language has promoted writing, creative enterprises, and a successful education system. A group of scholars and
teachers, the *ulama*, devote time to learning and writing. Literature, usually
in verse, expresses critical views of society and political discontent. The most
successful works are associated with the leaders of the Islamic jihad of the
nineteenth century.

Uthman dan Fodio's works are part of the great literary heritage of Nigeria.
He was a gifted scholar who composed close to 500 poems in Arabic, Fulfulde, and Hausa and over twenty books in Arabic. Many authors followed
in his footsteps. His daughter, Nana Asma'u, composed seventeen poems;
his brother, Abdulahi, wrote about eight. Most of these poems are short and
copies are made from the originals by students and disciples of the authors
who recite them in sermons and at other gatherings. The books are much
longer and do not circulate as much as the poems, since they are harder to
copy. The subject matter of these writings is broad and relevant: including
detailed critiques of contemporary events, opinions on leaders, didactic sto-

ries, religious lessons, and debates on the role of the state, religion, and leadership. To give just one example, the following is the translation of a poem composed by dan Fodio about 200 years ago:

> Oh God, the Forgiver
> Forgive my sins [committed] during the night
> Forgive also the sins I committed in the daylight
> The soot of sins has taken root on me and sunk deep
> Mohammad's esteem shall surely keep me clean.

The jihad movement was led by radical intellectuals, which explains their emphasis on writing. These leaders and many of their followers until today belong to the Qadiriyya religious order that enjoins its members to read, write, meditate, and share ideas. Dan Fodio and all the leading men of the jihad had believed that spiritual fulfillment and scholarship are interlinked. Controversial issues like anticipated religious changes and decisions should be predicated upon rigorous analysis explicated in books, pamphlets, and poems. Scholarship should inspire believers, strengthen their faith, and energize them.

If modern writings can be outdated or easily transcended by new ideas, many aspects of Arabic literature should be regarded as timeless. The Qur'an, a seventh-century holy book, is as vibrant as ever. A great poem by dan Fodio can be treated as a contemporary work to mobilize a congregation, as in the example cited above, known as the *Inna Gime* (the "Mother of Poems"). Such works acquire fresh meanings instead of being treated as "old" or "dated" as present-day scholarship comes to be regarded. "Every learned man," declared dan Fodio, "judges according to the knowledge of his age. Conditions change with the times, and the cure changes with the disease." A new age does not, however, reject the documents of old; for instance, dan Fodio continues to be cited, especially his injunctions on education and against the exploitation of women.

Writing in Arabic remains a strong tradition in Islamic areas. Teachers and scholars recite these works to their students in sermons and open-air services, and they are recorded on audiotapes for others to play. In these writings, political, economic, and social views are expressed in a religious language. The writers seek enduring values to sustain society, rejecting the corruption of secular authorities, advocating the rejection of materialism, and calling for a closer relationship with God.

The long-standing fusion of the Arabic and Hausa languages is the Ajami script, which is popular for literary compositions, mainly poems. Hausa, too, continues to be used: a written form of Hausa known as Boko uses Roman letters to write the Hausa language. Ajami has long been in existence and has been used to compose poems, letters, court records, and short essays.

Literature in Hausa began in the twentieth century, as the language became part of school curriculum. The government created a Translation Bureau in 1930 (the name was changed to Literature Bureau in 1933) to promote the emergence of new writers and the translation of works from Arabic and English to Hausa. Writing competitions were sponsored, and these led to the emergence of the very first set of five novels, now all treated as classics: Abubakar Imam's *Rvwan Bagaja*; M. Abubakar Tafawa Balewa's *Shehu Umar*; Bello Kagara's *Gandoki*, Mohammadu Gwarzo's *Idon Matambayi*; and *Jiki Magayi* by M. Tafida and R. M. East. These books narrate historical and imaginary stories that portray life among the people of northern Nigeria.

During the colonial period, a number of authors wrote anticolonial pieces, like the epics of Shehu na Salga or those of Aliyu dan Sidi, the emir of Zaria whose anti-British poems cost him his throne. Anticolonial struggles also received expression in poetry. Leading names include Mu'azu Hadeja, Aminu Kano, Sa'adu Zungur, Akolu Aliyu, and Aliyu Na-Mangi. Na-Mangi, a blind poet, composed various poems now published as a collection of twelve classics known as *Wakar Infraji*. Unlike writers of the previous generation motivated by Islam, poets such as Zungur were "secularists." Zungur was influenced by radical anti-colonial politics and he used his writings to mobilize the poor to join the nationalist movement. He was a revolutionary who challenged traditional authorities and abuse of power.

The most prolific and distinguished modern author from the north is Abubakar Imam who produced the three-volume classic, *Magana Jari Ce*, based on Hausa tales and in the style of *Arabian Nights*. In 1939, Imam became the editor of a Hausa newspaper, *Gaskiya Ta fi Kwabo*, that he used to foster creative writing in Hausa. The creation of schools and cultural councils by the various state governments in the north led to a massive production of literature in Ajami and Hausa.

In the south, the missionaries and the Nigerian elite were able to develop orthographies for a number of indigenous languages such as Yoruba, Igbo, Efik, and Nupe. All these languages have become vehicles for literature, the transcription of oral traditions, and the expansion of the frontier of creative writing. Among the Yoruba, the elite has increased in number at a rapid rate, and they are among the most published in the African continent. As early as the second half of the nineteenth century, they had started to produce historical and fictional works of great significance. Dreams about the future and views of current conditions were expressed in books, pamphlets, lecture notes, and newspapers, all of which witnessed considerable expansion and refinement during the twentieth century.

The most famous in this tradition is Daniel Olorunfemi Fagunwa, a Yoruba novelist who published six major novels between 1939 and 1961, and who has inspired a generation of writers. His best known work is *Ogboju Ode Ninu Igbo Irunmale*, which has been translated into English.[1] Fagunwa was a schoolteacher and a product of missionary education. He possessed a great ability to tell inspirational stories, drawing from his Christian background to create narratives that often offered moral lessons.

Developments among the Igbo parallel that among the Yoruba, although with a somewhat slower beginning. Efforts to create an acceptable written form of the Igbo language began in the second half of the nineteenth century, but it was not until 1933 that the first major work, *Omenuko*, was published. Written by Pita Nwana, the book dominated the market for almost thirty years and was widely read as a morality story. In the 1960s, the Varsity Press at Onitsha released Leopold Bell-Gam's *Ije Odumodu Jere* and D. N. Achara's *Ala Bingo*, both important works, but not as successful as *Omenuko*.

Production in Igbo has increased in quantity and quality since the 1970s, and the most successful author is Uchenna Tony Ubesie who is gifted in his use of language and his stylistic and thematic innovations. His books rely on Igbo oral heritage and language to capture a changing society, examining especially issues of contemporary significance such as the civil war, intergroup relations, and cultural survival.

Literature in Nigerian languages has successfully restored the practices and ideas of oral literature by borrowing communication techniques, language manipulation methods, themes, and stories. It has preserved the wisdom of old in proverbs, idioms, song, and methods of critiquing society.

LITERATURE IN ENGLISH

The successful spread of Christianity from the mid-nineteenth century onward, accompanied by Western education, produced a new educated elite. This elite continues to multiply and sees literature as one of the vehicles to express its identity and construct the vision of a new society. The growth of the newspaper industry has provided an added impetus and a space in which to publicize its ideas. Quite early in the nineteenth century, a literary and theatrical society emerged whose writers tried to imitate European ideas, which they regarded as a step in the acquisition of "civilization." Some works also have a moral tone, reflecting the influence of Christianity.

As the elite grew disappointed with British rule, cultural nationalists

And your dead Front
Lying on your laps
You'll no more be man among men.[4]

He advocates a synthesis of cultures and traditions.

The Ibadan Group is a collection of outstanding poets, university-based and working in a variety of literary forms. Soyinka, Okigbo (who died prematurely in the civil war), Clark, and Echeruo all had their poems circulated widely in the 1960s and 1970s, and they have dominated this genre. In creating new forms, their poems depart from indigenous ones, and not a few are disconnected from the local public who find them hard to read or understand.[5] The Ibadan poets capture the mood of the nation, the search for unity, identity, progress, and political stability.

J. P. Clark collected his poems in *A Reed in the Tide*,[6] a book that analyzes the traditional and modern currents combined in the author. "Two hands a man has," writes Clark who, on the one hand, celebrates African culture and frowns at the dehumanization of Western society. On the other hand, he laments his alienation from this culture that he cannot fully share and he is disappointed with postindependence politics.

Michael Echeruo uses poetry to reflect on spiritual values and cultural identity. In *Mortality*, (1968),[7] Echeruo examines Western culture and civilization with a focus on private issues, notably the importance of the individual. He is disillusioned with the West, yet Africa appears "innocent," and he is left without direction.

Christopher Okigbo's *Labyrinths* (1971)[8] is a quest for personal discovery and a biographical work. There is a political side to it as well, as Okigbo seeks means to achieve political liberation of Africa. He draws lavishly from his culture and his poetry has a musical prosody. He regards himself as an alienated, educated Nigerian who needs to return to his roots for redemption. "Into the soul the selves extended their branches," he declared, seeking reentry into indigenous culture. At the same time, he is aware that Nigeria cannot reject foreign culture.

Wole Soyinka published his poems in many outlets but collected many of them in *Idanre and Other Poems* (1967).[9] Some deal with local events and others with the larger themes of politics and the celebration of life and death. Others portray the tragedy of the nation. He is not much interested in the issues of European damage to African culture, identity crises, or personal history. He uses African gods, especially Ogun and Sango, to reflect on contemporary history. Regardless of the difficulty of the times, a pathfinder god such as Ogun will create new directions and possibilities.

The civil war that took place between 1967 and 1970 generated a genre of its own, in which the poets reflect on the country's unfulfilled expectations and the failures of military coups and regimes. Okigbo, Clark, and Okara all have something to say about the war. Soyinka published *A Shuttle in the Crypt* in 1973,[10] while Achebe gathered his thoughts in the poems of *Beware Soul Brother* in 1972.[11] These are all political poems, while a few narrate personal experiences of suffering. An army officer, Maman Vatsa, emerged as a soldier-poet, with his collection, *Voices from the Trench* (1978),[12] which also exposes the tragedy of war.

Many stars continue to emerge, building on previous traditions and expanding the horizons of poetry. Among respected talents are Pol Ndu, Odia Ofeimum, Tanure Ojaide, and Niyi Osundare.[13] A culture of "people's poetry" also developed; this uses simple language and is printed in local media.[14]

In both English and indigenous languages, poetry flourishes in Nigeria. Poets may entertain, as in the case of many of those who compose in local languages. Many speak to the public, but in a language that may not be accessible to it. Yet others have been able to speak to the public in a language and medium to which it can relate. Many creative poems have borrowed from indigenous languages and practices. As would be expected, the dominant issues still center around political and economic conditions. Many poems have been written on corruption, the decadence of the political class, the excesses of military rule, and the suffering of the poor. If the poets of the 1950s addressed clashes of culture, the contemporary ones dwell on the gap between the poor and the rich, the powerless and the powerful, and the hope for a better Nigeria.

POPULAR LITERATURE

Nonacademic literature flourishes in Nigeria in the form of books, newspaper stories, pamphlets, and poems. These can be expressed in indigenous and English languages or in pidgin, a combination of English and local languages. Ken Saro Wiwa is one of the country's celebrated authors in pidgin, with works that satirize social decay and abuse of power by the military.

The best known popular tradition is the "Onitsha market literature," a revolutionary intellectual genre that began in 1947 and was devastated by the civil war of the 1970s. This literature brings together writers, printers, journalists, readers, and students in the commercial town of Onitsha in eastern Nigeria. More than 200 works of fiction, biographical, political, ethical, and romantic literature were produced within a span of twenty years. Many of them deal with love stories, and the best read is *Veronica My Daughter*

(1956), by A. Ogali, which has been reprinted many times. Other famous authors include F. N. Stephen, O. Olisa, and Orlando Iguh. Cyprian Ekwensi, who contributed to this literature, is the only one who has crossed over to be counted among the "academic writers."

The fame of the Onitsha market literature derives from its simplicity. The language is accessible, the books are short, the prices are affordable, and the stories are appealing. This literature generated a considerable reading public fascinated with the stories and the power of the written word.

The domestication of the English language is carried further in the works of Amos Tutuola, the author of the famous *Palmwine Drinkard* (1952) and other notable books such as *My Life in the Bush of Ghosts* (1952), *Sinbi and the Satyre of the Dark Jungle* (1955), and *The Brave African Huntress* (1958). His fiction is unique in its ability to fuse English and Yoruba syntax to tell ghost stories—it is indeed appropriate to apply "marvelous realism" to Tutuola's works. The ghosts, magic, and legends of his stories are drawn from the Yoruba culture.

Popular literature is not necessarily dominated by the use of pidgin or other language combinations. There is a growing market in "youth literature," novels that deal with love, adventure, crime, money, and drugs. Known in some circles as "pace setter literature," these novels are addressed to high-school and college students and written by a younger generation of authors who believe in the simplicity of language and the integration of technology to reflect changing lifestyles. They capture the mood of the country in its mentality of fast money, flamboyant tastes, and opportunities to travel to all parts of the world. They also reflect the fast-paced lifestyle and individualism of city life. If oral literature talks about the witch, pacesetter literature talks about the Internet, both of which are forms of "magic."

FEMALE AUTHORS

Mainstream and popular literature is male dominated: male writers and critics deal with male heroes and characters. The lone feminine voice for a long time was that of Flora Nwapa, whose work, *Efuru* (1966), changes the image of women from the negative to the positive, from the faithless to the faithful, from the witch to the genius. She has also created liberated women characters in *One Is Enough* (1981) and *Women Are Different* (1986). After her came Adaora Lily Ulasi, who deals with the conditions of female exploitation and colonial domination in five novels.[15]

The "warrior" among them all is Buchi Emecheta, who is also the most prolific. She narrates a personal struggle to become a "woman" through liberation from her male relations in her autobiography, *Head Above Water* (1986). Her feminism shines through in many other writings where she explores the theme of female subjugation by society, parents, and marriage relations. After struggles, women become empowered, free to attain their professional careers and enjoy life more fully.[16]

Ifeoma Okoye and Zaynab Alkali are two other well-known novelists. In *Behind the Clouds* (1982), Okoye returns to the issue of childlessness, also addressed by Nwapa, to narrate the personal experience of a failed marriage. The husband of Ije, her lead character, pursues other women because she has no child and he is desperate for progeny. When these other women become pregnant, they move to the matrimonial home to humiliate Ije. As this complicated story progresses, it turns out that Ije's husband is sterile and his pregnant mistresses are carrying other men's children. By the end of the novel, the husband recovers, Ije forgives him, and the marriage is restored. Okoye turns to the issue of social decadence in her second novel, *Men Without Ears* (1984), moving beyond the issue of gender to address more universal themes.[17]

Alkali also addresses the theme of marriage, in the story of how an ambitious young lady, Li, waits for a man to marry, spends four miserable years with him, eventually leaves him and moves with her son to her father's house, goes to school, and becomes successful. Like Okoye, she resolves the story in reconciliation: ten years later, Li returns to her husband, although he is now crippled.[18] In her other novel, *The Virtuous Woman* (1987), Alkali tells the passionate and courageous story of a crippled woman who becomes successful.

Space does not permit the elaboration of the works of others: Mabel Segun, Funmilayo Fakunle, Zulu Sofola, Omolara Ogundipe-Leslie, Tess Onwueme, Catherine Acholonu, and a growing list of very talented writers and thinkers. It is common to describe all of them as feminists, in the radical tradition of the West, although not all of them would choose this label for themselves. Nevertheless, feminism raises important issues of equality of sexes in patriarchal societies.

Female writers are sensitive to their male-dominated environment, which may be one reason why some of them reject the label of feminism, that is, to avoid being criticized for excessive radicalism. In spite of the complications of marriage, some of the writers restore the relationship in their works, perhaps to suggest that they are not aiming at an alternative social arrangement but seeking respect and equality for women. The voices of these writers have acquired significant power, manifested in the attention given to them in school curricula, in the acute sensitivity of a number of male writers to female issues, and in the vigorous attacks mounted by critics on authors who either ignore women or assign them a less than dignifying role. The older generation has nurtured the younger, thus laying the basis for an enduring group of female authors.

NEWSPAPERS AND MAGAZINES

The Nigerian press dates back to December 3, 1859, when a missionary established the first Yoruba language periodical, *Iwe Irohin*, in order to "beget the habit of seeking information by reading." This newspaper publicized the activities of the Church Missionary Society and reported local events.

The idea of news reporting and the availability of printing houses led to the formation of several others in later years, especially during the colonial period. Six newspapers appeared during the nineteenth century: the *Anglo-African* (1862), *Lagos Times and Gold Coast Advertiser* (1880), *Lagos Observer* (1882), *Eagle and Lagos Critic* (1883), *Mirror* (1887), and *Lagos Weekly Record* (1890). The circulation was small, limited to a tiny elite in Lagos. The shortage of presses and printers created problems, and the papers could not appear as frequently as their publishers wanted. Nevertheless, they laid a solid foundation for their successors and demonstrated the possibility of this medium. New periodicals can easily be started, but they can fail just as quickly due to limited circulation, bankruptcy, or lack of patronage by the public.

A more interesting phase occurred in the first quarter of the twentieth century, when daily newspapers appeared. Herbert Macaulay, the hero of Nigerian nationalism, established the *Lagos Daily News* in 1925. Other contemporary newspapers included the *African Messenger* (1921), *Spectator* (1923), *Nigerian Advocate* (1923), the *Daily Service* (1933), *Daily Times* (1926), which remains in circulation and is now owned by the federal government. Nationalism was the primary motivation for establishing these and other newspapers of the period as they promulgated political ideas, demanded reforms and freedom, complained about colonial injustice, and attempted to instigate anticolonial movements. The papers of the colonial period did not generate much profit. Indeed, a few founders did not intend to make profit but to spread nationalist ideas.

There were many constraints on successful publication as the political environment was hostile, and colonial officers did not respect the journalists or their newspapers. Typesetting was done manually, which limited the number of pages, while the number of copies was restricted by the market. One editor would gather news, report, proofread, and handle marketing. In spite of the difficulties of the colonial period, outstanding pioneers emerged with undaunted energy, a facility with language enabling them to express opinions, and the ability to copyedit.

The newspapers of the post–World War II era continued with the nationalist orientation. However, Nnamdi Azikiwe, later to become Nigeria's first president, introduced in the 1940s a more combative, anticolonial newspaper, the *West African Pilot*, in the tradition of American yellow journalism. Another frontline politician, Chief Obafemi Awolowo, established the *Nigerian Tribune* in 1949. Azikiwe and Awolowo put their newspapers into effective use in building political parties and fortifying their power bases, mercilessly attacking their opponents. The connection between a newspaper and the political ambition of its founder had now become part of Nigerian media culture.

After independence, a host of government newspapers emerged, notably the *Morning Post, Sunday Post, Eastern Nigeria Outlook, Daily Sketch, Sunday Sketch*, and *New Nigerian*. Both the federal and the state governments retain strong control over the press. The government does not trust the private media to propagate its news; there exists the fear that antigovernment media will create instability and the need to inform Nigerians that the government continues promoting development policies. When independent editors remain committed to their ideals, government newspapers, like the *Daily Times* and *New Nigerian*, attempt to generate and maintain the people's trust. However, as these are most often progovernment, the people tend to prefer the privately owned press.

Private newspapers have also proliferated, essentially as profit-making businesses. More newspapers and magazines emerged after the 1970s as entrepreneurs sought opportunities for investment. Some are motivated by political considerations, using the print media to advance their agenda and popularize their names in the hope of winning elections or influencing those in power. The *Punch, Guardian*, and *Concord* are among the post-1970 newspapers established by successful entrepreneurs. M.K.O. Abiola, the late business magnate and politician, established the *Concord* empire that boasts a daily newspaper, a weekly magazine, community newspapers in several indigenous languages, and evening newspapers. Other prominent and aspiring politicians established various newspapers and magazines during the same period. Among the most successful have been the *Guardian* (daily and weekly) and *Newswatch* magazine.

There are now about forty daily newspapers, over thirty weeklies, and twenty monthlies. Evening newspapers are fewer and tend to do better in a few large cities. The Nigerian newspaper and magazine industry is successful and diverse. There is a progovernment group at federal and state levels, usually publicly owned. The private publications are adventurous and articulate and have wider circulation. The constitution ensures the individual's freedom of expression, including the freedom to hold opinions, receive and disseminate information, and establish newspapers and magazines.

All the newspapers carry news items, editorials, advertisements, and columns. Political issues dominate, but there is always a place for culture and customs. On Friday, they all devote a section to Islamic sermons and similar sections are provided on Sunday for Christians. Festivals are reported, as well as major cultural events. There are magazines devoted to popular culture, gender issues, religion, and other aspects of culture. The print media capture the changing Nigerian cultural scenes, in words, pictures, and cartoons. Similarly, foreign cultures are reported, mainly fashion and music trends in Western societies. Domestic and international fashions are displayed, and suggestions are offered regarding appropriate choices to be made in popular and elite culture with respect to taste and lifestyles. The most successful cultural magazine is *Nigeria Magazine*, established in 1927, which has continuously attracted young writers who contribute poems and short stories to its "Literary Supplement."

Military rule and political authoritarianism have created problems for the media. The government is able to control its own newspapers by appointing management personnel to oversee the behavior of editors. While government newspapers do criticize those in power, they do so in subtle language. The real tension has been between the government and privately owned newspapers. Many journalists and editors have been harassed, persecuted, and incarcerated, while newspapers and magazines have been proscribed. Under military regimes, the government is sensitive to critical comments, leakage of government policies, and other activities that they interpret as capable of causing a coup or public demonstration. Draconian military decrees attempt to limit the freedom of the press.

Nevertheless, the print media have survived political turmoil. Journalists with courage are numerous. In difficult political circumstances, some have survived by underground printing and using informal means of circulation. Soft sell tabloid newspapers and magazines exist side-by-side with business-oriented periodicals such as *Financial Punch, Financial Guardian, African Construction*, and the in-house magazines of different companies. Journalists are well trained, facilities for printing exist, and there is an extensive reading public, although many are unable to afford the dailies that now sell at high prices because of inflation and excessive production costs.

Regardless of the occasional troubles, the print media enjoy considerable influence. They are associated with all the major political changes. Publishers (and papers) try to shape events, present elite views of society, demand political change, and report news. A further testament to the important role of the press is the number of politicians that have come to power after using newspapers to build their image.

RADIO AND TELEVISION

Radio broadcasting began in 1932, primarily as a propaganda tool of the colonial government. Since then, radios have remained important and are the major means of obtaining news in many rural areas without electricity, since they can operate with batteries. There is also access to international news agencies such as the Voice of America and the British Broadcasting Corporation. There is no part of the country without access to radio. The most important development has been in the establishment of television stations, the majority of which also provide radio services.

In 1954, following protests by the nationalists, the federal government allowed the establishment of regional radio and television stations. In 1959, the Western Region took the lead by establishing the first television station in the country. Other regions followed in 1960 and 1962. The federal government created its own station in 1962. Since then, state and federal governments have both cooperated and competed in developing and maintaining their stations. In order to use the media to propagate its political agenda, the federal government has acquired many stations and has forced all of them to carry national programs, notably news items that are biased in its favor. However, a few private stations are now allowed to operate and there is access to a number of foreign networks.

The reasons for establishing the stations are similar: to educate, inform, and entertain. In the early years, limited funding and equipment affected the quality of production and frequency ranges were rather small. It took a while before technical and creative staff became available. Programming consisted of many foreign programs, the majority of which were movies. There were few other shows and these were only in English. Until the 1970s, television sets were limited to a small number of elite. The television was regarded as a "magic box" in those early years, a source of wonder that brought news and drama to the sitting room. A crowd would gather around one, including family members inside a living room and strangers outside peeping through the windows.

The expansion of the Nigerian economy since the 1970s, thanks to oil revenues, has made more television sets available, and they are now common household items, especially in the cities. The number of stations expanded with the creation of new states. Color transmission began in 1974. The Nigerian Broadcasting Corporation was established in 1973 as a means for the executives of all stations to exchange ideas and coordinate some of their activities. In 1976, using the excuse of the need to ensure national integration, the federal station acquired many state stations. Technologies were updated, and all the stations were required to simultaneously broadcast a number of similar programs, notably news and some important documentaries. Thus, they all show the national evening news at the same time. A national network has emerged, although the quality of reception varies from place to place, with people in major cities such as Lagos and Abuja enjoying the best reception.

As part of the federal government program of controlling as many stations as possible and creating a national network, the Nigerian Television Authority (NTA) was established in 1977 and granted monopoly power: "The Authority shall, to the exclusion of any other broadcasting authority or any person in Nigeria, be responsible for television broadcasting."[19] The NTA is charged with providing independent, impartial broadcasting, with the goal of maintaining the unity of the country. This organization divided the country into zones, each with its own board, and most stations came under the control of the federal government. Although the NTA created additional stations in new areas and was able to secure federal funding, it has become a means by which the federal government further extends its power.

Not surprisingly, many states were unhappy with this arrangement, and the Second Republic provided an opportunity for them to regain some control. The 1979 presidential constitution enabled both state and federal governments to own and operate stations. Between 1979 and 1983, many state governments established new stations to enable their governments to broadcast their own news and activities that would have been censored by the federally controlled NTA.

Just like other media, the television stations are victims of politics. Indeed, they have been created largely for political reasons and their principal executives are political appointees. The government regards them as the most effective way to reach the public and garner support for its policies. Consequently, the government owns most of them. Not only must they carry government news and regularly show the images of those in power, but they are not expected to antagonize important public figures. Programs are expected to favor those in power or at least desist from criticizing them. Staff can be removed because they do not display loyalty or are suspected of favoring political opponents. Key appointments go to those who favor the government of the day. There are cases when news presentation have been written by political parties or government agents and presented as independent; news anchors have been forced to broadcast false election results; and many journalists have been induced or compelled to exaggerate the benefits of government programs. Whenever the country is divided or political parties are at "war" with one another, viewers choose a station on the basis of their political affiliations. There have been many occasions when viewers in southwestern Nigeria have ignored or boycotted the news presented by the NTA stations that carry information about the federal government.

It is hard for journalists to satisfy governments, since what officials want to hear must be positive. If an accurate report of riots on a university campus is given, it can be interpreted as a deliberate attempt to incite antigovernment protests. If a documentary criticizes a government program, it can be misinterpreted as an attempt to insult public officers. Consequently, a number of television stations survive and employees retain their jobs only by becoming sycophants.

In spite of all difficulties, television has been very successful in many ways. It has contributed to the discovery of creative talents and the propagation of local drama and films. If the people distrust the news and government-related documentaries, it does not mean that they do not enjoy many other programs. Indeed, television has broadened the sources of leisure enjoyment.

In the beginning, television had to rely exclusively on foreign programs, such as *Superman* and *Lassie*, from either the United States or Britain. This did not satisfy the elite at a time when Nigeria was leaving behind British rule and scholars were talking of cultural revolution. Managers of the stations said that they were aware of the need to promote indigenous culture, but that the limitation of funds and the shortage of local sponsors created problems. Among the earliest attempts to broadcast local talents were musical performances, including piano recitals and choral programs. Orlando Martins emerged as the first television music legend. In the north, Kade Kade Mu was the earliest popular performer of Hausa music on television.

After this initial stage came attention to folk performers. Hubert Ogunde, a genius of Yoruba drama, staged a number of plays. The most successful program in the southwest began in 1965, following a talent hunt that produced Moses Olaiya, the first important television comedian. His weekly comedies, under the title of *Baba Sala*, draw considerable attention. A number of Ogunde and Olaiya followers established their own groups that also acquired television contracts, thus enriching the variety of available programs. In the north and east, a number of small dramatic groups also emerged, although not of the stature of Ogunde and Olaiya. Kukan Kurciya was the earliest drama group to record a major success in the north.

A few English language plays were presented on television in the early 1960s, limited to British classics based on the texts used in schools. Written texts have become abundant, but most do not succeed as television drama because actors are not creative or spontaneous in the use of English, and the number of trained people who can live on acting is rather small. However, plays in English as well as in indigenous languages are now common. The longest running English language drama is *The Village Headmaster*, which deals with various social problems in a rural setting.

The first drama series to be shown all over the country by the NTA is *Cockcrow at Dawn*, which is based on the emerging family culture. The most ambitious documentary is *Portrait of a Culture* which highlights various Nigerian festivals, while the most successful soap opera is *Mirror in the Sun*. In the 1980s, successful programs were exchanged among states, thus adding to the options for viewers. The Nigerian film industry has grown since the 1980s, and television has been able to exploit this by broadcasting many locally produced films. Religious organizations have gone into drama production to produce morality plays that are popular on television. Foreign movies continue to increase, and Nigeria now has access to a number of foreign stations such as CNN and CBN.

The television audience has grown, although it is concentrated in urban areas. For most families, watching evening programs is the best source of leisure. It is cheap, accessible, and diverse. Soccer programs and local drama top the list of interests, followed by action movies. The network controlled by the NTA has reduced the number of programs with foreign content to about 20 percent, and these are not even shown during prime time. However, local programs have to compete with those offered by foreign stations. When there is inadequate government funding, a station raises money through commercials (payments from government agencies to broadcast information), charging companies for carrying news items relating to them, and running unknown foreign movies to fill air time.

Television also reflects the intensity of religion in Nigeria. Christians and Muslims are well represented on a daily basis. All the major religious festivals are covered. In addition, organizations sponsor programs to preach and convert. The religious programs sometimes reflect the deep religious divide that causes tension in the country.

The government too, uses television as a device to encourage morality. Whenever the government launches a "morality war" such as the Ethical Revolution of the 1970s, the War Against Indiscipline of the 1980s, or the Movement for Social Justice of the 1990s, the television is recruited into service to transmit slogans, morality plays, and sermons.

In keeping with their role of service to the public, the stations also maintain school programs. In collaboration with educational agencies, important educational matters are covered, from the teaching of various school subjects to civic matters. The government donates television sets to schools as well, to encourage the viewing of educational programs.

The Nigerian television industry continues to grow and to seek the means to adapt to its local milieu. There is no shortage of staff, whether journalists or technicians. State-run stations have limited funding to develop a rich variety of programs, but the ideas and talents are there. Access to foreign stations has increased the options for viewers, but high maintenance costs mean that only the well-to-do can benefit. Of the foreign programs, the most popular are news, soccer and wrestling matches, and action films. Television stations make money from advertising and from showing clips of social events such as funeral and marriage ceremonies. Programs reflect the multiplicity of ethnic groups, cultures, and religions, although minority groups complain that they have not been adequately represented. Among national drama programs are *The New Masquerade, Samanja,* and *The New Village Headmaster,* all dwelling on contemporary issues and conflicts over money and love. The works of such celebrities as Chinua Achebe (for example, *Things Fall Apart*) have been turned into television series, adding to a growing list of "national programs." In big cities such as Lagos, Ibadan, Abuja, and Kano, there are many daily programs that give viewers a choice between local and foreign stations. The number of viewers, estimated at around 30 million by the NTA, continues to grow as more and more people gain access to television sets.

The role of government in the media will not diminish for a long time to come and it will continue to be more important than the role of the private sector. The reason is that, to the government, television is not primarily a source of entertainment but a public service agency to disseminate official information, garner support for policies, and maintain national cohesion. However, if the government-sponsored stations do not run exciting programs, they will lose viewers and money to the private stations and to satellite services that provide access to foreign stations.

NOTES

1. Wole Soyinka, *The Forest of a Thousand Daemons: A Hunter's Saga; Being a Translation of "Ogboju Ode Ninu Igbo Irunmale" by D. O. Fagunawa* (London: Nelson, 1968).

2. He later changed his last name to Bekederemo.

3. Gabriel Okara, *The Fisherman's Invocation* (Benin: Ethiope Publishing Company, 1978).

4. Okara, *The Fisherman's Invocation*, 6.

5. The most devastating critic is Chinweizu (he carries no first name), who accuses them of elitism and obscurantism. See Chinweize et al., *Toward the Decolonization of African Literature* (Enugu: Fourth Dimension, 1980).

6. J. P. Clark (Bekederemo), *A Reed in the Tide* (London: Longman, 1965).

7. Michael Echeruo, *Mortality* (London: Longman, 1968).

8. This was published posthumously (London: Longman, 1971).

9. This book is now included in Soyinka, *Early Poems* (New York: Oxford University Press, 1998).

10. (London: Rex Collins, 1973).

11. (London: Heinemann, 1972).

12. (Enugu: Fourth Dimension, 1978).

13. Paul Ndu, *Songs for Seers* (New York: Nok Publishers Ltd., 1974); Odia Ofeimum, *The Poet Lied* (London: Longman, 1983); Niyi Osundare, *Village Voices* (Ibadan: Evans Brothers, 1984), and *Songs of the Market Place* (Ibadan: New Horn Press, 1983).

14. See, for instance, Osundare, *Village Voices*; and Chinweizu et al., *Toward the Decolonization of African Literature.*

15. *Many Thing You No Understand* (London: Joseph, 1970); *Many Things Begin for Change* (London: Joseph, 1971).

16. Among her novels are *In the Ditch* and *Second Class Citizen* now combined in *Adah's Story* (London: Allison and Busby, 1983); *The Bride Price* (London: Allison and Busby, 1976); *The Slave Girl* (Oxford: Heinemann, 1995); *The Joys of Motherhood* (New York : G. Braziller, 1979); *Destination Biafra* (Oxford: Heinemann, 1994); and *Double Yoke* (New York: Braziller, 1983).

17. Okoye, *Men Without Ears* (London: Longman, 1984).

18. *The Stillborn* (Lagos: Longman, 1984).

19. Federal Military Government, Decree No. 24 (1976).

4

Art and Architecture/Housing

ART

ALTHOUGH "ART" is a foreign word to many Nigerian groups, its objects and meanings are not. Examples of art include tools, weapons, utensils, musical instruments, carved doors, house posts, and various sculpted masks and items used for social and religious ceremonies. The most common art productions in Nigeria include rock paintings and engravings; decorated pottery; sculptural representations in bronze, clay, stone, wood, and ivory; and ornate forms of decoration.

Objects of art reveal the level of specialization in the country, the dedication of time and energy to creating them, and the number of people making a living as artists or working in media organizations. Many young people go to formal schools to study various art media, while others serve as apprentices to traditional wood-carvers, leather workers, or gourd decorators.

Art appreciation provides people with leisure activity as they visit museums and monuments. Furthermore, it contributes to modern living and the economy, as people decorate homes and offices with artwork. Traditional and modern forms coexist and are also combined as elements of creative modern art. The religious significance of art continues to be maintained as important objects are utilized in indigenous and other religious rituals, as in the public display of masks in masquerades, and in the ornamentation of churches.

Nigerian and African art is not limited to wood sculpture, which is the form generally displayed in Western museums and often appearing on the covers of books and magazines on Africa. The genres and forms are multiple and diverse, each having traditional and modern styles, reflected in architecture, body adornments, and the various performances associated with religion, law, agriculture, and other ceremonies.[1]

Traditional Art

There is evidence of Late Stone Age art in the country, notably in pottery, stone, and figurative art, for example, the rock paintings and engravings in Birnin Kudu (near Kano).[2] Excavations in the north (Dutsen Kongba in Jos and Rop) and in the south (Akure and Afikpo) have yielded decorated pottery shards and polished stone axes, many dating from between 3,000 B.C. and A.D. 100. Early Iron Age art also exists in places such as Nok, where stone and iron tools and terra-cotta figures have been found.

There is also an enormous amount of evidence of art being used to celebrate cultural heroes, ancestors, and kings, as in the bronze objects of Igbo Ukwu.[3] In Ile-Ife, bronze busts, a full-length figure of a king and his wife, and terra-cotta figures similar in style to the bronzes have been collected. They all testify to the wealth and prestige of kings, the worship of gods, and respect for ancestors. There are many ritual and religious objects associating art with festivals, sacrifices, and worship. Benin art works are equally famous, including pots and bronze representations of kings, queens, palace officials, commoners, Europeans, and animals.

Traditional art forms share numerous characteristics, many of which have been retained into modern times. For example, artists have drawn materials from local resources: from plant materials such as wood, calabashes (gourds), fruit stones, raffia, cotton, and bamboo; from the earth, including stones and clay; from animals, including feathers, shells, teeth, and hides; and from available metals, notably iron, gold, brass, and bronze. Regardless of the simplicity of the tools utilized, the artist's imagination has remained rich and fertile through the ages.

The continuous production of artifacts in various regions show that certain families have been dedicated to certain types of art production, transmitting skills from one generation to another. Each generation makes appropriate changes to reflect the history and aesthetic judgments of its time.

Through their work, artists represent the people's worldview and aspirations, the ideas of creation, the legacy of the ancestors, the community ethos, and local histories. Many traditional art forms are connected to religion: they are used to express beliefs in the power of gods and spirits; they represent objects of worship to reach the spiritual forces; they serve as symbols of witchcraft, ancestors, and gods; as symbols designed to maintain law and order in religious communities; and as divination objects. Indeed, Nigerian art has flourished best through its religious use. Art works are collected as ritual objects and have proved useful and appealing not because of their historical or aesthetic value but because they continue to be necessary in reaching spiritual beings.

Art also has an integral connection to social life, and many works portray the relationship a person has with kin group, family, clan, and village. Rites of passage are captured and celebrated in art depicting important life moments such as birth, marriage, death, circumcision, and initiation.

Politics play an important role as well. Several important art works are symbols of power, such as the crown, the royal stool, and the beads used as bodily adornments. Political and social organizations use art to represent them and their authority within the community. Thus, members of a secret society may have a symbol that only they can use.

Art is also associated with many trades and occupations. Not only are tools made to sustain economies, but skilled artisans such as leather workers, calabash decorators, and woodworkers depend partly on the sale of their artwork for their livelihood. Artists often emphasize the need to distinguish between works created for utilitarian purposes and those for leisure. Regardless of the artists' intention, their tools and their products reveal the state of technology of a particular time and region.

Finally, Nigerians have always used art as a means to play and to embody shared communications. There are musical instruments to facilitate song and dance. Masks and other objects are used to enhance performances. Various games carved from wood (such as *ayo*[4] among the Yoruba) facilitate leisure. There are artists who make toys for children, such as the *omolangidi* (carvings in the image of humans and animals) of the Yoruba. In general, traditional art tends to radiate energy outward, which lends itself to play and communication. The making of a mask may be a contemplative exercise, but its use is directed outward.

Thanks to efforts at preservation and adaptation, traditional art is very much alive in a variety of ways: bronze casting, wood carving, and painting. By and large, concerns with aesthetics now overshadow objects' ritual and religious significance. Contemporary kings and court officials have revived the custom of commissioning bronze workers, wood-carvers, and bead and crown makers to supply objects of royalty that they continue to use as symbols of power and prestige. The Catholic mission has a proud history of encouraging local artists, especially in wood carving. There is also a foreign market and a growing number of Nigerian educated elite for which traditional artists produce.

Traditional crafts can be found everywhere, in cities and villages alike. They include the making of domestic utensils, such as cooking pots and serving spoons, furniture, and decorative items. These days, materials may not be wholly local: for example, the yarns and dyes for local cloths can be imported; and the thread and materials for hairstyling can come from local or foreign sources. In the areas of fashion and hairstyling, the elite do consume products of local crafts but local products, especially domestic utensils, are used with more frequency in rural areas.

Producers of traditional arts and crafts are underpaid and undervalued simply because they lack sufficient numbers of patrons with money. While the techniques of production are integrated into some school curricula, not many students develop an interest in them. Nevertheless, traditional art has endured a century of great changes and many of its aspects have been carefully integrated into modern art.

Contemporary Art Forms

Contemporary art has been driven by the need, first, to retain the essence of traditional art; second, to blend traditional art with modern; and third, to create abstract works. While modern artists borrow tools and techniques from different parts of the world, many among them still talk of the need to preserve African artistic traditions, retain Nigerian identity, and project an "African personality." Traditional art, modern two-dimensional art, sculpture, painting, architecture, graphics, textiles, and fashion designs are among the most popular art forms. As in other aspects of Nigerian culture and customs, the arts have had to respond to the spread of Islam and Christianity, the imposition of colonial rule, and the rapid spread of Western culture. What follows is only a brief description of some of the more widely used media and the most celebrated artists.

Sculpture

Traditional sculpture has already made Nigeria famous in the international art scene. Many artists continue to build on this tradition by reproducing Ife, Benin, and Igbo Ukwu art, notably busts of kings and queens and various objects depicting royalty. A notable traditional carver of wood objects is Lamidi Fakeye, who for many years was resident artist at Obafemi Awolowo University. His masterpiece, *Oduduwa* (a carving of the Yoruba ancestor), graces the main theater of this campus. A group known as the "Osogbo artists" carves Yoruba gods and goddesses. One of the most celebrated of this group is Susanne Wenger, who is famous for carvings that exaggerate the characters in size and form.

New paths have also been charted. Felix Idubor, the great sculptor of the 1950s and 1960s, is a master of optical illusion, borrowing extensively from the Yoruba and Benin naturalistic bronzes. Ben Enwonwu, too, is famous, for his realism. His famous work, *Sango*, is a representation of the Yoruba god of thunder and it is appropriately displayed at the National Electric Power Authority Headquarters in Lagos.

Many artists are creative in their works. A number do paint portraits in different colors. A few work in the abstract form, notably Isiaka Osunde. Some combine traditional and abstract forms, as in the works of Uche Okeke and Demas Nwoko.

Churches, government bodies, and private individuals patronize artists and have contributed to sculpture and painting through their commissioned pieces, especially carved panels, cement relief screens, metal relief, and portraiture. Artists have worked on pews, chairs, recliners, and various decorative items. Such objects may represent indigenous tradition, imported traditions (as in crosses and figures of Jesus Christ in churches), or a blend of different traditions.

Painting

Painting is probably the most creative and vibrant area, in which the country has produced a long list of distinguished artists. Chief Onabolu and Akintola Lasekan pioneered a new field in illusion representation. In the 1960s, groups known as the "Yaba school" and the "Zaria school," including such notables as Bruce Onobrakpeya, Uche Okeke, Simon Okeke, Yusuf Grillo, and Demas Nwoko, developed new pictorial styles that emphasize Nigerian and other African characters. Highly individualistic, these styles are meant to appeal to an elite with a taste for high art. Ben Enwonwu carries this style further in a series of paintings, entitled *Nigerian Theme* and *African Dances*, which express spirit and religion through dance.

At Osogbo, an informal school has given rise to a small number of highly talented non-university-based artists, notably Twins Seven Seven and Jimoh Buraimoh. Now international figures, the Osogbo artists choose themes from Yoruba folklore and legends. A work of painting becomes a window opening on past culture and history. Bruce Onobrakpeya, trained in a formal system, takes a similar approach. In one painting after another, he elaborates on the legends of the Urhobo, a major ethnic group in the southwest, in addition to his inspiring decorative details and motifs. Segun Adeku of Ife is another successful member of this school.

Since the 1970s, the trio of Kolade Oshinowo, Shina Yusuf, and Dele Jegede, all members of the "Zaria school," has made considerable impact on expressive styles, linear elements, and the creative use of the circle. After them has emerged the "Abayomi Barber school," which recreates the old Ife tradition, in a naturalistic style added to modern two-dimensional works. The themes treated by members of the Barber school are dominated by local lifestyles, making them appeal to many people, and the styles they use pay attention to technical details and surrealism.

Institutional and individual demands for murals and portraits sustain a number of talented artists, most notably in major cities.

Graphic Arts

Some artists have become popular through creative designs used to make newspapers attractive or to promote cultural or government policies through mass media. The most appreciated of these designs have been the cartoons by such distinguished artists as Dele Jegede, Bisi Ogunbadejo, and Kenny Adamson, all of whom dwell on politics and contemporary social issues. Graphic artists, combined with prominent photographers, have contributed to the popularity of many magazines and have shown that resources and talents are available to enhance the quality of the growing graphics industry.

Textiles and Fashion

Textile arts are a lively and creative form that has developed over centuries. The old weaving technology of the horizontal and vertical looms continues today as well as the production of various hand-made designs. Wax prints and fabrics reflect local tastes for multiple colors. Adaptations have taken various forms: the old tie-and-dye (*adire*) textile is now adapted to modern apparel, window blinds, and table covers. Nigerian textiles are sewn into Western styles, as in the use of *akwete* and *adire* fabric to make jackets or coats. Clothes are elaborately decorated and embroidery reflects great talent. Nigerian clothes are now exported, since there is a growing market among African migrants and their hosts who love the colors and elegance of the exotic and extraordinary. The economic downturn since the 1980s has benefited the local textile industry, as people reduce their purchase of imported textiles and clothes. Local designers have emerged, seizing the opportunity to actualize themselves, and many have shown that they are talented and versatile.

Body decorations are drawn from established cultural practices and are also borrowed from the West. The use of cosmetics, permanent scarification, and various coiffures are widespread. Hairstyling is a major industry, and there is no limit to the ingenuity displayed in this craft.

Other Functional and Aesthetic Crafts

As in the case of textiles and fashion, there is a large body of art expressed in terms of both function and aesthetics. A decorated cooking pot can be used both to cook and to please the eye. An entrance door to an office can provide both security and beauty. Houses, furniture, and even household tools bear the imprint of artists as they seek to create a market for their works.

The creative genius of Nigerian artists is evident in the construction of buildings, such as churches, and the artwork that decorates them. Representations of Christ, Mary, and various angels adorn the inside of many churches, while elaborate wood carvings are displayed on the pulpit, pews, and chairs.

Like churches, a number of residential houses are ornamented, a reflection of the social and political standing of their owners. Palaces and residences of chiefs can boast carved wood posts and panels. Horizontal wall flutings can be found in the palaces of the Benin king and chiefs. Wall paintings abound in different styles and colors throughout the country.

Local smithies use both old and new forms of metalworking to make such old tools as hoes, machetes, and axes. These tools have their functional use, but they can also be for decoration, allowing the maker to make a creative aesthetic judgment. Tourism keeps promoting a rich industry in brass casting, representing traditional subject matter such as animals, as well as more contemporary subjects like cars and airplanes. Sheet metal is also converted into bowls, cups, and other utensils that are often given as gifts.

Pottery satisfies the needs of rural communities for functional objects such as cooking pots, drinking bowls, and water vessels. At the same time, pottery satisfies those who need it just for decoration. Pots are decorated with incisions, etchings, and paintings. Even more popular than pots are calabash decorations, which can be used as wall hangings or table centerpieces. Cut from gourds into different shapes and sizes, they are then engraved with different patterns or painted. Basketry is yet another item found in many homes, made by coiling and stitching or by spoke construction and weaving.

Leather work has always been a highly specialized craft, with products widely circulated within the country and traded abroad. Leather specialists can be found in the north and among the Oyo-Yoruba group in the south, making leg rests, bags, poufs, sheaths, and equestrian gear. Hides are treated and dried, then sold to leather manufacturers for sewing and appliqué work.

Beautiful leather items, especially from northern Nigeria, can be found in many homes and are among the official gifts presented to foreign dignitaries.

Contemporary Art: Practices and Presentation

The first set of modern artists, notably Aina Onabolu and Akinola Lasekan, discovered their talents in elementary school and later went to Britain to receive professional training. These pioneers were interested in the representation of their society, rather than the presentation of abstract traditional art, which their missionary and European teachers had condemned. Lasekan was Nigeria's first famous cartoonist, producing mainly satirical works directed at the British government. He was also a renowned painter. Onabolu was a painter and educator, and he painted many portraits of Lagos celebrities. Onabolu was a member of the pressure group that fought for the appointment of Kenneth Murray as an art teacher in 1927. Murray in turn became famous in the preservation of Nigerian antiquities and was a mentor to Ben Enwonwu, who became the country's first art adviser to the government. Although a formal Western education was important to an artist's success at one time, there are many, like Twins Seven Seven, who have acquired international recognition without it.

Art is now part of the established formal education system in Nigeria, taught at all levels of the educational system. Among the great educators have been Ulli Beier, a German, Yusuf Grillo, Solomon Wagboje, and Uche Okeke, and important art schools have developed at Yaba, Zaria, Benin, and Nsukka. In the 1960s, the Mbari Club provided opportunities for a number of artists without much formal education to practice their art in summer workshops. The Society of Nigerian Artists brings artist-scholars together to reflect on the discipline. While there are students interested in art, the difficulty of finding good jobs after graduation forces many of them to explore other careers. Many find gainful employment in advertising, the media, and education, but only a few can survive primarily on the sale of art works.

The modern artist is an "eclectic personality." He or she works in a studio or workshop, uses imported tools and materials, presents themes from indigenous and Western cultures, and uses both traditional and modern techniques. If sculpture was the most popular art form in the precolonial period, painting is becoming the most important in the modern era. Inspiration is drawn from multiple sources: local culture, imported cultures, Islam, and Christianity.

There are museums in a number of cities like Ile-Ife, Lagos, Benin, and Jos that house traditional and modern pieces. Art councils operate as governmental agencies to sponsor competitions and promote new talent. In 1977, the country hosted the Second World Black and African Festival of Arts and Culture, which enabled Africans and Blacks in the diaspora to display their heritage and to emphasize that culture is relevant to national development. Opportunities for artists to display their work have also increased and include occasional exhibitions on university campuses and in various cities, in lounges and foyers of major hotels, and in private galleries and homes.

Patronage has depended on a few sources: the local elite, foreigners, and the government. In the view of the local audience, the best works are naturalistic, with meanings that are clear; but foreigners prefer the abstract. Commissioned works reflect the interests of the representatives of funding agencies, and rather than the feelings of the artists. When mass production has a market, artists respond to the demand. Thus, many workshops reproduce masks by copying traditional motifs and use staining to age them or make them more attractive.

Nigerian arts tend to take one of three major orientations. First, and among the most popular outside the country, is the adaptation of traditional motifs. Thus, there are carvings and paintings of ancient masks, representations of traditional warriors, kings, queens, and figures on horseback. New masks and ancestors have been invented to keep the ideas of the past circulating. Similarly, there are prints based on legends and folklore. Igbo body painting (*uli*) has provided various ideas for artists to use in representing the past.

Second, there are artists who capture routine and peculiar experiences of life, social and political events, the environment, and public figures. This naturalistic art is popular in Nigeria, as people can easily relate to it. Examples include the paintings of market scenes by Akinola Lasekan, the sculptures of Ben Enwonwu (for example, *Sango* the god of thunder), the ritual scenes portrayed in the paintings of Yusuf Grillo, and the emphasis on landscape in the works of Joshua Akande. No important object has escaped the attention and brilliance of the artists.

Third, abstract works are numerous and appear in virtually all art forms. The artist makes an object, gives it a name, and attaches a story to it. Thus, a number of famous sculptors have made many figures that are hard to interpret. Painters are probably the most adept at this technique, using lines and colors to depict complicated meanings. Some abstractions appropriate the natural world, as in cases when the artist projects an individual or animal invested with some power and idea. Thus a lion in the forest can wear the crown of a Yoruba king to show that it governs the forest.

The Nigerian art industry has attained great maturity. Talents abound, trained and untrained in the formal school system. Their ideas, vision, sentiment, and thought draw from multiple sources and reflect changing politics and society. Most of the glorious and dark moments of Nigeria have been captured in various forms, ranging from the vibrant picture of Herbert Macaulay, the great nationalist, to the picture of the hungry child that reflects the devastated economy of the 1990s. The "big names" are internationally known and are creating role models for others to follow. Nigerian artists will benefit from the expansion of the market and an enhanced standard of living, as more and more people purchase decorative objects to add beauty to their homes and offices. Artists continue to search for authenticity, to create what is distinctively Nigerian in a modern world.

ARCHITECTURE

Rural Settlements

The majority of the Nigerian population lives in rural settings, although cities have grown at a phenomenal rate. Rural settlements vary a great deal, due largely to differences in ecology, culture, economy, and pace of modernization. A casual observer focusing merely on environmental beauty may not see the differences in rural settlements. There are dispersed compounds, each composed of an enclosure containing the houses of married couples and their dependants and relatives. There are hamlets, which stand apart from the regular houses and are closer to farmlands or vegetation. Then there are villages, each a group of many hamlets and compounds with a population that can be as big as 5,000 but as small as 200.

In southern Nigeria, settlement types fall into five major categories: fishing camps and hamlets; nucleated rural settlements; dispersed, small, walled villages; dispersed rural settlements; and "satellite" farm villages and hamlets. Changes are inevitable, and a village can grow to become a town over time as a result of economic development.

Fishing camps and hamlets are located along the coast, among the Kita, Ijo, and Itshekiri, to mention a few groups occupying the coast of the Bight of Benin. In these areas, people congregate in rather small clusters, owing to the nature of the terrain and their occupation. The Ijo and Kita take to sea fishing and find it convenient to stay in hamlets or camps on coastal sands. Communities that engage in lagoon fishing, notably the Ijebu, Ijo, and Ilaje, build their hamlets along the edges of lagoons and creeks. Migrants among these people, notably Urhobo and Igbo, take to cassava farming and inhabit small farm camps of less than twenty people.

Nucleated rural settlements can be found in the southeast, notably around Ogoja, northeast of the southern forest, in the Owerri area, and in different parts of the Niger Delta. These settlements fall into three major types. In the Ogoja type, people live primarily in small nucleated villages. Houses are organized into compounds on both sides of a narrow street. Larger settlements have not emerged because of the preference for living in small villages and the relative peace in which people live, which does not require them to consider defense or security. In the second type, the Owerri nucleated villages, the compounds are arranged in a circle, with their walls joined to create a common screen. Within this outer area are small compounds. In the third, Niger Delta–type, many houses are packed into a small dry area above the flood level, thus promoting a greater degree of affinity among the inhabitants.

Moderately dispersed, small, walled villages exist among the northern Igbo and are also scattered over a wider territory. Each settlement is differentiated from the other by fallow land, or oil palm trees. Where population density is high, villages are clustered with smaller farmland areas separating them. Within a village, compounds are built close to each other, a sort of defensive arrangement. As new roads pass through the area, many compounds move close to the roads to take advantage of commerce and accessibility.

Dispersed rural settlements are found among the Ibibio and Igbo in the southeast, with hamlets or compounds scattered in various locations. This arrangement is probably a consequence of the disintegration of nucleated settlements. Among the Yoruba in the southwest, one can also find "satellite" farm villages and hamlets far away from the cities. This arrangement enables farmers to work in the village and travel to the city for social events.

In the north there are two settlement types: nucleated and dispersed, each associated with one ethnic group or another. Nucleated villages comprising hamlets and compounds dominate the northern half of the savanna, and long distances separate the villages. The rural Hausa live in nucleated villages (known as *gari*) with many dispersed compounds (*kauye*), a combination of two distinct types that probably reflects the history of their long habitation. Many huts and granaries that reflect the dominance of farming in their lives can be found in a compound. The compound has one entry and is enclosed by a fence. A village is walled for security reasons. A number of compounds (*unguwa*) can now be found located outside of a walled village either because of a recent population increase or because of better maintenance of law and order.

The Kanuri to the northeast live in nucleated settlements that resemble those of the Hausa. The Kanuri village comprises round houses arranged into compounds that are surrounded either by mud walls or by mat screens. Among the Nupe, located southwest of the savanna, the villages are more closely nucleated because of higher population density. Villages are large and many have *tungas*, "daughter settlements," located three to five miles away from the parent villages. A *tunga* is a hamlet that farmers use to explore fertile farmlands. It serves essentially as a mobile home that can be dismantled when harvests are disappointing. Because a *tunga* is not served by markets or government, the farmer must always return to the parent village.

In the southern half of the savanna, notably in the middle belt, people live in dispersed settlements. Among the Tiv, who live in an open landscape, can be found many thatched farmsteads bounded by farmlands and trees, as well as thousands of isolated hamlets, huts, and compounds. Members of the same lineage occupy the compounds. The dispersal of rural settlements has been very common, even among groups that traditionally live together on hills (for example, the Gwari) but who have now taken to compounds located on the plains.

Urban Settlements

Nigeria has three major types of cities: traditional, modern, and a combination of both. Some traditional cities were founded many centuries ago, others as late as the nineteenth century; modern ones are of twentieth century creation; and cities combining both are older cities that have been transformed by new changes. Traditional cities include Badagri, Ile-Ife, Ogbomoso, and Oyo among the Yoruba; Kano and Sokoto among the Hausa-Fulani; and Maiduguri among the Kanuri. All these and others survive today and their histories reveal their adaptations to the environment, culture, and changes in politics and economy. Sokoto and Oyo serve as good illustrations.

Sokoto (with a population of about 150,000) was founded in the early years of the nineteenth century, as the capital of the Islamic empire established by dan Fodio. It was walled for defense and built on a plateau to benefit from the Rivers Sokoto and Rima. It has always been an important religious center, the seat of the sultan, the most powerful king and spiritual leader in Islamic areas, and home to many Muslim scholars. It is a center of crafts production, notably of leather work. The impressive Sokoto city wall has gates with roads that lead to the most important architectural area: the Sultan's palace, the mosque, and a huge open space for religious and social events. Tall buildings are not common in the old city center due in part to the effort to protect the privacy of women in their private compounds, and to the difficulty of building large structures on shaley soils. A typical house is rectangular, low in height, built with mud walls and high thick roofs. The compound is large and spacious to tolerate weather changes and extremes.

In the first half of the twentieth century, Sokoto grew partly because of expansion in trade and a road system connected with a railway station 99 miles (160 km) away. The River Sokoto prevents expansion to the north, so that most new buildings are to the south. Among the notable additions are the government reservation areas for modern buildings, the Usmanu dan Fodio University, and many commercial centers. The old part of the city maintains the identity it created during the nineteenth century.

Oyo (with a population of over 120,000) was also founded early in the nineteenth century, following the crises that led to the fall of the famous Oyo Empire. The layout of the city is modeled on many older Yoruba cities. The central part is the major arena of economy and politics. Here can be found the major market (the Oja Akesan) attended by the city people and those from outlying villages. The market is a vast open space with stalls, and it is the venue of important festivals and political functions. There is also the *afin* (palace) of the king, with its enormous walls and gates that open to the market space. Within the palace are various compounds to house the king, palace staff, and wives and children. There are also temples and shrines to various gods, and an extensive open arena for public events. The next major units are those of the chiefs, also with large spaces in front, and roads leading to elaborate compounds that house members of the chiefly lineage. The majority of houses in the older part of the city are family compounds. These are built with mud walls, covered with thatch or corrugated iron sheets, and rectangular in shape. A compound has a row of rooms that open onto a large courtyard. The courtyard often serves as a playground and can also contain shrines to the family gods. The major occupation of the family is also conducted here, especially crafts. Families are noted for their specialization in certain occupations such as drumming, singing, farming, dyeing, and carving, and they reflect this in their organization of space. A number of small farmlands exist within the city to grow vegetables and food crops. When modern expansion has taken place, it has occurred outside the traditional city's walls.

Among the major modern cities are Port Harcourt, Aba, and Enugu in the south and Kaduna in the north, all built during the twentieth century in response to the changes of the colonial era. Some grew as railway centers, others as administrative headquarters. They have many of the hallmarks of Western cities: administrative buildings, hotels, night clubs, cinemas, large markets, modern houses, an army of poor people, and a minority of the very wealthy. All of them attract migrants from rural areas who come for jobs or to share in the pleasure of city life.

Port Harcourt in the southeast is one example of a modern city originally developed as a port and railway terminus. Founded in 1913, it served as a provincial capital for a while. It grew as a center of commerce and industry, as the oil industry grew and thousands of people connected with it moved to Port Harcourt. In 1967, it became a state capital, drawing even more people, so that in the 1990s it was a city of half a million people. Commercial buildings and residential houses are modern, and the streets are well engineered, despite the sudden growth.

Kaduna in the north, another example of a modern city, was built close to the River Kaduna by the British. Founded in 1917 as the capital of Northern Nigeria, it grew very rapidly as a result of the railway, economic changes, and the influx of many people to staff the colonial government. With a population of 3,000 in 1919, Kaduna grew to 150,000 in 1963, and to half a million in the 1990s. Still a state capital, it is a hub of commerce and industry, and a center of educational activities. Kaduna's economy reflects the characteristics of a modern city: about 30 percent engages in commerce and 40 percent in manufacturing. This working population necessitates a myriad of services, generating thousands of small shops, large department stores, and hotels. Houses are generally modern, except for the "slum section" where the working class lives. The poor live in the south in a gridiron area known as the Sabon Gari. The industries are also located in the south for easy access to labor. To the north, separated from the southern area by a river, is the most modern part, originally known as the "European zone." This is the seat of power, home to huge modern buildings, a stadium, military and financial institutions, and the real estate most desired by the rich.

A combination of traditional and modern features can be found in Zaria and Kano in the north, and Ibadan, Benin, and Lagos in the south. They can be described as "twin cities" that include both old and modern sections. The old section is like the traditional one described above. The new has modern residential areas, industries, office blocks, apartments, hotels, nightclubs, and restaurants. The old established traditional elite including kings, chiefs, priests, diviners, and Islamic scholars maintain their visibility in the "old city" while the modern elite controls the "new city." The educated people and the youth prefer to live and play in the "new." However, there is integration, as roads and markets unite both, festivals and ceremonies are celebrated together, and the king in the "old city" commands respect in the "new."

Ibadan began as a war camp in the 1820s, rising to become the largest indigenous city in Africa. It sprawls endlessly, and its large urbanized area spread over 174 square miles. It is often described as the biggest village in the world, partly because its night life is limited, but largely because it has retained most of the features of traditional Yoruba cities. The old city was enclosed by a wall and situated to take advantage of regional trade, while extensive farms are located outside the city wall. Some parts of the older area form the foundation of the "new city." The "new city" consists of modern high-class residential areas, the University of Ibadan, the sprawling secretariat of the state government, plus hotels and businesses. The "old city" appears unplanned and chaotic, compared to the "new." In both the "old" and "new" cities, streets are lined with small shops and trade can interrupt traffic flow in the densely populated areas. The most active commercial center, that seemingly runs for miles on end, lies to the west and north and is adjacent to the railway station and the roads that lead to the port city of Lagos.

Benin, with a population of over 135,000, is the famous center of the old empire of Benin. It grew slowly in the first half of the twentieth century, mainly because of the absence of railways. In 1963, it acquired the status of a state capital and rapid expansion has followed. New developments have concentrated in a concentric manner to surround the "old city"; thus there is no sharp demarcation of "old" and "new." The core of the old city is the palace and market but, unlike Ibadan, it is also the business district of the modern city.

Zaria in the north, with a population of over 110,000, is a "double twin city" with four major units. There is the walled "old city" that was founded in the fourteenth century and became the capital of a major kingdom. It continues to be populated by the Hausa and Fulani and many old spaces of the past are retained. There is also a "new city" (Tudun Wada), which has grown because of the railway and the cotton trade. Many industries are located there, with a large population of factory workers. A third unit is the Sabon Gari, a modern area located north of the old city and inhabited by nonindigenous people and foreigners. The fourth is Samaru, characterized by a university, an agricultural research station, and modern city planning and housing.

The most active traditional-cum-modern city is Kano, which has been a great center of commercial and industrial activities for centuries. Kano continues to retain its importance as a metropolis of commerce, manufacturing, and industry, and it is connected nationally and internationally by road, rail, and air. In addition, it is a center of excellence in both Islamic and Western education. The "old city" is still very much under the influence of the powerful emir, a Muslim king. Expansion has occurred outside the old city wall with various residential districts having developed their own unique character. Citizens of Kano who desire modern living live in Fegge, where "new money" is displayed in grandiose buildings. Immigrants from the other parts of the north, including Hausa and Fulani merchants and workers, live in Tudun Wada and Gwargwarwa. Southerners live in Sabon Gari with their stores, churches, and restaurants. The affluent, educated middle class live in Nassarawa, while the industrial area is located at Bompai. Thus, Kano is segregated by both income and ethnicity.

Lagos stands in a class by itself as the most industrialized and fastest growing city, the major entry point to the country, the center of political protest and media activities, and the home of diplomats, wealthy investors, and crime syndicates. The annual growth rate is above 15 percent, due mainly to a constant stream of new immigrants that has created a population of over 3 million. The city contains a diverse variety of houses, from the old to the most modern. Division by social classes is very marked, from the poorest who have no homes to the wealthiest who live in architectural masterpieces.

Traditional House Types

As previously indicated, Nigeria comprises well over two hundred ethnic groups and a variety of settlement patterns. House types reflect this diversity, as well as differences in taste, customs, and environment. One house adds to another to create the broad settlement type already described. The architectural style of the houses reflects the social system. The Ijo fishing people along the coast require a different type of house from the hinterland Yoruba city-dwellers. Construction is affected by income, climate, and available building materials. Even when the houses look alike, differentials in income can affect the type of materials used. For instance in the far north, the urban-based wealthy build flat-roofed mud houses, with thick walls and roofs of timber plastered with mud. The poor build houses with conical thatched roofs and circular mud walls. Whether in the villages or the cities, one will see a limitless variety of structures and their respective decorative accents.

However, one can also discern a pattern in traditional houses. They all reflect the need to satisfy the requirements of large families and their occupations, the local resources available for building, the skills of the builders, established religious and cultural practices, and considerations of privacy and security. Building materials consist mainly of mud, wood, raffia matting, palm fronds, and straw. In the south, the common roofing materials are mats and straw from raffia palm leaves. In the north, the Saharan roof-type is a flat, mud roof, placed on square, box-like structures.

Materials are chosen to withstand the weather conditions of the region. In the north where heat is intense and trees are scarce, the walls and mud roofs serve as insulation. In the middle belt where the heat is less intense, the people use more wood than mud. Among the Igbo, lateritic soil is preferred as a building material, because it is cohesive and it requires only minimal foundations. Wooden poles support thatched roofs of raffia palm leaves. The Yoruba use mud for the walls and grass or raffia leaves for the roof.

If building materials are locally available, so too is the labor for building as construction is traditionally organized communally. Volunteers gather to build on a set date and are lavishly treated to food and drinks by the future dwellers of the house. Such labor is reciprocated since a house is considered an important individual and communal asset. In rural areas, houses are owner-occupied and rarely change hands. They can be regarded as belonging to many generations of a family, and some groups, such as the Igbo, have a feast in honor of the house either when it is built or annually. The house provides shelter, enables a family to function, and shields individuals and their problems from public view.

Many traditional houses have four important design components and utilitarian functions. First, a compound includes multifamily housing units within it to accommodate many households of people, sometimes over a hundred people, belonging to the same lineage. Thus, a compound should not be confused with a modern, freestanding housing unit for one nuclear family.

Second, many compounds are rectangular in shape, with large walls. The walls are high to allow light and air but also to prevent neighbors from seeing inside. In the south, the compound is divided into many rooms or small housing units. Among the Yoruba, the rectangular compound is known as the *agbo-ile*, and the housing units within it, the *oju-ile*, are constructed around the open courtyard. Most compounds have one entrance, which leads not to the housing unit or the living room (as in most American homes) but to the courtyard. In the middle belt, the housing unit is round in shape, with clay walls and a conical thatched roof.

Third, many have a reception room for guests, called the *zaure* among the Hausa, which prevents guests from proceeding directly to the courtyard. The reception area is also used for relaxation and to view the public without leaving the compound. The Hausa also add an antechamber, a second reception area that is intended to give privacy to the residents. Guests are rarely allowed to venture beyond this area, in order to give privacy to the women who live and work within the compound. The reception rooms can also be used for storage and as the connection between the compound and the street.

Finally, the courtyard serves as an important common space used for a variety of social and occupational functions. Among the Yoruba, the court-yard is big, its verandas providing additional space under which to sit, cook, and relax in the shade beneath their overhanging roofs.

Urban Housing

Modern houses, found in the cities of all regions, borrow from designs from other parts of the world, modify traditional styles, and combine various regional elements. This trend began in the nineteenth century with the build-ing of churches, offices, and houses for Europeans, and Brazilian-style houses for the Lagos elite who imported the techniques from Latin America. The colonial period saw a rapid increase in building to meet the needs of growing numbers of European residents and expanding governmental bodies. Many Nigerians began to imitate these new buildings in materials and designs.

In areas with developed cash-crop economies and new, income-generating occupations, corrugated iron sheets and cement have become standard ma-terials in residential buildings since the 1940s. In the 1960s, many offices and homes were built with concrete and steel. The prosperity brought by oil money since the 1970s has led not only to a massive expansion in building but to a limitless number of designs. The architects are creative in the use of space and building materials, but it cannot be said that a distinctive modern Nigerian architecture has fully matured. National architecture has also yet to fully capture the vitality of Nigerian arts: many houses and homes do not benefit from the artistic resources of the country.

Urban homes are commonly two or more stories in height, and freestand-ing houses are generally bigger than those found in rural compounds. Behind the houses of the rich are "boys-quarters" for domestic staff and drivers who live there on a permanent basis until they move to other jobs. These houses also have security gates, which may be manned by dogs and security guards (called "watchnights" or "meguards"). In areas with high crime rates, the guards work around the clock; in others, they are on duty only during the night.

The modern house is designed for the Western ideal of a nuclear family. It has a "master bedroom" for the husband and wife, and other rooms for guests. In most houses, the emphasis is on the living room, which contains all the objects that define urban/elite living: refrigerator, television, video-cassette recorder, art work, good-quality furniture, and decorative items.

Most cities have the "neighborhoods of the rich," called government reservations areas (GRAs) in some cities, and Victoria Island in Lagos. The houses here set the standards in taste and beauty. The floor plans and designs are similar to those found in wealthy areas of Western countries. Home owners build and decorate their homes primarily to give the impression of success and prosperity. At the same time, they seek privacy and security, especially in high-crime areas. Where the land is scarce and expensive, the creation of harmony with nature is a minor consideration.

Places of religious worship are an impressive aspect of the Nigerian architectural landscape. Churches and mosques are everywhere and frequently are the largest buildings in small communities. Public buildings, mainly offices and residences for senior public figures in major state capitals, are also located in conspicuous places. These are constructed to accommodate the high volume of people that utilize them during the weekdays.

Urban building materials are derived from local sources (e.g., bricks and cement) and are imported from abroad (e.g., marble) as well. The wealthy prefer to use a variety of imported items, even when local equivalents are available. The cost of some of these items is beyond the means of the majority of the working population.

All cities have housing problems. The population increases faster than the availability of houses and facilities, causing overcrowding and inflated rents. In places like Lagos and Port Harcourt, the working class spends as much as 80 percent of its monthly income on housing. To reduce expenses, many will crowd into a single room. In low-income areas of Lagos, the occupancy rate is as high as eight persons per room. People can often be seen sleeping outside the house, on verandas and in corridors, either because there is no space in the room, or because it is too hot or poorly ventilated. Sleeping outside invites mosquito attacks and, ultimately, malaria and other diseases.

Where available, low-cost housing, both private and public, lacks adequate space for recreation, efficient drainage, and maintenance. Rental properties are found everywhere, especially in the cities, and can be expensive single units or blocks of apartments. High-rise apartments are a prominent feature of Lagos where land is scarce.

The environmental quality of most cities is poor. Major streets are congested and noisy. Drainage and refuse disposal systems are substandard, creating ugly sights in various places. Inadequate water supplies make the flush toilet systems undependable, creating difficulties in disposing of solid human waste. In cities like Ibadan, a high percentage of houses do not even have any formal waste disposal system. Development efforts will include alleviating urban housing problems and using the abundant local resources such as clay and timber to provide low-cost housing for the urban poor.

NOTES

1. For works on African art, including illustrations, see, R. S. Wassing, *African Art: Its Background and Traditions* (London: Greenwich, 1994); Christopher Spring, *African Arms and Armor* (Washington, DC: Smithsonian Institution, 1993); Robert Brian, *Art and Society in Africa* (London: Longman, 1980).

2. For details of these various examples, see C. O. Adepegba, *Nigerian Art: Its Tradition and Modern Tendencies* (Ibadan: Jodad, 1995); and Thurstan Shaw, *Nigeria: Its Archaeology and Early History* (London: Thames and Hudson, 1978).

3. The major work is by Thurstan Shaw, *Igbo Ukwu: An Account of Archaeological Discoveries in Eastern Nigeria*, 2 vols. (London: Oxford University Press, 1977).

4. *Ayo* is a complicated game played with forty-eight seeds on a board with twelve holes divided into two rows. The seeds are divided into groups of four and placed in the holes. To win, you must capture the twenty-four seeds of your opponent in a series of moves that rivals chess in its use of intelligence.

A Nigerian king in a meeting with chiefs and guests. The seating arrangement indicates power and prestige: while the king sits on a huge chair, others sit on the floor. The man standing is addressing the audience. Photographs on the walls decorate the living room, a typical feature of most Nigerian homes.

Group photograph of king, chiefs, and guests. The king and chiefs adorn themselves with special beads, and they all wear traditional attire. To the left of the king is an educated elite, wearing a long-sleeved shirt and pants, which do not always confer prestige in a setting such as this. The background shows a modern two-story house with a verandah that enables the occupants' view of the public. The main door is left open to allow ventilation and the use natural light.

An audience with the King of Kano. All are wearing huge *babban-riga* and turbans. An Arabic inscription in praise of Allah and artwork permitted by Islam decorate the wall. Although the emir understands English, a translator may still be required to serve as an intermediary between a guest and the emir, who prefers to communicate in the Hausa language.

Group photograph of elementary school children in uniform. The teachers stand on both sides.

Youth Corper. This young woman wears a cap and T-shirt that bear the logo of the national youth service. Service in the first year following college is encouraged in an attempt to create a patriotic culture.

One of the country's many churches.

A mosque, another common feature of the landscape.

A client (standing) consults with a spiritualist (hidden from view). Objects and symbols that confer religious power are scattered around the room. This modern spiritualist, an occultist who draws objects and ideas from India, is different from a traditional diviner.

A market scene; most markets are held in the open.

An old house with corrugated iron sheets. The gutter is an open sewage system that occupants cross to reach the house, which can be built of mud or bricks. The rooms are arranged in two rows, with a long passage in the middle. The kitchen and toilets in the back are shared by all residents.

Modern architecture: high-rise offices in Lagos. Because official electricity and water supplies are often erratic, buildings such as these have their own back-up systems.

Modern house. The landlord lives on the top and the tenant on the first floor.

Clay folk art for sale. The designs of the people in the back row capture the elegant traditional dress from various parts of the country. The two heads on the table are reproductions of ancient archaeological figures.

Clay pots for sale at the market. Pottery is a traditional craft industry in Nigeria and has survived in spite of the now-common use of metal utensils.

Cottage industry for food processing, also serving as a kitchen for cooking traditional meals. A notice advertises the products for sale, mainly food items.

An educated couple wearing expensive, locally made, hand-woven textiles for a social engagement. The woman wears a head-tie made of the same material as her main attire. She holds a long scarf, which she may also tie around her waist or over her shoulder.

A successful couple by the side of their modern building; the two parked cars represent further evidence of their success. The traditional dress is well-embroidered, another mark of affluence. Because of their ages, they would generally be called "Papa" or "Mama" by their relatives and neighbors.

Weaving and braiding are popular hairstyles for Nigerian women and girls.

A crowd marching to a social event.

Modern nuclear family.

Children playing under a tree in a village. Outdoor activities are very common. In the evenings, an adult may entertain them with moonlight songs and stories.

Three children of an elite with their family car.

5

Cuisine and Traditional Dress

NIGERIAN CUISINE and eating habits differ in a number of significant ways from those of Americans. One-course meals are popular, and a serving tends to be big, sometimes limited only by what the stomach can take. The soup (also called stew or sauce), with or without vegetables, goes with many meals that include rice, yam, and a host of carbohydrates such as *eba, fufu,* and *iyan.* Most people drink water with their meals instead of other beverages, although it is becoming more common to see the urban elite eat a heavy lunch or dinner with a bottle of cold beer or soda. The fingers of the right hand are used to eat, rather than a knife and fork. In some areas, eating with knives and forks is associated with elitism, and many believe that these utensils take away from the pleasure of eating. The majority of Nigerians hold to their age-old cuisine and eating habits.

In farming and rural communities, the tendency is to eat the big meal of the day in the early evening, in order to leave time for digestion before sleeping. In the morning, rural dwellers can have a bowl of porridge and later snack on fruits and nuts to tide them over until dinner. Diners often sit on the floor or at a table and eat in the company of other relatives. Among the elite and in cities, three meals (breakfast, lunch, and dinner) are common, in addition to snacks and fruits. The sedentary elite tends to eat more than the active farmer does! The use of dining tables and cutlery is common among the elite. The majority of the population eats most of their meals at home, but the cities have hundreds of eating places, from five-star restaurants to small eateries, known as *bukas*, that specialize in local foods.

Some important customs persist in both traditional and modern families. Visitors expect to be invited to eat and the host is obliged to cook more than necessary in case additional guests arrive. Generous meals indicate affection to visitors. Elders and heads of household eat the best parts of the meal. In communal eating, the young are expected to take their share of beef or fish after the elders. Among some groups, a guest is not expected to finish all the food served to him, and elders are supposed to leave a portion on their plates for the children to finish. When respected persons are lavishly treated with food and drinks, they are expected to reciprocate with some gifts either on that day or on another occasion.

Cooking is done on a hearth in rural areas and among the poor, while middle-class families have electric and gas ranges. Kerosene cookers are fairly common and economical. In modern houses, the kitchen is part of the house, while in rural areas, it is often in a separate shed. Three stones may serve as a tripod to hold a pot set over burning firewood in an open space. Regardless of the technology, all kitchens have facilities to boil, fry, roast, grill, steam, and bake. Even in rural areas without modern ovens, water can be boiled or steamed in pots; food can be toasted by the fire; palm oil is used to deep-fry; and baking is accomplished by wrapping food in moistened leaves and putting it in hot ashes. Local utensils are products of the environment: pestles and mortars are made from local trees and used to pound nuts, yams, and other plants; cooking and storage pots are made from clay; knives, spoons, and forks come from local smiths; banana leaves serve as pot covers and baking pans; hollowed gourds are used as containers, jugs, and mixing bowls; and the delicious meals are served in clay bowls and gourds. Today, plastic and aluminum are often used instead of clay and wooden utensils.

Culinary duties are gender-specific as young girls are expected to master the skills of cooking and serving dishes through observing their mother. Nigerian women hardly consult recipe books or use precise measurements of salt, water, and spices. Everything, including timing, is learned by rote. The most skilled cook is the one who can make a fine soup and have relatives and friends commend her. "The way to the man's heart is through good food," is one popular saying praising good cooks, and it reflects suitors' preference for women with outstanding cooking skills. Among some groups, wedding presents to a woman from her mother may include a long-handled spoon[1] that serves as a blessing and a reminder that good cooking will keep the marriage stable.

By and large, Nigerians prefer to eat the food inherited from previous

but the cities have hundreds of eating places, from five-star restaurants to small eateries, known as *bukas*, that specialize in local foods.

Some important customs persist in both traditional and modern families. Visitors expect to be invited to eat and the host is obliged to cook more than necessary in case additional guests arrive. Generous meals indicate affection to visitors. Elders and heads of household eat the best parts of the meal. In communal eating, the young are expected to take their share of beef or fish after the elders. Among some groups, a guest is not expected to finish all the food served to him, and elders are supposed to leave a portion on their plates for the children to finish. When respected persons are lavishly treated with food and drinks, they are expected to reciprocate with some gifts either on that day or on another occasion.

Cooking is done on a hearth in rural areas and among the poor, while middle-class families have electric and gas ranges. Kerosene cookers are fairly common and economical. In modern houses, the kitchen is part of the house, while in rural areas, it is often in a separate shed. Three stones may serve as a tripod to hold a pot set over burning firewood in an open space. Regardless of the technology, all kitchens have facilities to boil, fry, roast, grill, steam, and bake. Even in rural areas without modern ovens, water can be boiled or steamed in pots; food can be toasted by the fire; palm oil is used to deep-fry; and baking is accomplished by wrapping food in moistened leaves and putting it in hot ashes. Local utensils are products of the environment: pestles and mortars are made from local trees and used to pound nuts, yams, and other plants; cooking and storage pots are made from clay; knives, spoons, and forks come from local smiths; banana leaves serve as pot covers and baking pans; hollowed gourds are used as containers, jugs, and mixing bowls; and the delicious meals are served in clay bowls and gourds. Today, plastic and aluminum are often used instead of clay and wooden utensils.

Culinary duties are gender-specific as young girls are expected to master the skills of cooking and serving dishes through observing their mother. Nigerian women hardly consult recipe books or use precise measurements of salt, water, and spices. Everything, including timing, is learned by rote. The most skilled cook is the one who can make a fine soup and have relatives and friends commend her. "The way to the man's heart is through good food," is one popular saying praising good cooks, and it reflects suitors' preference for women with outstanding cooking skills. Among some groups, wedding presents to a woman from her mother may include a long-handled spoon[1] that serves as a blessing and a reminder that good cooking will keep the marriage stable.

By and large, Nigerians prefer to eat the food inherited from previous generations, made with ingredients drawn from local farms and food industries. If a plant or animal is considered edible, most parts of it will not go to waste. To take a few examples: apart from intestines and scales, all parts of a fish, including the head, are consumed; and all parts of an animal, including the head, skin, and feet, are eaten. Some plants are similarly treated. Roughage and various parts of animals or plants have additional uses. For instance, in the past, cattle urine was used for medicine and dung for insulation and the making of dye sealant. The palm tree is perhaps the most useful plant, as nothing is thrown away: the leaves are used for brooms and thatch, the stem for poles, the fruits for oil; and it is incised at the top to collect palm wine, an alcoholic beverage.

Despite its vast resources, Nigeria has had a long history of incorporating ingredients and crops from other regions. Pineapples, sweet potatoes, cassava, and a variety of types of corn were introduced from the New World after the fifteenth century. Many of these can resist locust damage, thereby minimizing the dangers posed to the harvest. Some new crops and new varieties of already-known crops came from Asia, including cocoyams, plantains, papayas, and rice. These have been successfully incorporated into local diets and have helped to improve nutrition and the range of available food items. There is an extensive trade in food items within the country. Sea salt travels from the south to the north; rock salt (natron), a tenderizer, travels from north to south. Smoked and dried fish produced along the coast travel all over the country. Yam is traded to the west from the middle belt and east. Kola nuts move north, and cattle move south.

Major local crops include starchy tubers (for example, yam, cassava), grains (maize, millets), vegetables (okra, spinach), and fruits (bananas, oranges). Most are harvested by small-scale farmers who use hoes and machetes. Wild plants supply a variety of fruits, vegetables, and mushrooms. The palm tree supplies palm oil, used most widely in the south to fry and make soup. Vegetable oil also comes from peanuts and melons. Many foods are seasoned with salt, pepper, onions, shallots, and garlic. The leading staples remain yam, cassava, beans, and rice.

In most parts of the country, the yam is the "king of crops," a tuber that provides the most esteemed dish: the pounded yam, consumed with stew and vegetable soup. Yam is an indigenous crop, one of the very oldest, with the exception of two less popular varieties introduced from elsewhere, the cush-cush and water yam. Like other food sources, no part of the yam is wasted. The yam itself is high-quality starch and contains large amounts of protein. Dried yam is converted into powder to prepare a solid starch, known as *amala* among the Yoruba, which is also consumed with vegetables and stew. Like potato, yam can be boiled, roasted, fried, and mashed with vegetables and other ingredients. Yam can also be used to make porridge, bread, and fritters. Even the dried peelings are used as animal feed. In many parts of the south and the middle belt, the yam harvest is accompanied by celebrations. Among the Igbo, the eating of new yam is an important occasion to rejoice. The status a farmer holds in the community is proportionate to the success of his yam farm and the size of his storage barn.

Corn is another major crop that is mashed, boiled, roasted, and eaten alone or in combination with other food. Small "industries" turn corn into powder, porridge, cornstarch, fritters, cakes, and gruel. Beans of various types (cowpeas, black-eyed, and pigeon) can be steamed, boiled, baked, and mixed with other products (such as yam, banana, and plantain) to make porridge, stews, and fritters.

Cassava has been a major crop since the end of World War I. It grows faster than yam, it requires less tending and little weeding, and its yield is greater. Also a tuber, it can be grated and roasted into powdery starch (*gari*) and dumplings (*fufu*). The less acidic varieties can be boiled and consumed, as is done in the north. Cassava is one of the cheapest sources of carbohydrates. *Gari* is consumed in most parts of the south. It is low in crude fiber and fat, and it is quick to prepare: when cold water is added it can be eaten as a cereal; with hot water, it becomes solid and is eaten with soup.

Black-eyed peas and other types of beans are used for fritters, stews, snacks, and desserts. Beans provide the majority of the population with their main source of protein, as they are cheaper than fish and meat. Storage is easier, as beans require no refrigeration, which most people do not have. Beans can be cooked and spiced and consumed alone or in combination with fried plantain, rice, and yam. Beans can also be roasted and served as snacks. They can be converted into cakes and fritters to produce tasty and nutritious treats.

Rice is grown locally and imported. It is very popular everywhere as it can be easily prepared and consumed with soup and vegetables. Like the other staples, it is put to various uses, for example, rice porridge and rice *tuwo*, a sort of dumpling. *Jollof* rice, a combination of rice and sauce, is the most popular ceremonial meal.

Fruits are abundant, notably oranges, pineapples, papayas, bananas, guavas, and sugar cane. By and large, they are eaten raw and as snacks, not as fruit juices. Fruits and vegetables are cheaper in the countryside, thus providing the poor with the opportunity for a healthier diet than their urban counterparts.

Notable snacks and desserts, many sold by street vendors, include roasted peanuts, meat on skewers, fried plantain, *chinchin* (a crispy pastry made from wheat flour), and *kulikuli* (baked nuts). Many have been part of the Nigerian diet for centuries, including *kulikuli*, corn on the cob, coconuts, peanut butter, *gurudi* (coconut biscuits), *mosa* (corn fritter), *dundu* (fried yam), plantain chips, yam balls, *suya* (meat on skewers), and grilled meat. Many others are modern, combining European ingredients with local techniques: these include doughnuts, rice pudding, coconut toffee, queens' cupcake, carrot cake, sausage rolls, rice cake, tropical fruit salad, potato balls, meat pies, and "puff-puff" (a flour, sugar, and yeast mixture that has been allowed to ferment, then deep-fried).

Throughout the country wild game and fish are consumed. Domestic animals are reared in small quantities, notably chicken, ducks, pigeons, turkeys, guinea fowls, goats, sheep, pigs, and rabbits. Large-scale animal husbandry is concentrated in the north, practiced by nomadic Fulani who keep cattle for subsistence and sale. Cattle are traded all over the country, as are goats, sheep, and sacrificial rams. Fish and animal proteins are also imported, as in the examples of frozen fish and chicken, tinned meat, and stockfish (from Norway), a major delicacy, especially in the eastern part of the country.

Wealth and status are indicated by the consumption of fish and meat. Except for the hunters and fishermen who are sustained by their catch, others must rely on market purchases. Fish is more available than red meat, but good fish is expensive, and some (like catfish) is reserved for the rich because it is so expensive. Game is even expensive and considered a delicacy. Beef is widely available, sold in major street market and butcher shops. Recently, however, beef has become very expensive, as the cattle industry has recorded only slow growth. Because of the high cost, fish and beef are consumed in small quantities. Thus, a meal consists of rice and sauce and two small pieces of beef or fish. Many Nigerians are vegetarians, not by choice but by necessity, since they cannot afford to buy meat or fish. Consequently, there is a high dependence on legumes and vegetables as alternative sources of proteins.

Domestic animals are not regularly slaughtered as they are meant for festivals and communal sharing. A chicken can be cooked in honor of a valued guest. Many people consider the consumption of domestic animals to be connected with special occasions, such as weddings, naming and funeral ceremonies, and religious celebrations. In rural areas, a farmer is successful if he can afford to slaughter many goats for one ceremony. To have the ability to buy a cow or a big ram is to be counted among the well-to-do or "blessed" among community members. A member of the lower class cannot afford to buy a cow for ceremonies that traditionally require one, such as the funeral of one's parents.

Meat and fish can be dried, fried, roasted, or grilled, and all these methods of preparation are very popular among Nigerians. *Suya*, roasted beef or chicken with a combination of savanna spices and served on skewers, is a great delicacy and a delight in nightclubs and hotels. Meat and fish, even in small quantities, are also the main ingredients in soups, a necessity for many meals.

The soup is a combination of many things: meat, fish, shrimp, pepper, onions, tomatoes, cloves, garlic, oil, and different types of leafy greens, always fresh and nutritious. The combination varies from one culture to another. The Yoruba like palm oil and hot pepper. "The body that does not consume hot pepper," a popular Yoruba adage says in celebration of the pepper, "is a weak one." Another proverb pays homage to oil: "The face of the soup is oil." Even people that use less hot pepper still sprinkle on enough to give the soup its distinctive flavor and aroma.

It is widely believed that pepper is important in order to improve the flavor and taste of foods, but it does more than this. It is an antibacterial agent that acts as a natural preservative to prolong the life of foods, especially of meat, even more effectively in combination with oil. Although the climate is hot, those who consume hot pepper actually think that it reduces their body temperature. Certainly, one is forced to drink plenty of fluid to replace the fluid lost to perspiration. As the body has to flush out some of this liquid, antioxidants go with it, and the pepper thus acts as a diuretic.

The soup is consumed in combination with starch dishes, which have been mistakenly classified in the literature as generically *fufu*. In Nigeria, *fufu* refers specifically to the dumplings derived from cassava starch. Other starch dishes include *eba*, also from cassava, *amala* from yam, a variety of related starches made from rice (*tuwo*), plantain, corn, sorghum, and pounded yam, the most famous of them all. Many of these starch dishes resemble mashed potato dumplings. They are shaped to resemble a ball; pieces are slowly pinched off, each small one dipped into the soup and then popped into the mouth. "Pepper soup," which is taken as an appetizer, dessert, or snack, needs no companion—it is a thin soup, rich in beef or fish and a variety of spices that can sometimes be very peppery.

Nigeria does not have a single national dish, although habits and ingredients may appear similar and some food, like *jollof* rice and pounded yam, can be found everywhere. Different ethnic groups and regions have their preferences for recipes based on their customs, religions, and available food resources. In the southeast, among the coastal communities, the choice meals are seafood and yam stews. Among the Igbo, yams and *gari* dumplings are the favorites. In the north, the staples are based on sorghum, brown rice, and beans. The Yoruba in the southwest prefer pounded yam, *amala*, and *eba* consumed with stews and vegetable soups.

Soups, too, reveal ethnic varieties. To the Urhobo, the best is *owo*, a combination of meat, smoked fish, crayfish, red pepper, salt, the local spice *egidje*, cassava starch, periwinkle, and salt. It is commonly served with boiled yam, another starch, or plantain. To their neighbors, the Itshekiri, the preferred soup is *banga*, made from local spices, *atariko*, *rigije*, and *beletientien*, with shrimp, beef, fish, and crayfish. *Banga* is also served with starch and plantain. The Hausa cherish *miya yakwa*, a mix of beef, peanuts, onions, tomatoes, *yakwa* leaves, or collard greens. *Miya yakwa* is generally served with rice dishes like *tuwo acha* or *fufu*. Among the Yoruba, the favorite is *efo elegusi*, vegetables cooked with melon seeds, dried fish, shrimp, spinach, red pepper, garlic, and beef. It goes with rice, pounded yam, *eba* (from cassava), and *amala* (from yam). Among the Igbo, *ofe owerri* is the soup that goes with pounded yam. *Ugu* (pumpkin leaves) and *okazi* vegetables are added to beef, fish, crayfish, and spices. The *edikang ikong* of the Efik and Ibibio of the southeast is gradually becoming both national and international, served with rice and *fufu*. Assorted vegetables (*ugu*, spinach, and bitter leaf) are cooked with fish, beef, stockfish, and spices.

A number of other foods reflect the changes in tastes during the last one hundred years. Tea, bread, and cakes made from flour are some of the additions of the nineteenth century that came with European contact. During the twentieth century, they were first consumed as elite items, and later by all. Various food items are now imported, such as rice, wheat, milk, sugar, flour, and vegetable oil, primarily to overcome the problem of food scarcity as agriculture declines, but also to meet the growing taste for foreign food. Meat pies, baked flour stuffed with meat, and eggs prepared in several ways are popular snacks in the cities. The love for beef has been incorporated into European-derived foods, as meal choices are based on beef (as in different types of pies). Western fast food has not been able to invade much of Nigeria, and in the few places where it does exist, it is very expensive.

Beverages

Alcoholic beverages have traditionally been made from guinea corn, maize, bananas, and sugar cane. Palm wine, which looks like milk, is obtainable in the south, where palm trees grow wild. Palm wine is obtained by tapping the sap of palm trees, which contains yeast that gives the wine its alcohol. As the wine ferments, it becomes more potent and vinegary. Water serves as a dilutant, especially in areas with fewer trees. Sugar is also added to sweeten the wine, although this offends discriminating consumers. Gin is made in coastal areas and sold in bottles that do not announce their alcoholic content.

Modern brewing is one of the best established industries. Beer is produced from wheat and corn, and the popular brands include Star, Rock, Gulder, and Trophy. Guinness Stout is available everywhere. Wine and spirits are also produced, although of inferior quality compared to those that are imported.

Muslims are expected not to drink alcohol. In the north, sales of alcohol are restricted to areas inhabited by southerners. Drinking is a common pastime in most other places, and drinking establishments exist in thousands of locations. At parties and ceremonies, guests are lavishly entertained and are urged to drink more and more. Palm wine and beer are most frequently consumed, followed by stout. Spirits are taken straight. Drunkenness is criticized, and women are expected not to drink or smoke in public.

Nonalcoholic beverages include tropical fruit punch (made from a combination of pineapple, guava, mango, orange, and lemon juices) and juice drinks extracted from the pineapple, papaya, ginger, and banana. As in most other countries, one can find Coca-Cola, Pepsi, and 7-Up. Tea drinking is common in the north, and coffee is associated with educated people. Cafés are not common, but a number of restaurants serve tea, coffee, and hot chocolate.

Cuisine and Ceremonies

There is a high consumption of food and drink during ceremonies; a multidish feast is prepared with all the staples and delicacies of the community. In some ceremonies, men and boys can be seen eating together, while girls and women eat in a different corner of the house. Traditional ceremonies coincide with seasonal changes and harvests. Thus, feasting is reduced in the period from March to May, known as the "hungry season," and the rest of the months, known as the "season of plenty," are traditionally filled with celebrations.

Almost all groups sacrifice animals to God or the gods. This is to thank the spiritual beings for all their support, praise them, request additional blessings, and express gratitude for prosperity, including good harvests. Muslims sacrifice once a year, in a major festival (described in Chapter 7). The symbolism of sacrifice is more important to members of traditional religions who want to show respect and devotion to their gods. Some animal organs (heart, liver, kidneys, and gizzards) are believed to have spiritual force and are consumed mainly by priests and chiefs. Some gods require special animals, as in the example of Ogun (the Yoruba god of iron) who demands that the sacrifice be a dog.

Large feasts are associated with marriages, naming ceremonies, and funerals. Among the Hausa, millet porridge and red sorrel are prepared for guests at a traditional marriage. In naming ceremonies among the Yoruba, certain food items are used to pray for the new baby: honey and salt for a joyous life; kola nut for long life; and gin for respect. These and other items such as pepper, water, and salt are placed on the tongue of the baby (in the most minute quantities) or of the mother if the item is considered strong (for example, gin, pepper) to welcome the baby to the world. All guests partake of these items, in addition to the big meal that follows. In many areas, it is also an occasion to eat sweet "puff-puff."

Food is also consumed for its medicinal benefits. The power of food to benefit the body is privileged far and above the aesthetics of food presentation. Some groups associate an inadequate intake of pepper and oil with bad eyesight. Excessive consumption of some foods, such as peanuts, is discouraged among some groups who associate them with hemorrhoids. Certain food items are considered taboo in some families. Pregnant women and sick people must alter their diets to suit their conditions. In short, a number of health conditions may be affected by the consumption or avoidance of some food items.

Traditional healers may also prescribe certain foods for sick people to eat, based on the belief that some foods can weaken the body while others can give it strength. When death is anticipated, struggles to prevent it may entail the inclusion of specific items in the medication, and a traditional healer may prescribe the consumption of parts of the tortoise, snake, or other "strong" animal. Various plants are used to make herb drinks, consumed as medicines and beverages by the sick and weak.

Nigerian Cuisine in America

Nigeria (and many other African areas) have exported some of their foods and cooking techniques to the United States. A number of southern dishes in the United States show the impact of the African diaspora in the use of such items as okra, gumbo, black-eyed peas, and a variety of desserts.[2]

The impact of Nigerian food in the United States dates back to the time of slavery. Enslaved Africans and their descendants successfully retained some aspects of their cultures while assimilating new ones. As in Africa, food remains important for ceremonies and sacrifices. Africans are associated with the spread of peanuts, okra, sesame seeds, and black-eyed peas. For years, they were the leaders in growing these crops in slave gardens and other small farms. Over time, their hosts also accepted some of these cooking techniques and foods.

Africans have made creative substitutes: if there is no palm oil to give the soup its red color, tomato paste and sauce substitute for color, and lard for oil. A variety of grain alcohols replace palm wine. Okra soup gave birth to Cajun gumbo, and corn and bean cakes have become popular alternative snacks. The established cooking techniques of slow stewing and deep-frying are now traditional in the Americas.

New combinations have also been created. Animal parts discarded by the hosts became materials with which to be creative. Pig's intestines (chitterlings), ham hocks, bacon, and various organs are valuable, and "side meats" such as animal fats and salt pork enhance the flavor of vegetables. If yam is not available as a starch to build energy, cornmeal, onions, and seasonal vegetables can act as substitutes. Commonly found ingredients and poor-quality meats were converted to delicious meals, as Africans created new combinations that are now part of the southern, Creole, and soul food cuisines.

Nigerian and African-American communities continue to eat most parts of fish, pigs, and chickens. Peas and beans are desired staples, in addition to rice and grits. Vegetables, stalks, and roots remain important parts of their recipes. Soups and stews are flavored with ham hocks. A big, one-pot dinner with beans, rice, and potatoes remains popular.

Nigerian and African restaurants and groceries can be found in major American cities, a reflection of the growing diversity of the United States and the interest in cuisines from various lands. Groceries carry many African foods and spices that the U.S. government allows to be imported. Restaurants sell refined traditional meals, with reduced pepper and oil, to meet the taste of Americans.

TRADITIONAL DRESS

As in the case of food, Western culture has not undermined the preference for traditional dress in Nigeria. The majority of the population wears traditional dress or a modified version on a routine basis. Even the elite that wears Western attire in the workplace prefers traditional garments for ceremonies and special occasions. Clothing styles tend to retain established basic themes, but differences are marked in materials, patterns, and colors. High-quality handwoven cloth from local weaving industries is still available, although mass-produced, manufactured textiles are more common and less expensive. Cloth has traditionally been made from cotton, other organic materials, and silk, but synthetic fabrics are now added to the list of available materials. Silk is woven by the Yoruba (*sanyan*) and the Hausa (*tsamiya*), but not as frequently as cotton, which is more abundant. There are two basic dress forms, the poncho and the wrapper, which will be discussed below.

The Poncho

Examples of the poncho forms include the *danshiki* among the Fulani, *buba* among the Yoruba, *babban-riga* among the Hausa, and various related styles usually called "gowns" in the literature. More widely known as the *boubou*, this garment resembles a poncho sewn at the sides. Although *boubou* is a French word, it has nothing to do with the French, who merely adapted the Wolof word *mboubou* to describe the ample garment. The Fulani use the word *maboube* for a group of makers of wool blankets and *khasa*, which are handwoven, embroidered cloths.

The most simple way to make the male version of the *boubou* is to sew bands of handwoven cloth together, each band between three and four feet wide. A hole is cut in the middle for the head. To prevent the sides from flapping, they may be held in place by tabs or sewn to look like a shirt without sleeves. Pockets are added in the center either for decoration or utilitarian use.

The voluminous type, the *babban-riga*, was originally associated with the Hausa and later the Nupe and Yoruba but is now widespread all over the country. This is a big robe whose skirts reach the floor and whose width extends well beyond the wrists. A central piece is cut from long bands. Sleeves are attached to the central portion at right angles. There is a front pocket, so large that it extends below the knees. The beauty of the cloth is in the pocket, usually embroidered in silk. The embroidery reflects status as well, as only the well-to-do can afford much silk. These robes are generally large and can weigh as much as eleven pounds. Worn with a fitted cap, the outfit lends the person wearing it an air of importance and ceremony. In tropical climates, the *babban-riga* does not offer comfort, as it can be hot, but the compensation lies in the prestige it brings. To this day, it remains the preference of many chiefs, kings, politicians, and merchants, as it confers great prestige on them.

The *babban-riga* has been adapted to modern living, and one can see Nigerians wearing smaller, lighter versions to their offices. Many are now made with a cotton-polyester blend, either imported or locally manufactured, which makes them lighter. The embroidery can be scant, found only on the small pocket and the neck opening.

Women also wear the *boubou* in different styles. These include the large version, the *grand boubou*, either knee- or full-length. The wide round neckline allows a generous display of necklaces and other adornments. The garment is suited to the weather, allowing air circulation, but very unsuitable for housework as it slows down movement. For wealthy women, the *boubou* can also serve as an additional layer, on top of the blouse and wrapper. The *boubou* placed on top of another garment has to be in materials, such as lace, that will reveal the under layers and show off contrasting colors.

There are smaller types of *boubou* as well, including the Yoruba *buba*, a type of blouse which must be worn with a wrapper. The *buba* has a slit in its middle, like a T-shirt without the collar; it is round-necked and has tubular sleeves. The Hausa wear an embroidered blouse called the *taqua* that traditionally has wide tubular sleeves, while modern versions have smaller sleeves. The sleeve is joined to the main part of the garment around the upper arm and usually extends to the wrist. Among the Kanuri, the *buba* resembles that of the Yoruba in the top, but it is floor length and the rectangular tubular sleeves extend to the waist.

Dozens of other styles exist for men and women, many along the same line. Some versions are gusseted, that is, triangular pieces are added to make the garment stronger and roomier. The nomadic Fulani group wears the *danshiki*, a flowing robe, for festivals and on market days. The Yoruba, too, have the *gbariye alapan-adan*, bigger than that of the Fulani, as they enlarge the size of the sleeves.

The Wrapper

Non-tailored clothes wrapped around the body in various ways are very common throughout Nigeria. In some areas of the middle belt, men wear such in a toga style. In the past, the Yoruba men's ceremonial dress was also a toga made of handwoven materials. Men often wear short wrappers at home.

Most women wear the wrappers in various sizes. The quality and texture of the materials may reflect class and wealth. Many now wear blouses with a shirt-type wrapper, but there are variations. For instance, among the rural Fulani, the handwoven wrapper is tied to cover the body from above the breasts to the ankles (or slightly above the ankles). Other beautiful, smaller wrappers are tied around the body and can be removed and tossed on the shoulder or head. Among the Yoruba, three wrappers of matching colors can be used. One is tied on the head, to cover the hair and provide an elegant headtie. The second is the largest one, a floor-length wrapper called *iro*, which is wrapped around the entire lower half of the body. The third is worn as a stole or tied around the upper torso to hold down the large wrapper and provide color contrast.

Yoruba Dress

The clothing of the Yoruba of the southwest brings out the richness of traditional dress.[3] The Yoruba put great emphasis on dress, and people are expected to wear appropriate clothes to attend different functions and to visit important people. Farm workers are allowed to dress scantily, but to wear farm clothes or dress of poor quality to the market or city is considered to be uncivilized. Formal wear is elaborate and ample, and it is generally traditional rather than Western.

Traditionally, the Yoruba wear gowns, like those described above. When they are not wearing gowns, they throw a piece of cloth (about three yards by two) under the right armpit and over the left shoulder to cover the body, in a style similar to the Roman toga. Today, when this is worn, as it is by a prominent Yoruba king, the Ooni of Ife, another garment can be worn underneath, so that the thrown piece becomes more of an adornment. This style was probably preceded by the simpler one found in most parts of the country, the *bante*, which is a piece of cloth wrapped around the body. The Yoruba urban culture rejects the use of the *bante* outside the compound: "only a bush man will come to the city in *bante*," as the saying goes.

More often than not, men wear gowns, vests, and *sokoto*, an ample pair of long pants. For centuries, Yoruba weavers have produced handwoven cloth. Men weave narrow bands and women weave broad bands. A tailor sews the bands together to make a variety of cloth, for rich and poor alike. In the past, the common covering for the low class was the *elegodo*, a plain material of inferior quality.

Traditionally, the Yoruba have four types of vest, the *kukumo, ewu, dandogo*, and *togo*, often now modified in one way or another in a simplified *buba*. A vest is worn under the gown or toga. Usually made of different materials from the gown or toga, it has no sleeve or collar. The vest of the wealthy can be made from *alari* (crimson dyed silk) or rough silk (sanyan) and this can be worn by itself. Today, a factory-made T-shirt or singlet has replaced the *kukumo*. The *ewu* has sleeves and a collar and was only made in white in the past. Today, the *ewu* can be in any color, worn by itself or under a gown. The most expensive vest used to be the *dandogo*, meant only for the rich. It has pleats that reach the calves, and the sleeves are long, ample, and wide at the end. It can be worn by itself, as a substitute for the gown. The fourth type of vest is the *togo*, a sleeveless garment smaller than the *kukumo*. It was the occupational dress of the soldier who would use a long, narrow strip of cloth, also twisted around the waist to serve as a belt. A shirt and shorts now replace the *togo*. Of all the vests, the most popular today is the *buba*, a tunic with short or wide sleeves that can be made of any material.

The gowns of the Yoruba are of three types: the *suliya*, *girike*, and *agbada*. The lightest and smallest is the *suliya* (often also called a *buba*), which reaches just below the knee. It is open on both sides, and the sleeve is ample. The *girike* is the biggest gown: large, heavy, and well embroidered, it is strictly a ceremonial dress. The *agbada*, today the most popular gown, is equally large, reaching below the ankles, embroidered at the breast and neck, open on both sides, and fully covering the arm. The *agbada* can be made of many different materials, local or imported. The material and embroidery can be very expensive, to reflect the wealth and status of the owner. A popular gown among the Yoruba, and indeed all over the country, is the *kaftani*, a long gown that reaches the ankle but is narrow and reveals the body shape. It is suitable for office work, which makes it popular among educated people. The *kaftani* is lightly embroidered on the chest.

The pants, known as trousers in Nigeria, come in different lengths and shapes, but all are held at the waist by a cloth cord. They are worn below the vests, which hide the waist and cord. Although the generic name is *sokoto*, pants vary a great deal, and some types are no longer in fashion. The *ladugbo* and *aibopo*, "free" pants that fit snugly around the knee where they terminate, are both out of fashion but may reappear in youth culture. The *alongo*, tight all the way down like a bishop's gaiters, is more of a sports garment. Warriors used to wear the *kafo*, tight-legged pants that reach the ankle. Nobles and wealthy people prefer the *kembe*, embroidered at the leg cuffs and still in vogue. The *efa* is like European trousers, but terminates below the knee. The last type, the *agadansi*, stretches from the waist to the ankles, and is well embroidered at the ankles. Traditionally, it is voluminous between the legs, like the Indian pant. The *agadansi* is still in fashion, but the voluminousness between the legs is now much reduced.

Women traditionally wear an undergarment, the *tobi*, now replaced by a variety of Western underwear. The *tobi* is like an apron, tied around the waist with a band and reaching the knees. The most common traditional dress for women is the wrapper. There is a short top, the *buba*, made of a light material, and a large wrapper, the *iro*, tied around the waist or above the breasts. A third piece can be added, the *iborun*, a shawl covering the back or head or simply tied around the waist. All can be of the same material and color, but this will be in its most simple form. For ceremonies, the combinations are elegant and beautiful. The *iro* can be handwoven, the *buba* can be an imported item, the *gele* or, headtie, is in bright colors and can be made of imported or local cloth.

Adornments

The head is covered as part of traditional dress with turbans (worn by Muslims), headties (by women), and caps (by men). No formal Yoruba dress for a man is complete without the cap. The most common is the *fila*, a close-fitting cap, slightly bent at the top. It can be plain or embroidered in the same color as the gown or vest or in a contrasting color. There is an older design among the Yoruba, the *abeti-aja*, with flaps to cover the ears. Caps are generally made of textiles, although straw caps are worn as protection from the sun. In the southeast, caps of European designs are widely used. The cap in the north is fully embroidered, in multiple colors and motifs and in complex shapes and lines. The Hausa caps now display such modern symbols as cars, airplanes, and the country's coat of arms.

While elite women wear hats like Europeans, Muslim women wear a veil that covers the head and face. Scarves can be used to tie back the hair and for decoration. The *gele*, or headtie, is common among the Yoruba. It is a band of cloth about six feet long and one foot wide, wound twice around the head and tucked in at the side. The cloth can be plain or expensive, depending on status and wealth.

Headties and scarves do not disguise the elaborate hairdos that emphasize beauty and femininity. Women's hairstyling is both an occupation and an art, learned informally at home or in many of the modern salons in various parts of the country. Skilled hair braiders and hairdressers can be found in most parts of the country.

Hairstyles say something about the person or event and there are established traditional styles such as *suke* and *kolese* among the Yoruba. Each style is fashioned in rows, with furrows, lines, and ridges. Some styles reflect the changes of the time, including the design called "skyscraper," which shows that high-rise buildings are now part of the landscape. A few styles are reserved for princesses and royal wives, while some are for religious devotees and priestesses (for example, the *agogo*). In the north, the Kanuri, Fulani, and Hausa adorn their hair with a variety of ornaments such as beads.

Rings, necklaces, bracelets, and earrings in silver, gold, and other metals are popular body adornments especially among women. The material and craftsmanship are indicators of status. Shoes and sandals are worn by all, and bags (cloth and leather) are an essential feature of women's fashion.

The European Impact

European elements have been incorporated into some types of traditional dress. Women's blouses can be made in European prints. "Empire style" designs reflect the importation of foreign ideas. Educated women can wear an "up and down," an outfit that modifies the big wrapper and blouse and incorporates various types of European blouses and skirts. In some areas along the coast women are seen wearing bell-shaped skirts and tight bodices, again an adaptation of European styles. One can also see bodices decorated with lace and ribbons imported from Europe. The *boubou* has been produced in European textiles as well. A variety of the male *boubou* is the long-sleeved shirt and trousers, the adaptation of the *babban-riga* to a European dress style.

European dress is also worn, notably short and long pants, shirts, T-shirts, and coats. European dress was first worn as work dress in the formal sector (for example, banks, government offices), as Sunday dress to attend church, and as school uniforms. Today, European-style clothes have become fairly common. Hats of European designs are available, and imported textiles are used to make local styles.

Textiles imported from various countries can be found in Nigeria. The manufacturers meet the taste of Nigerians in colors and patterns. Desiring to capture a large share of the market, European merchants have regarded indigenous textiles as competitors. For years, they imitated their colors and patterns, if not their quality. The imported textiles have allowed people of small means to enjoy imitations of the more expensive traditional cloth. Exact European copies have not been possible in most cases, as in the intricate designs of the Yoruba handwoven *ofi* and the indigo *adire* cloth.

A number of imported materials have become so successful in the Nigerian market that they are now treated as essential to the wardrobe. Kings, chiefs, and wealthy individuals use imported lace, satins, velvets, brocades, damasks, and silks. There was a time before colonial rule when kings and chiefs prohibited their citizens from using these materials, so as to establish a monopoly for themselves. Those who wanted to show that they shared in European civilization desired English woolens in the first half of the twentieth century. These were totally unsuitable in the hot weather, and those who used them were criticized as slavish in imitating Europeans. As more and more people traveled abroad or gained access to imported items, the association of imported English woolens and coats with prestige diminished.

Not all imports feed the needs of status. The majority are actually lower-quality, affordable materials. As the Nigerian economy declines, the market for secondhand clothes continues to expand, with much of these coming from Europe. These clothes are originally donated to churches and then imported in bulk and distributed in street markets in different parts of the country.

Europe no longer enjoys a monopoly of the textile import trade. Batik prints now come from successful local industries. Asian and Japanese materials are also available. These materials are used to make traditional garments.

Factory-made materials have contributed to the decline of traditional textiles. As factory textiles are cheaper and easier to get, fewer people pay attention to the more laborious, traditional ways of weaving and decorating cloth. In aspects of life where the Westernization of fashion has been successful, there is no need to use local counterparts. Producing locally woven cloth is labor intensive and the common, plain styles do not appeal to the middle class and wealthy and have declined in importance and sales. Also, the occupational clothes of the past are now considered cheap and meant for the poor. Unmodified traditional garments can be found in rural areas, where the users are regarded by the elite as backward and uncultivated. Appliqué cloths are not selling as much as before, either because they are expensive or they do not satisfy the tastes of the elite. Competition with factory-produced textiles has forced many traditional textile makers to reduce their prices, thereby making the business less lucrative. Whenever alternative employment is available, many abandon their crafts, thus reducing the pool of people with the skills to weave and decorate and the teachers to pass on the knowledge to a new generation.

Nowhere has Western influence been greater than in the workplace. European-style shirts, pants, and business suits define workplace dress in the south. The north is more resistant, and the majority of people still go to work in a simplified *babban-riga*–style garment. Thousands of local tailors can make Western clothes more cheaply than they can be imported to meet individual needs.

Fashion

Nigerians are creative and talented in changing fashions and dressing according to the occasion. Traditional textiles have responded to the market in order to satisfy the tastes of those who need them for ceremonial use. Handwoven cloth now comes in a variety of colors and lighter materials to satisfy urban consumers. Traditional styles also respond to changes. When dressmakers see a preference for short skirts and small wrappers, they will make them, and when the taste changes to bigger ones, they will change accordingly. In the Yoruba *buba*, the sleeves that reach the waist have been reduced just to arm length to cater to the need to drive a car, write, and do other work. When occasions demand less work, a *boubou* can be designed to reach the floor. Embroidery patterns have changed considerably, and some consumers even personalize orders.

There are various types of fashionable imported textiles. Lace is the most favored choice, and each new type is always expensive, although it is sewn into the same traditional styles. Even traditional weavers make holes in hand-woven materials to look like lace-holes. Chiffon lace, embossed lace, and many other types have come and gone. Textile motifs change to appeal to different generations. In some years, textiles will carry glittering rhinestones; in other years, flower motifs will be popular. Color choices, too, can change to capture a historical moment or event. Images of political leaders or patrons can be embossed on commemorative cloth. Politicians use such designs during election campaigns.

Hats and other headgear also respond to changes, and certain designs are dropped in favor of other, more trendy ones. With respect to European hats, the television and fashion magazines provide ideas for traders or local designers. Hairstyles are so adaptable to fashion that something new turns up each year. Traditional patterns are modified, while foreign styles are imported and quickly spread among the younger generation.

Although Nigerians live in a global world and many of them travel freely, their rapid and creative response to fashion and ideas from the rest of the world will continue to enrich their traditional dress and the ancient styles that now define the taste of the wealthy members of society.

Dress and Identity

Dress fulfills the essential need to protect the body. It is also associated with the desire to appear good and "civilized." "Clothes are the glory of the body," declared a Yoruba saying; "but for cloths, many people will look like the monkey, others like the baboon." But dress does more than this, as one volume about dress in many cultures shows.[4] Clothing choices reveal education and taste, as the elite reshapes many traditional styles and adds new designs to meet the challenges of the workplace and a fast-paced lifestyle. Dress reflects wealth, as the materials and embroidery of an elaborate gown will show. Modern living now includes wearing "designer dress" as the successful individual tries to personalize his/her fashion.

The way people dress yields information about culture and the environment. Cultural codes define how to dress correctly in public. Many frown at a blouse that exposes the breasts or a skirt that is too short. Muslim women are expected not to expose their heads.

Dress is connected to socialization and status. Dress and adornments separate girls and boys at a young age. Children's clothes are modeled after those of their elders, including the colors associated with their cultures, such as the preference of the Yoruba for blue and of the Igbo for red. Children can wear accessories for protection, such as charms, or for good luck, such as cowries, a currency of the past.

As people's status improves in life, they change to more expensive clothes. As people get older, they abandon European-type dress and opt for the traditional dress that confers respect. Chiefs and kings wear traditional dress to project the image of authority. Thus, a Yoruba king will wear an *agbada*, instead of an English coat that will make him look like a government clerk.

As in all modern societies, clothes distinguish members of certain occupations, such as members of the army, police, navy, fire-fighters, and prison officers, each with their own particular uniform. Students in primary and secondary schools wear uniforms to distinguish them from other youth. Traditional styles have borrowed uniform designs to create nonprofessional clothes. For instance, the "French suit" style is inspired by the uniform of an army general.

Specialized and ritual attire is associated with all religions. Islamic and Christian clergy have their particular robes. Traditional worshipers of certain gods have their own particular dress and adornments. For instance, a male priest of Sango (the god of thunder) plaits his hair like a woman. Mourning clothes are black. The costumes of the masquerade, the representative of the ancestor, can be made of raffia, to differentiate them from the clothes of the living.

Dress also documents historical changes. Textiles and hairdos have captured many historical moments and events. Cloth is made to commemorate specific historical changes such as the country's independence in 1960, the end of the Nigerian civil war, and the new currency of the 1970s. The cloth of the period is named after the historic moment, just as the fashion of the 1960s was called *ominira* ("freedom" in Yoruba). Hairdos can be named after people, like the Gowon-style, named after Yakubu Gowon, the head of state in the late 1960s and early 1970s. A popular cap among the Yoruba is the "Awolowo cap," named after Chief Obafemi Awolowo, the foremost Yoruba politician and statesman. The economic crisis of the 1980s has given names to inferior textiles. Secondhand clothes are called *tokunbo* to separate them from new items. Developments in music, drama, and films can be linked to those in dress, either in naming or in the adoption of a style popularized by a particular artist.

Finally, dress reflects the place of Nigeria in the international community. This is a two-way street, in which Nigeria receives and gives at the same time. Ideas about designs and textiles come from the United States, Europe, and Asia. Western textile companies study local preferences and trends to know the materials to send to Nigeria. Youth dress culture, shown in sneakers, sports apparel, jeans, and other items, is not much different from that of the United States, but lack of accessibility and high cost turn these items into dream objects for many Nigerian youths.

Nigerian traditional dress and color preferences are also exported. Not only do Nigerians wear their clothes in major ceremonies, they now market them in a number of stores in major American cities. Nigerian hairdos have been extensively borrowed by the African-American community, and Nigerian dress styles will continue to make an impact on their American hosts and ultimately find their way into the leading department store chains.

NOTES

1. Helen Mendes, *The African Heritage Cookbook* (New York: Macmillan, 1971), 27.

2. See, for instance, Ellen Wilson, *A West African Cookbook* (New York: Evans, 1971); Iyanla Vanzant and Cassandra Webster, *Mother Africa's Table: A Collection of West African and African-American Recipes and Cultural Traditions* (New York: Doubleday, 1998); Angela Medearis, *The African-American Kitchen* (New York: Macmillan, 1971); and Diane M. Spivey, *The Peppers, Cracklings, and Knots of Wool Cookbook: The Global Migration of African Cuisine* (Albany: State University of New York Press, 1999).

3. Information for this section is mainly derived from Samuel Johnson, *The History of the Yorubas* (Lagos: C.M.S., 1921); R. Galleti, K. D. S. Baldwin, and I. O. Dina, eds., *Nigeria Cocoa Farmers: An Economic Survey of Yoruba Cocoa Farming Families* (Oxford: Oxford University Press for the Nigerian Cocoa Marketing Board, 1956); and personal observation of the modified traditional styles in contemporary society.

4. See May Ellen Roach-Higgins, Joanne B. Eicher, and Kim K. P. Johnson, eds., *Dress and Identity* (New York: Fairchild Publications, 1995).

6

Gender Roles, Marriage, and Family

THE INSTITUTIONS and ideas of gender, marriage, and family reflect the impact of modern changes and the survival of traditional social organization. Migration, new occupations, Western education, and foreign religions have had significant consequences on gender roles, marriage, and the family. For example, the educated elite increasingly favor small, monogamous nuclear families. But the majority of the population continues to cherish children; men are the heads of most households; large families are common; and polygyny (having multiple wives)[1] is still practiced in many parts of the country.

The family is a universal social institution and both a biological and a social unit. The members are related by blood, marriage, and adoption. It is a social unit where members share not only a residence but the maintenance of the household, the management of economic matters, and the reproduction of the next generation through approved sexual relationships. Members are expected to support and protect one another. Each family is known by a system of self-identification by name and residence, as well as by other signs such as family religion, totem, taboos, facial marks, and titles. As in other parts of the world, the family reproduces and socializes children. However, in rural areas and traditional occupations, the family also serves as the primary economic unit to produce and consume goods and sell their surplus to meet their other needs. Whether traditional or modern, the Nigerian family serves as a welfare and insurance agency to the needy, the jobless, the elderly, and the sick. Where public services do not exist or are minimal, the family organizes and distributes resources to help its members. The family is equally a social organization. As with families the world over, members can partici-

pate in organized events such as recreational activities and religious ceremonies. But the family accomplishes more than this by serving as the basis
of social organization itself, responsible for creating the opportunities for
ceremonies, leisure, and education. As a social organization, the family defines
roles on the basis of gender, age, and generation. Discipline and cohesion
must be maintained. The Nigerian approach has been to use a system of
patriarchy, which gives more power to men.

A family can be classified on the basis of authority figures; extendedness,
as defined by the number of those who are considered relations; and residence
patterns. A family is usually formed by marriage, but in Nigeria, the size is
generally defined as bigger than the American conjugal or nuclear family of
a man, his wife, and their children. As an extended family, a Nigerian family
will contain people of different generations living together or close to one
another, or believing that they are united by a single ancestor. It is common
in many parts of Nigeria for family and kinship to be synonymous. Kinship
binds two people, through marriage or birth. When individuals are joined
in a marriage, this is called an affilial relationship. When they are joined by
blood, it is consanguinous. Nigerians combine both to define the significance
and expectations of the family.

LINEAGE

In consanguinous relationships, where the emphasis is on descent or ancestry, a family tree shows how a present generation is connected to the
previous one, back to the founder of the lineage. Descent is traced in one of
four ways. The most common in Nigeria is patrilineal descent, which traces
one's descent through the male ancestors, especially the father. Less common
is matrilineal descent, which traces descent through the mother. These are
both examples of unilineal descent, that is, through just one parent. The
third type, common in the United States, is bilineal or duolineal, which traces
descent through both parents. The last type, found among the Hausa, is
bilateral descent, which traces the ancestors through one's grandparents in
both the father's and the mother's families. Irrespective of the type, the members of a line of descent are known as a lineage. It is common for a Nigerian
lineage to share a common ancestor. When two or more lineages claim the
same ancestor, they are a clan. Bifurcation can occur in a clan or lineage,
when one member breaks away or relocates, thereby becoming the founding
ancestor to his offspring. Among the majority of Nigerian people, members
of the same lineage cannot marry one another.

Although one may have a wife and children, as in a nuclear family, one's relations also include the other members of the lineage. Even today, a lineage member can expect a share in inheritance; a cousin may contest a piece of property with the son of the deceased, especially if there is no will. One may be expected to treat one's daughter and one's sister equally. Descent affects one's identity, inheritance, access to land, and, in traditional settings, where one can live and farm.

In a patrilineal system, men have inheritance rights, and women may receive only a small share or nothing. In a patrilineal system, when a woman marries she changes her last name to that of her husband and becomes a permanent member of the husband's lineage. All children, irrespective of gender, belong to the father's kinship group. The children will treat their father's cousins as brothers and sisters and may refer to them as such. The man is a patriarch, seeking resources to support his large family and many dependents. His ability to cater to the needs of many people is interpreted as a measure of success.

MARRIAGE

Marriage is one of the most important social customs. Through it, kinship is formed, the lineage is maintained and expanded, and new household units are created. Reproduction is so important that many consider it the primary function of marriage. Of course, there is affection and love. Marriage confers respect and status, such that single men and women are pressured to marry, and a woman will tolerate a number of lapses in her husband rather than divorce him. Agrarian communities place a premium on large families in order to build communities and provide a work force that is hard to recruit by other means. A married couple without children will pursue all legitimate means to get a child, especially through religious and medical agencies. When marriages are in trouble or children are dying or falling sick, someone in the community may be suspected of being a witch. So strong is the desire for marriages to endure.

A marriage unites not just the couples but their lineages and clans. It is conceived as an instrument to join two extended families, forming alliances among different kinship groups. The role of families is reflected in the choice of partners, the religious ceremonies that accompany marriages, the bride-wealth, and the intervention of members of the lineage to resolve marital problems. When a couple wants to divorce, the two people involved tend to consider the feelings and roles of other lineage members.

Arranged marriages are becoming less common. In the past, a daughter could be engaged to a man chosen by her parents. Important dignitaries, such as chiefs and kings, priests, imams (prayer leaders of mosques) and respected Islamic scholars, diviners, and others, may be persuaded to take on additional wives, usually girls from families who have received, or anticipate, favor from them. Even when the choice is made by the partners themselves, the families still become involved in information gathering to ensure that the other family has a good reputation and a tolerable medical history. Where certain diseases are thought to be hereditary, a family in which such a disease appears is avoided in order to prevent possible contamination.

While arranged marriages have declined in importance, men and women still announce their choices and decisions to their parents and other family members, with the hope that consent will be granted. Parents ask questions regarding ethnicity, town of origin, religion, and occupation to ensure that a good choice has been made. Most parents still prefer that their children marry a member of the same ethnic group as themselves.

Nigerians do not necessarily express love in the ways Americans do: a couple in love may not go to movies, eat out, hold hands in public, or kiss one another time and again. Emphasis is placed on responsibility and respect for one another, attention to the moral upbringing of children, attention to the education of the children, fidelity in monogamous couples, and caring for the needs of the extended families.

Traditional marriages record a low divorce rate. Indeed, it was assumed in the past that all marriages would last forever. It is true that marriages experienced greater stability in traditional societies than modern ones. Coping with a bad marriage carried less social stigma than divorce. Members of the kinship group were involved in conflict resolution and they applied pressure to prevent a divorce.

Attitudes toward divorce have adjusted to profound societal changes. While it is still frowned upon, it is no longer a social stigma in urban areas. Many couples also separate without formal divorce in the hope of becoming reunited at a future date. In Islamic areas, there are rules for divorce based on adultery, mutual incompatibility, and the man's failure to meet the basic needs of his wife. Court and Christian marriages follow the British legal system in separating couples. Divorce occurs, and now more regularly than in the past, although not at a rate as high as in Western societies. Barrenness is a cause of tension in a number of cases. Where male children are highly valued, a man may be pressured by his kin to marry another wife, one who can produce sons. Where one of the parties exhibits antisocial behavior, like criminality, the shame arising from it may terminate the marriage. Where a couple lives among a large number of relatives, the wife may find it difficult to manage them, as she is pressured to choose between satisfying herself, her husband, or her in-laws. The husband's relations may intrude unnecessarily into their affairs, to the extent that their meddling may anger the woman. Adultery on the part of the woman constitutes a ground for divorce. In polygynous settings, men justify adultery as an attempt to seek their next wife, but women do not put forward similar reasons.

Where divorce is agreed upon, the process is not very complicated but it is costly. In most cases, attorneys are not involved and the man retains most of the property. In elite marriages, property sharing may be discussed, but it is generally agreed that children will stay with their fathers. If they are babies, the mother takes care of them until they can go to their father unless he makes no claim. In traditional marriage, divorce never stops the woman from visiting the house of her ex-husband to see her children. She can even live with her grown-up male children a short distance away.

Bridewealth

Whether traditional or modern, a marriage requires the exchange of bridewealth and religious ceremonies, both of which involve many people as participants in an important social institution and contract. The customs are also designed to ensure the survival and stability of the relationship.

Erroneously described as "dowry" in some of the literature, bridewealth involves the transfer of property from the lineage of a man to that of a woman. In other words, unlike what is called dowry in some other cultures, it is not passed from a woman to a man, nor is it a gift expected from a woman's family. It is never interpreted as commodities in exchange for a woman or as a form of payment for services or obligations. It is merely the use of symbols and wealth to cement a contract, to announce to the community that the relationship is legal, and that the couple is free to engage in socially approved sexual practices. It ensures that the children of the marriage belong to the lineage of the father. Some also interpret the practice as compensation to the family that has raised the woman and who is now losing her presence and labor to another family. Since a lineage contains both men and women, what is given when a man marries is returned when a woman takes a husband. Thus, bridewealth is a form of social payment that allows a community to circulate wealth. Where the bridewealth is significant and has to be paid back if there is a divorce, it serves to ensure some stability in the relationship since it may be hard to renegotiate the refund. In areas where bridewealth is high, marriage is postponed until such time that the groom can raise sufficient resources to marry.

The goods involved reflect what is available in an area, and the quantity varies from one area to another, from very little, as among the Yoruba, to something bigger, as among the Igbo. Among the objects used are the food staples in the region (for example, yam), cattle in some areas, drinks, clothes, and money. They also include items that are used to pray, such as religious holy books or kola nuts among many groups in the south. Where they involve cattle, as among the pastoralists, the movement of the animals must be carefully negotiated.

Bridewealth is still part of modern marriage, even when the couple marries in the church or court. A traditional wedding precedes that of the church or court, and during the traditional wedding the bridewealth is offered. Bridewealth's survival and the widespread compliance with the custom, even among those who marry outside the country, means that the traditional ceremony remains an important aspect of culture in the modern world.

Procedures and Ceremonies

The payment of bridewealth is accompanied by a religious ceremony that concludes the traditional marriage. In Islamic, Christian, and court marriages, other ceremonies will follow to legalize the marriage. In the traditional ceremony, the gods and ancestors are invoked to bless the marriage. The parents of the bride will attest to the character and chastity of their daughter, her ability to cook, manage the household, and have children. In the past, virginity was very important, to the extent that a discovery that the woman had previously had sex could bring shame upon her and her family. During the ceremony, the family of the bridegroom will make statements of affection and promise to take care of the bride and her children and to meet all expected responsibilities to their new in-laws.

Ceremonies take different forms from one area to another. Among the Ibibio in the southeast, part of the marriage preparation is for women to go to a "fattening house" where they eat large quantities of food to add to their weight and increase their good looks. At the same time, they receive training in home management, cooking, and child rearing. In the north, among the Fulani, a month is devoted to selecting and courting a partner. In this Gani ceremony, every evening is devoted to singing and dancing. Available men line up in front of women of their age. After a period of dancing, the man approaches the woman he likes. If the woman accepts the offer, they will begin a courtship that will end in marriage.

The Ibibio and Fulani examples represent the customary types of marriage. They vary extensively from place to place; but all groups recognize the importance of kinship, bridewealth, community responsibility, and the joining of two families through marriage. The major ceremonies occur in the residence of the bride. A customary marriage is based on the assumption that the man may take yet another wife.

A different arrangement is seen in Islamic practices. Using the Hausa example, the society mandates that all Muslims must be married, even as a condition for sexual relations. In the past, and in a few areas today, arranged marriages involve teenage girls being married to older men, not by their own but their parents' choice. As a forced practice, it is now unpopular and not a few women have run away from their husbands. Yet another arranged form of marriage is known as the *sadaka*, a practice that allows a father to give his daughter in marriage to either a poor man lacking resources or to a learned Islamic teacher. Also dying out, this practice enables a father to force a reluctant woman into a marriage or to use his daughter to build a network of powerful allies in the community.

The common practice among Muslims is more elaborate. After courtship, the religion prescribes four stages in which the relationship is legalized. The consent to marry is the first important stage. The man and his friends visit the girl's house many times to talk and exchange presents. At some point, the man's parents approach those of the woman. If the woman's parents accept their presents, it is a firm indication of their consent. Relatives and neighbors may then be informed of plans for the betrothal.

The imam leads the betrothal ceremony, the second important stage. A representative of the girl, known as the *waliyi*, who can be her father or her guardian, must consent to the marriage before the imam proceeds with the religious ceremony. Bridewealth is exchanged before witnesses. An elaborate prayer follows, and the betrothal is affirmed. Among the Hausa, this signifies that the woman cannot have another suitor and the lovers can see each other but not engage in romantic exchanges or sex. Muslim groups may regard this ceremony as enough to finalize a marriage.

Four to five weeks later, a date-fixing ceremony (the *sa rana*) is arranged to choose an agreeable date for the wedding. Sufficient notice is given to relations who live far away to attend or send their presents and apologies.

The last stage is the marriage ceremony itself. More women are involved than men, and the groom and bride's fathers are less visible. The ceremony can last for eight days, but it is now frequently condensed to three or four days because of the need to cater to the demands of modern occupations. The traditional eight-day format is filled with various activities:

Day 1: The *Kamu*. The bride is secluded in her parents' house with a number of visitors, including those of the groom's relatives. This is to introduce her to the Islamic life of seclusion, if she is to follow the traditional Islamic lifestyle.

Days 2 and 3: Public rejoicing. Relatives and neighbors rejoice by dancing and singing.

Day 4: The *Ranar iyayen ango*. The groom's parents, relatives, and friends appear to participate in the rejoicing. Many poets, drummers, and singers attend to mark this, thus far, the most important day.

Day 5: The *Kamun ango*. The groom appears in the evening. Friends and relatives sprinkle milk and perfume on the groom. The bride's gifts are displayed and packed to be transferred to her new home.

Day 6: The groom is officially presented to the public and presented with gifts, including cash. The public display of the gifts encourages competition between families to see who can afford to part with more resources.

Day 7: The bride goes to the groom's house, accompanied by a young maiden. The groom and friends will visit. For three days, the groom will sneak nightly to the bride's room.

Day 8: The *Yawon tasani*. This is a thanksgiving ceremony consisting mainly of visits to the parents of the couple. Other relatives may be visited and guests are generously entertained.

Christian practices allow for local bridewealth customs and other traditional ideas about the family. However, the legality of the marriage is provided by the license issued by the church. Such a legality assumes a monogamous marriage, unlike that of Islam. The preacher stresses love but still accords patriarchal power to the husband. The Christian marriage type has borrowed Western ideas of wedding gowns, bridal trains, the exchange of rings, and the reception.

Finally, people can marry in court—a "civil marriage"—with the couple signing a marriage contract. However, Nigerian liveliness is added to a foreign legal practice. Families are still expected to be present. The contract goes with a vow that gives the couple the option to make their oath using the Bible, the Qur'an, or the symbol of the local gods. The celebration that follows entertains guests with local food and drinks, and small pieces of cake, in an imitation of the European style.

Marriage Forms

Monogamous marriage—one man, one wife—is not the only marriage form that exists, although it is the most popular among the educated elite.

Polygyny remains widespread among traditionalists and Muslims. A marriage in church or court disallows it, and an antibigamy law exists to deal with its violation in these cases. However, a number of men are known to keep mistresses if their marriages are in trouble or they are not blessed with children.

Although the statistics cannot be confirmed, almost one-third of the married population in Nigeria is polygynous.[2] Customary and Islamic laws allow it, thus enabling the traditional practice to survive. Traditional agrarian economies encourage polygyny. A large farm requires many hands to tend; so, too, does food processing. There are duties at home and in the village, and social expenses to meet. The most secure way for a man to obtain more labor is to have many children, produced and raised by many women. This is closely associated with the function of the family as an economic unit of production.

There are also other reasons for accepting polygyny. In areas with more women than men, it allows every woman who wants to marry to have a husband. The social pressure for women not to remain single lends itself to polygyny as well, since being a second wife carries a higher status than being single. The practice allows women to marry at a younger age than men, which means that a man may be far older than his wife, especially his second or third. In practice, it is often hard for men who want to be polygynous to find women to marry or to gather the resources for the ceremonies and other expenses. Each marriage has to be sanctioned by custom to make it legitimate.

From a medical perspective, polygyny has been seen as an answer to the problems of a high infant mortality rate. Until medical services improved, a large number of children were lost to a variety of diseases. To ensure that a family would have children to keep the kinship line going, one solution was to have many children born to a man by two or more women. Not unrelated is the need for an heir to bear the family name and continue the reproduction of the lineage. If a large kinship group is desired, more sons may be necessary, thus providing a justification for additional wives. Among groups where pregnant and nursing women are forbidden to have sex, marrying another woman solves the problem for a man who does not want to wait for three years. Finally, wealth can be counted in people—the more children and wives a man has, the higher his social status. Thus, a number of chiefs, kings, and wealthy merchants increase the size of their families because of the prestige this brings. Some can boast about their virility, their ability to create a large kinship group, and the enormous resources needed to support many people. Those who own business enterprises can rely on their wives and children as managers and workers.

There are other forms of polygyny that are well adapted to the needs of society. Widow inheritance—the practice of marrying the wife of a deceased brother—is practiced in a number of areas. The woman is not forced into this, but it is a form of insurance, taking care of her and her children. The lineage is able to retain the wife and the children as members and to care for them.

Polygyny requires rules and diplomacy to function. The husband is careful in disbursing his resources to his wives and children. He avoids excessive discrimination so as not to trigger too many rivalries among his wives and children. The senior wife enjoys some power over the younger ones. Where the system works, the women support one another in raising their children and managing their businesses. Where it does not work, especially in modern times, the man may end up losing his wives.

There are a few exceptions to the widespread rule that the members of the same kinship cannot intermarry. Some nomadic Fulani groups allow inter-marriage among clan members. This seems to be a device to perpetuate the nomadic lifestyle by rejecting as partners people from sedentary or urban populations. A junior brother can marry the wife of a deceased brother, a system known as the levirate, although the senior brother cannot marry his junior brother's wife. When a wife dies, the husband can marry her sister, if she is single. A number of Fulani clans also allow some types of marriage between cousins, that is, a man can marry the daughter of his aunt, or a person can marry his or her uncle's child.

FAMILY AND GENDER ROLES

Whether monogamous or polygynous, most Nigerian families are ex-tended in size. A household may contain not just the couple and their chil-dren but uncles, nephews, cousins, and children of friends and relations. People rarely complain of loneliness. The family members promote the values that will unite them, so that a feeling of belonging is cultivated. In traditional settings, a joint economic enterprise such as farming serves to integrate the members, and each person has a set of tasks to perform. There is family property with rules that govern its uses and inheritance. Families are also united by the same religion. In the past, ancestor veneration united them.

A nuclear family has, on average, between four and six children. A child is so important that without one, a marriage is regarded as incomplete. For a newly married couple to be expecting a baby carries great significance: both of them are fertile; the reward of the marriage is immediate; and two families become more closely united. In traditional custom, diviners are contacted to predict the future of the child and to anticipate problems so that appropriate sacrifices can be made to prevent them.

The preparation to receive a child includes protecting the woman's health and acquiring all the items necessary to care for the baby. Many customs protect the pregnant woman so that she will enjoy good health and the baby will be secure and protected. For delivery, there are specialists in both traditional and modern medicine. Husbands, in general, are not allowed to observe the labor and delivery.

Delivery is followed by an immediate celebration. It is an occasion to eat, drink, exchange gifts, and pray for the child and the parents. The celebrations are regarded as both civil and religious events. All religious traditions have established ceremonial procedures.

Where names carry great historical meanings, as among the Yoruba, the couple and their extended families pay attention to the signs that will produce the names for the child. Names can also extol the virtues of the gods and ancestors. Among Muslims and Christians, names can be drawn from the holy books. To take the example of the Hausa, a child can be named in one of three ways. First, it can be associated with an important event, such as the Ramadan fasting period (Azumi for a female and Danazumi for a male). Second, names can be derived from the day of the week. A baby boy born on a Friday is called Danjuma, and a girl is Jummai. Third, religious names are common: boys receive any of the names associated with the Prophet Mohammad and his attributes, while girls can receive those of the Prophet's wives or daughters (for example, Aishatu).

Mothers spend a considerable amount of time with their children, many on a full-time basis in the first three years. They are expected to breast-feed for a long period. In traditional families, sexual intercourse is prohibited during the breast-feeding period, the belief being that disease can contaminate the milk and kill the baby. Weaning takes place between the ages of two and four. Most mothers prefer to carry babies on their back and have them sleep in the same bed. When they are able to walk and fend for themselves, children are allowed to interact with the other household members much more fully. Thereafter, they learn the rules relating to societal values, education, occupation, and customs.

A family blends into community life, especially in rural settings. "It takes a village to raise a child," is a common adage, as relations and neighbors keep an eye on each one. A child is expected to respect not just his or her parents but every older person in the household and neighborhood. Children can be voluntarily and happily sent away by their parents to live with relations who can best give them necessary training or discipline. Parents who can afford it also send their teenagers to boarding schools where education and discipline can be rigorous. In the past, missionary schools were noted for their well-run boarding houses and schools, where religion and values of hard work were instilled in children.

In traditional families and economies, the division of labor is gendered. Among the Yoruba and Hausa, men are farmers and women help during the harvests. In the southeast, women engage in farming as well. Among the Fulani nomads, men keep livestock and women maintain the animal shed and sell dairy products. When Fulani boys and girls are young, they do similar things, like herding cattle. Roles begin to change when they become teenagers and even begin to separate in play: girls milk cows, prepare butter and cheese, and engage in trade; boys handle the security of cattle, the clan, and administration. Yoruba women are great traders, traveling great distances in search of profits. Both men and women can perform religious roles, although more men serve as diviners than women. Among Muslims, the imams and religious scholars are mainly men. Such occupations as blacksmithing, hunting, carving, and others that involve heavy physical labor are considered male jobs. In most areas women do the household chores, including food preparation and house cleaning.

Among the Muslims that practice female seclusion (purdah, or *kulle* among the Hausa), the women stay within the compounds and wear their veils whenever they venture outside. Being homebound is not being jobless, as a compound can also be a factory. The women can practice various crafts and sell their products to fellow women traders or middlemen.

Women are integrated into the management of households and the community. They dominate many craft industries and local trade. As they become older, they acquire greater respect and authority. In some indigenous political systems, they have a share of the power. For instance among the Nupe, women can be influential court chiefs and each village has its "chief of women."

Modern occupations are less sex-based. Schools admit both sexes to the majority of programs. However, more men can be found in the modern sectors of the economy, they hold the executive positions, and they dominate the political arena. There are two reasons for this male domination. In the first place, the education of women is a recent development. It was not until the second half of the twentieth century that more secondary schools and universities were created to meet the demands for the education of both sexes. Secondly, there is a preference for educating boys rather than girls, especially where job opportunities are limited. In areas where the primary role of women is still child-rearing, investments in girls' education may be consid-

insurance for its future. To ensure full participation, there are sanctions, almost curses, to punish delinquents who ignore elders. Elders will soon become ancestors; it is important to seek their favor while they are still alive. Before the transition, they serve as mediators between the living and the deceased ancestors, and their blessings are, therefore, important. From a practical point of view, taking care of them is compensation for their past contributions to their lineage, clan, and community. And the elders, too, take part in raising their grandchilden and other children in the community. When other people go to work, the elders remain at home. They mediate marriage conflicts, discourage excessive punishment of youth, notice and discipline children with anticommunity habits, administer medication, and tell moonlight stories.

Families stress the importance of membership in a kinship group and community, primarily to prevent people from regarding themselves solely as individuals who do as they wish without considering members of the lineage, clan, and community. Both traditional and modern societies continue to socialize children with this communal ethos. This is a carryover from the past, when commitment to a group ensured collective survival. Group interests are now being eroded, as well as the sense of responsibility to the kinship group, but the basic ideas of socialization still reject individualism. Now, as in the past, identity is defined through membership in a lineage, clan, and community. In the past, the sins of a member might be visited upon a whole extended family, for example, expelling all of them from a village if a member committed theft or adultery. Religious law and practices subordinate the interests of the individual to those of kinship.

As this aspect of Nigerian society is very different from the emphasis on the individual in a number of capitalist cultures, it is important to say a word about its original motivations. Why punish a whole group for the transgression of one person? Why does one wage earner in Lagos feed ten mouths, six of whom are not his children? Agrarian societies need the commitment of every member of the society to survive in the difficult task of building houses, harvesting crops, coping with food shortage, and protecting the young when adults are in the fields. If insecurity is a problem, members need to cooperate to fight or protect themselves. Raising large families means that younger members have to rely on older ones and that a man who has children when he is at a ripe age will not live long to take care of them; and without insurance policies, people have to depend on each other for support. Although some of these needs are no longer felt in a modern world, a culture of community, sharing, and philanthropy has survived.

ered a waste of money. The government provides free elementary sch(
everywhere, but girls are not compelled to attend.

SOCIALIZATION

Children are socialized to accept a number of values and practices as aspe
of culture that should not be challenged or questioned. Growing up in la
households and families, they accept the reality of extended families a
kinship. Their cousins and other relations are as important to them as th
parents. Nieces, nephews, and uncles will mingle with aunts and brothers
the same space. Many children see their grandparents and accept the real
that they will be obliged to take care of their own parents at an old age. Th
attend funeral ceremonies and see their parents spend a great deal of mon
on the burial and subsequent entertainment. They will hear the standa
wish that parents be blessed to live well during old age, taken care of aɪ
buried in dignity by their children. The kinship group must continue aɪ
survive. The children will quickly realize that they stand in the circle ᵢ
history: their ancestors represent the past, their parents represent the presen
and they represent the future. While they listen to ideas and lessons aboɪ
the future, they are trained to cherish the past and respect the present.

In the past, without formal school systems, the home was the place t
learn everything, including a number of occupational skills. Where famil
occupations exist, as in hunting or crafts, children become apprentices t
their parents, senior sisters and brothers, and other relations. Where th
children are interested in occupations that are not practiced at home, they
are sent to other places where craft masters are expected to treat them ver
well. In the case of formal education, both Quranic and Western, children
follow the rules their educational institutions prescribe.

Not a single Nigerian group compromises on the belief that elders must
be protected and treated with respect. "He who mocks an elder forgets that
he too will one day grow old," is a proverb that reminds youth to show
deference. Elders must always be addressed in polite language and saluted as
customs dictate. All groups have rules and codes for greetings and forms of
address based on age and sometimes gender. Among the Yoruba, men pros-
trate and women kneel to greet those who are older than them. When this
is not possible, a deep bow may be allowed. Among the town-Fulani, a son
addresses his father as Baffa, his mother as Ummi, his sister as Yaya, and his
uncles as Kawu. Where a man has many wives, a senior wife has a special
name, as Yaya, to express deference to her.

Taking care of the elderly guarantees the welfare of the society and provides

The transition from one stage of life to another is oriented toward making the individual a responsible member of the kin group and community. Many transitions are marked by celebrations that bring the community and kinship group together. Such celebrations bind families and individuals to the community. The birth of a baby is announced far and wide with great fanfare. The kinship group has expanded, the mother is not barren, the marriage has fulfilled its primary condition, and the creation of a next generation is assured. Names are given to reflect the circumstances of birth and the wishes and aspirations of the society. In the past, and still among some groups today, the child would be given facial marks (skin scarification) to show to the whole world the kinship group to which he/she belonged.

Adulthood can be marked by initiation ceremonies, followed later by a publicly celebrated marriage signifying the creation of a new household. Among the Igbo, the male initiation ceremony (between the ages of twelve and eighteen) involves circumcision. The Yoruba and Hausa use marriage as the transition to adulthood. Some nomadic Fulani groups perform circumcision ceremonies for people of the same age group over a two-week period.

With respect to women, the transition to adulthood is also marriage. Some groups, such as the Hausa, believe in female circumcision (clitoridectomy). Where circumcision is practiced, the failure to perform it is socially costly, as the person will be denied a marriage partner and regarded as socially inferior. In the case of female circumcision, it is meant to minimize sexual desire, but it is also painful, medically risky, and makes childbearing a problem. The practice is dying out in most parts of the country.

Children are expected to grow into adults as members of non-kinship groups as well. The idea is that civic culture is important for survival. In the past, this would involve membership in age-grade associations and participation in ceremonies of initiation into adulthood. Children born during the same period would bond in an age-grade association. As they grew older, they would move into another grade together, thus allowing for multiple grades in a community. Age-grade associations were involved in public works, peace maintenance, and some political work assigned by chiefs and kings. Where circumcision and initiation ceremonies were practiced, members of an age-grade would undergo these rituals at the same time.

Older adults could also bond as members of a secret society. In traditional secret societies, membership was closed, and it was granted only after the performance of necessary rituals. Members swore and kept an oath of secrecy, circulated relevant information, formed political alliances, and governed in collaboration with chiefs and kings. They were often called upon to perform legal duties, administer punishment, and guarantee social control. Secret societies still exist, with practices and rituals known only to their members, although their role in public affairs has become less important.

Occupational groups are important to children and adults alike. Skills have to be acquired to make a living. In the past, people were expected to join trade or craft guilds to learn the techniques and politics of different occupations. Many choices were available; for example, the Hausa have more than thirty craft guilds (for example, hunters, blacksmiths, and musicians). The secrets of occupations such as divination, witchcraft control, rainmaking, and medicine were never revealed to nonmembers. This is an area where old practices are still strong. These traditional occupations and guilds remain. Even government officials pay rainmakers to stop the rain from falling when an important ceremony is to be performed. It is believed that a competitive game, like soccer, can be won with charms. These and related beliefs contribute to the survival of occupations and guilds. Female vendors in modern markets still form guilds to control prices and argue with a single voice in matters that affect them.

Modern education and governments have undermined the functions of the age-grade associations. New associations such as the Boy Scouts and Girls Brigade have replaced them. Attendance at formal school means that elaborate initiation ceremonies are no longer necessary for children to become adults. The power of chiefs and kings has been taken over by modern officials, and there is thus no need to train citizens in the art of governance and public management according to traditional ways. Secret societies have survived, but the network is now designed to maximize the opportunities offered in various modern occupations and provide help in moments of trouble. The modern doctor now does many of the jobs of the traditional healer, but attempts have been made to integrate both practices. Modern industries produce cheaper items than those of the blacksmiths, although smiths are still working in many places.

SOCIAL CHANGE

Various elements of gender roles, family, and marriage have changed to new or modified practices due to Western education, new formal occupations, the impact of other cultures, and changing lifestyles and habits. Economic modernization keeps transforming rural areas as more and more people earn monthly wages, work far away from their places of birth, migrate out of Nigeria, and meet people of various ethnic and racial backgrounds. The major changes include the declining importance of extended families in favor of nuclear ones, especially among the elite; the reduction in the number of children a couple has; the increase in the participation of women in formal economic and political systems; the emergence of new child-rearing practices and emphasis on Western education; rural-urban migration; and a more democratic, rather than partriachal, method of managing the household.

Urbanization, Western education, and modern economies make the monogamous marriage the most common arrangement among the elite and the younger generation. Educated Christians are encouraged by their religion to have one wife. Problems arise if the woman is barren and the man is pressured by kin members to take a second wife. However, it is no longer regarded as advantageous to have many wives and children because of the need to maintain an elite status—living in a beautiful home in a good area, driving nice cars, and wearing good outfits all cost money. Having fewer children enables the elite to send them to private schools and even to colleges in Western countries. The number of children has been reduced even among traditional families, due in part to better medical facilities which enable more children to survive and diminishing economic opportunities which mean that many people cannot afford many children.

The rise of nuclear families means the decline of extended families. As people live in smaller families adaptable to smaller houses, the significance of the extended family is diminishing. A newly married couple is no longer obliged to live among extended relations or even in the same city with them. The members of a kinship group are no longer united by religion, occupation, or culture. Nuclear families do not, however, mean that extended ones no longer exist, even if the members do not live under the same roof. Many members of nuclear families still regard themselves as belonging to a wider kinship group.

The functions of modern nuclear families are becoming different in major ways from those of traditional extended ones. The modern nuclear family is a unit not of production but of consumption. Other agencies have taken over the family's role in the production of basic goods. The family is no longer a security unit needing many people in a clan to defend the community. There are now the police, the army, professional firefighters, and other security agencies. Many more families are either Muslims or Christians rather than followers of traditional religions, thus affecting the ceremonies to which they attach importance.

Bridewealth remains a crucial element of communal culture, combining traditional and new goods, for example, kola nuts and imported textiles. A noticeable trend is to increase the amount demanded, sometimes far beyond the availability of the best products. The justification for this has been based on the greater cost of raising children and paying for their education, rising inflation, changing tastes, and the need to use bridewealth to establish prestige. If the groom's family is rich, that of the bride can be greedy. Demands can be made for larger amounts of cash, textiles, food, and drink. In some areas, as in the eastern part of the country and among the Tiv, local authorities and the church are so opposed to the increasing costs of bridewealth that they have embarked upon a vigorous campaign against it. A number of families and women are also contemptuous of the rising demands and refuse to follow the trend. High bridewealth is now seen as a cause of problems for many in securing loving partners while those with cash can keep acquiring additional wives.

Within the household, working mothers are spending as much time as their husbands in their professional occupations, making it difficult to continue a traditional division of labor. Those with good incomes have live-in maids and other domestic help to do routine chores. Professionalism is highly valued as it brings prestige to the family. The enhanced economic power of women has translated into more democratic household management. In elite homes, children have a voice, women have authority, and traditional values of patriarchy have been eroded. In such democratic arrangements, the children consider the occupations that suit their needs and later select lovers and friends with little or no parental interference. Many engage in premarital sexual intercourse, a growing phenomenon that bothers their parents and those who believe in the purist values of old.

Educated elite nuclear families give property to both girls and boys. Indeed, the obsession with having male children, as in traditional societies, is now curtailed as women are found in most occupations and taking care of their elderly parents. A woman can now inherit from two families. A small number of elite women are now hyphenating their last names, to show their connections to two families, especially if that of their parents is more important than that of their husband.

Western education has also become an agent of socialization. Many Nigerians are happy about the skills acquired in schools. However, many blame the moral lapses in society on the weakening role of the family in the socialization of children and on what they perceive as negative trends in Western education. Many Nigerians, notably representatives of religious organizations, have complained about Western dress, films, pornography, literature, and ideas that they consider immoral for people to use or assimilate. High divorce rates, teenage pregnancy, and sodomy are also blamed on the impact of foreign culture.

Aspects of marriage have changed as well. Among educated people and many others, the choice of partners is based on love and emotional stability, rather than on parental blessings. A couple fearing parental disapproval can elope, relocating to the city to start a new family. Nigerian migrants in other parts of the world engage in interracial marriages, many informing their parents after the fact. It is common for such migrants to travel home much later to perform the necessary obligations of bridewealth and religious ceremonies. Nowadays, marriages can even be celebrated without the presence of the couple: people pray for them, eat, drink, and dance, to mark the occasion in their honor.

In cities, houses and apartments are not designed for large families, and they are scarce and costly. In other words, new residential patterns are unsuited to polygyny. Perhaps the most important agent of change is the refusal of women, especially elite women, to enter into polygynous relationships. Poverty is also a major issue, particularly in the cities where family income is barely sufficient to pay the necessary bills. This creates a source of tension and worry in most homes, most notably regarding the financing of the children's education and the ever-growing cost of commitments to extended families.

Most modern economies do not require the services of one's children, thus reducing the need for a large family. Raising children, especially if they have to go to formal schools, has become so expensive and competitive that those with many wives and children find it difficult to make ends meet. The youth abandon their villages, migrating to cities to find new opportunities. They create a variety of youth subcultures in music and leisure, but those without job opportunities can also take to crime. Older people, too, abandon the villages and move to the cities. Where wages are low, many men leave their wives behind in the villages (as in the example of low-income families in Abuja). The wives do more work in the villages as they take on the tasks abandoned by the men and they suffer the consequences of separation. At the same time, the men live in poor conditions in the cities.

Despite the changes, the communal ethos of the village and society is recreated in the cities. People form associations on the basis of their ethnic groups, cities, or religions to help one another. The associations help new members to find housing, obtain jobs, and negotiate the complications of city life. The successful serve as credit institutions advancing loans to their members. The commitment to age-grades and traditional occupations is weakened where alternatives exist. Some new alternatives, such as cooperative societies and savings clubs, are modeled after indigenous customs. As in the past, members of the same generation, sex, or age still come together to celebrate, wear the same dress for certain functions, and pool their savings in order to invest, buy land, or build a house.

Commitment to kinship and ethnic group still exists, but its importance is diminishing among the new generation of youth. An individual-oriented wage earner living in Sokoto or Owerri, or a Nigerian migrant living in Austin or Seattle, may feel no need to depend on kin support and refuse to share his income. If he is arrested for crime in any of these cities, his case will be tried in a modern court, and he may lack the network to mobilize resources to defend himself. There are certain obstacles that a kinship or other support group cannot overcome and that require the individual to seek help in the formal sector or among non-Nigerians. And there are those who think that their income is so limited that commitment to fellow members of an extended family may bring them to ruin. Although older collective values are being eroded, however, the majority of Nigerians still do not regard themselves as motivated by individualism. They still connect with their community to celebrate, share jobs, build houses in the village, take titles, and sympathize with those in trouble.

Old age is still respected, but certain functions associated with it, such as performing initiation and circumcision rites, are diminished. Hospitals have taken over some of the functions of traditional healing homes controlled by guilds and elders. As village settings change, the role of elders changes as well. With television and radio available, there is less incentive to listen to endless moonlight stories told by the elders. Nevertheless, elders are still cared for at home. There are no nursing or retirement homes; elders live with their children or relatives until they die.

In spite of all the changes and new trends, many long-established cultural practices are still retained. Nigerians remain family-oriented, pray for children, spend resources within their means to raise their children, adore and respect the elderly, and are firmly committed to the institution of marriage. The majority still prefer to identify with their kin and to reject an alienated, individualistic lifestyle.

NOTES

1. Generally called polygamy in many works, but this has two forms: polygyny (one man married to two or more women) and polyandry (one woman married to two or more men).

2. Diane Kayongo-Male and Philista Onyango, *The Sociology of the African Family* (New York: Longman, 1984), 8.

7

Social Customs and Lifestyle

AMONG the widespread social customs in Nigeria are ceremonies that celebrate aspects of family life; festivals that unite the community; major religious festivals and holidays; sporting competitions; and events that promote nationalism in order to build a united country. Current lifestyles reflect the retention of traditional practices in occupations and culture, as well as emerging Western-oriented way of life in careers and tastes.

In general, Nigerians are outgoing and friendly. Salutations communicate warmth and, while kisses are uncommon, people may hug, shake hands, and hold one another. It is not regarded as vulgar to speak loudly in public, although the qualities of a gentleman are appreciated in certain quarters. Whether in a bus or an airplane, Nigerians openly discuss their country's or their own aspirations. Their knowledge of other parts of the world is very impressive indeed, with many following international events on a daily basis.

Community life is important and Nigerians enjoy social gatherings, celebrations, and parties. Many ethnic groups turn various occasions into parties, enabling their relations and friends to enjoy good food, music, and dancing. A successful person may invite a live band to his home, parade women and men of high social status, and provide food and drink in greater quantities than the guests can consume. For instance, among the Yoruba, a party is called to mark all important ceremonies. The celebrants and others will dance, having money pasted on their foreheads, till the early hours of the morning. The musician will praise each important dignitary in turn, and each will reciprocate with money.

Nigeria has a highly developed oral culture. With telephone access limited to a minority of the population in the cities, most discussions and negotiations take place on a "face-to-face" basis. It is not a sign of dishonesty, but of respect, for a younger person not to make eye contact with an elder or a person in authority when the elder or authority figure is talking. Even if other forms of communication, such as the telephone and computer are available, it is still regarded as polite and courteous to arrange a meeting to talk over a very important issue or a business contract. A person may travel over a hundred miles just to report a conflict with an associate or wife. In such meetings, participants show respect to people of rank and age by allowing them to dominate the discussion. In addressing an older person, a younger person uses the "third person," such as "they" and "he," instead of "you." Gifts may be required to facilitate some meetings if they are political in nature or involve the intervention of a third party to resolve a matter. A few kola nuts, a symbol of respect and best wishes for longevity, or a bottle of spirit are enough in most cases.

The ability to use proverbs, analogies, and stories to support a case is highly valued. Elders are respected for their skill to use appropriate local proverbs. All situations have proverbs and idioms relevant to them. Where an issue is very delicate, an elder may settle it by using idioms and proverbs that the parties have to interpret in an appropriate manner. There is also a religious belief in taboos, that is, actions and expressions that are disallowed in certain circumstances. One may not be allowed to use the fingers of the left hand to eat; a pregnant woman may be prevented from traveling at night; and members of a particular kinship group may be prevented from eating snake. Strangers and visitors are not compelled to follow the taboos, while many educated citizens also disregard some of them.

SOCIAL RELATIONS

Interpersonal relations are characterized by a code of behavior that places emphasis on respect. In many ethnic groups, seniority demands respect. Elders have to be respected; a junior brother respects the senior; a senior wife expects deference from junior wives; and a senior officer at work demands respect from his subordinates. Wealth, power, and titles also confer respect. A king, irrespective of his age, must be treated according to the dignity of his office.

Respect can be shown by the manner of greeting (for example, bowing) and the forms of address (honorifics) and other expressions approved by the culture. In many areas, one must never address elders and senior people by their first names. Morning greetings are mandatory in many areas, and one

up an independent household. Sexual identity is confirmed and role differentiations are affirmed. Survival of the endurance test, including the painful removal of the foreskin, is a source of pride and self-esteem. When the new adults join peer groups, it is something they boast about and use to claim seniority over the junior members of the community.

Ceremonies for the dead mark the last of the life-stages. Burial is a reflection of the rank and status of the deceased and that of his/her children and other relatives. Some burials are not celebrated, like those of children who die prematurely and whose deaths cause great agony. Some individuals may be considered so shameful that their death passes in silence, like those executed for a crime. Those who commit suicide are not entitled to a decent burial. Others require special ceremonies, as in the funerals of members of secret societies.

To receive the most elaborate burial, one must grow to an advanced age, have children, and be regarded as having lived a good life. The burial of such a person becomes an occasion both to mourn and to rejoice, as the deceased will become an ancestor. Among the Nupe, however, there is no rejoicing, as the death of even the oldest member of the lineage is regarded as a great loss. The entire Nupe community is involved in mourning but only adult males attend the burial. The same village casket is used for all burials, to carry the body to the cemetery, "the land of the ghosts," located far away from living areas.

For all groups there are rules to follow regarding the preparation of the body. As would be expected, the burials of kings and chiefs are much more elaborate than others. Among the Igbo, the family will take a deceased chief to the *oto kwbu*, the "funeral compound," to be cleaned. The water and washcloths must never touch the ground. The washed body is clothed in a special costume by the wives and sisters of the deceased. Then the brothers and sons take the corpse to a room filled with the shrines of ancestors. There is wailing and drumming, not to announce the death but to inform the ancestors that another worthy person will soon join them. The wives sit around the body, arranged in order of seniority, each holding a broken knife. The daughters and sisters also sit on both sides of the corpse. Guests come and go throughout the night.

Children and widows sing in praise of the dead. Known as the *kala ekkpe siaba*, the performance is dramatic. The wife stays in a room for three days, her body painted with camwood and black dye. She sings special songs in praise of the dead. The deceased is buried with a variety of material objects— gin, plates, knives, tobacco, beads, and ornaments—things that are believed will be used by the dead in the next world. A pot is placed on the burial ground where food is placed once every eight days for a few months during which time the dead will join the ancestors and later be reincarnated. Women are not allowed to weep at the burial in order not to prevent the spirit from leaving the corpse. If anyone cries, sacrifices must be made to purify the tears. Cannons are fired to tell the spirit world that a new member is on the way to join them. Mourning follows the burial. Mourning attire can be worn for ten months. Widows and female relatives wear black dress or the white baft and *okuru* cloth, and other relatives may wear baft, blue for men and white for women. Male and female relatives will shave their heads and wives will leave their heads uncovered for ten months. Ten months after the burial comes yet another ceremony, the *kopinai*, a great feast that will show how influential the deceased was during his lifetime, as all his great friends and allies are invited and entertained.

Ceremonies for the dead are continued in ancestor veneration and the masquerade festivals described below. In cultures that believe in resurrection (such as the Tiv), arrangements are made to welcome the departed soul. Through *tsav*, a spiritual power, life after death exists. It is believed that resurrection occurs in the first three nights after burial. In those three days, one must chant a series of incantations to call the dead to life.

FESTIVALS

Most cities hold an annual celebration either to mark their foundation or to celebrate a religious event. Thus, not only are there many festivals, but they are celebrated in most parts of the country, exhibiting great drama, creative songs, and intense dancing.

Festivals have social, political, and entertainment objectives. They bring members of the community together. They are intended to give pride to the people; to set a particular community apart from others and give it a sense of loyalty and identity through what is peculiarly its own; and to provide amusement and happiness. All gods have festivals that are occasions to offer praise and appeal for blessings.

Festivals reveal the power structure of each community. Many are indeed designed to reflect (and elicit) the power of the kings and chiefs. In such celebrations, the history of the establishment of a dynasty can be recreated. Ancient conflicts are reenacted, and the victory of the ancestors becomes the justification for singing and dancing.

Some celebrations are carnivals that enable the public to speak their minds about the government, kings, chiefs, and the wealthy. People who are believed to have done something bad or to have acquired illegal wealth are publicly insulted. In some, as in the Okebadan festival in Ibadan, sexual jokes are allowed.

Finally, a festival can be an exercise in crime control, as in the case of Oro among the Yoruba, during which people already found guilty of certain offences can be punished. In some of these festivals, those who have been condemned for violating laws or customs are paraded in public and lampooned. This happens in the Osuru festival among the Otunja, a Yoruba group. As offenders are paraded, the public will sing condemnatory songs; for example:

> It is the cult festival that we are celebrating
> You ought to know the thieves
> The thieves shall give birth like rats
> I am not a cursed person
> Those who stole yam seedlings shall suffer
> It is the fornicator that would suffer.
> The fornicator ought to be publicly disgraced
> We will disclose the identity of the thieves
> We will expose the adulterer

The festival strikes fear in the guilty, as they may not even know that the public will come to their houses to ridicule them. Statements made in such carnivals are not considered libelous or defamatory. The only protection one has is to behave according to community norms and values.

The most widespread festival, especially in the south and middle belt, is that of the masquerade, a celebration of ancestors. Among the Yoruba, such celebrations are called *odun egungun*. The masquerade signifies that the deceased have risen from the dead and the ancestors are present among the living. The masquerade speaks in a disguised but understandable voice. He wears a robe of cloths and a huge mask. He dances in public, prays, receives gifts, and entertains. Some masquerades are accompanied with acts of violence and masculinity, such as beating other participants with lashes. Many of these clashes attract hundreds of spectators as the masquerades wander through the city. Some ceremonies, such as Oro and Agemo among the Yoruba, forbid the participation of women. Oro is the cult of a secret society and is celebrated at night. Agemo is a masquerade known for bringing together the people of a city.

Good harvests also provide occasions to celebrate. These may involve religious celebrations in honor of Mother Earth and fertility. The Igbo celebrate the "New Yam Festival" (known as the *Iri ji Ohuru na Igba Nta*), a thanksgiving festival to mark the abundant harvests of yam and grains. This takes place around July shortly after the first yam is harvested. Sacrifices and praise are given to the ancestors and earth goddesses who make abundant harvests possible. Masquerades appear, and people make sacrifices and pray for better harvests. So important is the "Yam Festival" that it has been modified by Igbo Christians, who celebrate it as part of the Christian "harvest festival." In recent years, the event is sponsored as the Ahiajoku celebrations, by the state governments. Igbo intellectuals also present erudite lectures on aspects of Igbo life and culture.

The federal and state governments now promote many of the leading festivals in occasional competitions on a state or national level. Performances in halls and stadiums have led to their "modernization" by educated people who have choreographed them for a mixed audience. In competitions such as this, the religious significance of the festivals is lost and the focus is on entertainment value. Not only do the festivals bring out the country's rich heritage, however, they reveal new talent and serve to unite various communities and their artists.

NATIONAL AND RELIGIOUS HOLIDAYS

Holidays are national celebrations. They are both secular and religious, and people enjoy the days off even when the celebrations do not concern them. The secular ones include such universal holidays as New Year's Day (January 1), which can be marked on its eve by social events and religious services. May 1 is Workers' Day, which allows labor unions to organize rallies and talk about the problems of workers and poor people. A special holiday for school children—Youth Day—comes on May 27 and is generally an excuse to stay at home. Independence Day is marked on October 1. Free of school or work, the day is marked by a national address by the head of the federal government and public parades in all the state capitals and the federal capital, Abuja.

Christian holidays include Easter (Good Friday and Easter Monday), marking Jesus' death and resurrection. Easter is an occasion to worship and the weekend is filled with events, which end on Monday in public displays of dancing, picnic feasts, and fine dining. Christians mark Christmas with long prayer sessions on the night of December 24. There are also services the next day and a day full of celebration. Cards are exchanged, but lavish gifts are not expected. December 26 is called "Boxing Day," and it is also a holiday, used mainly for picnics and outdoor events.

Muslims celebrate Ramadan and Eid-el-Fitr around March and April.

Ramadan is a thirty-day fasting period, which begins when the full moon appears. It is a major annual event among Muslims, requiring that they abstain from sex, food, and drink during the day. Ramadan brings great joy and is a time to enjoy various games. Although it is a fasting period, it is actually associated with the consumption of a variety of fruits, with a large meal and desserts in the evenings.

The youth prepare for Ramadan by assembling the musical instruments that they use on the day the moon is sighted, to sing around the city in the early morning and wake people to prepare their meals and pray. (Muslims use this, instead of the calendar dates, to know when to begin Ramadan.) Among the Hausa, a song-drama is added, as bands of boys look for single girls and boys to mock for their unmarried status and divorced couples to criticize. Also among the Hausa, on the tenth day of Ramadan, young boys and girls sing from one place to another and receive presents that they later share. Known as the *tashe*, this is a religiously approved drama designed to entertain people in front of their homes. Boys disguise their voices, color their faces black, and carry the skulls of donkeys. They make jokes in order to collect more presents. Small fights occur, as a stronger band overpowers a weaker to dispossess it of its collection. To collect presents is one thing; to be clever enough to save them until one gets home is part of the game of *tashe*. From this Ramadan singing tradition has emerged notable musicians such as Ayinde Barrister and Kollington Ayinla, two outstanding Yoruba who play *fuji*, a modified Islamic musical form that is now a national genre.

The Eid-el-Fitr marks the end of Ramadan. Special prayers are organized to thank Allah in designated praying grounds. Important Muslim kings and dignitaries use the occasion to display their grandeur and generosity. In the north, the emirs and chiefs will ride horses back to the palaces where they are received by poets, singers, and drummers. A *durbar* (parade or carnival) is presented to pay respect to the king. An annual address is read, and massive feasting follows. All Islamic households are drawn into the celebration. Among the Hausa, the day will start with almsgiving, usually of grains, to the poor and needy. Thereafter, people dress in new clothes and they head for the prayer ground. When they return home, they eat, visit friends and relatives, and enjoy themselves. Many may also visit the palace to see the equestrian events.

The second major Islamic holiday is the Eid-el-Kabir, held for two days in June. The holiday marks the end of the hajj, when Muslims perform the pilgrimage to Mecca. The killing of rams is important to this holiday, a big source of additional fun for children who play with the animals and dance to their own songs. Other forms of entertainment are added, such as equestrian displays and races. The Eid-el-Maulud is celebrated in September to mark the birthday of the Prophet Mohammad. This involves prayer and giving alms to the poor; in the north, it can also be marked by displays of horsemanship.

AMUSEMENT AND SPORTS

Festivals and ceremonies are associated with dancing, singing, and song-dramas that involve people of all ages, women and men alike. Many rituals and festivals encourage play and games. Children and adults compete in wrestling, games, and poetry. Storytelling and moonlight plays are traditional activities that are supplemented with television and radio. Films, television, and radio continue to rely on traditional stories to entertain their audiences. All societies have tales to narrate events, preach morality, or present riddles. Many stories have a pattern. For instance, Fulani tales are divided by generation: some are for children and some are for adults. Children's tales use animals, fairies, and tricksters to teach values. Tales for adults deal with life and its problems and offer warnings to avoid bad luck and destructive vices.

Children play both indoors and out and can be seen using clay, cornstalks, and paper to make toys of various kinds. Adults engage in all sorts of sports, including boxing, basketball, table and lawn tennis, field hockey, and handball. Wrestling is an old sport in many areas and has developed into a culture of its own. Among the Hausa, wrestling is one of the activities during major celebrations. Communities can compete, as well as individual children and adults. A challenge to a neighboring group can be initiated by a community, and a day is set for the competition. Led by a group of small boys, the competitors will arrive at the neighboring village and will be fed by various households. Drummers will circulate to alert the villagers to the presence of the wrestlers. Mats are spread for elders and referees to sit on; a large crowd gathers; the wrestlers appear in their uniforms, and each spends time praising his prowess. A fight begins when a wrestler makes a challenge with hand signals and agrees to wrestle someone of the same age. The wrestlers' knees and hands must not touch the ground. If both fall on their sides, it is a draw; if one falls on the ground, he loses; and if both fall on the ground, the one on top is the victor.

Soccer is the most popular sport in the country. During a major soccer event, people forget politics and problems to support the national team. Soccer's popularity brings all segments of the population together in the stadium or in living rooms where they are glued to television sets. At all levels, one can always see youth playing soccer and engaging in competitions. Nigerians may disobey traffic laws, but not the rules of soccer. Violence can end a game if rules are broken or the referees are partial. Talented Nigerian players make fortunes in Europe, but they are quick to respond to the call to play for the Green Eagles, the national team. Nigeria is yet to host the World Cup, but it has hosted the junior world cup and has won both continental and other international trophies.

Changing Leisure: Cinema

Cinema complements television as a modern source of leisure. It is a rich medium that acquires everything possible from abroad but also produces local films that capture indigenous and emerging cultures, social values, and decadence.

Cinema came with British rule, primarily as a source of propaganda to spread government policies and to obtain people's support for new measures. Through films, the British also hoped that they could spread their civilization. Early films in the 1930s were directed to a new generation of Africans who would, it was hoped, accept Western education and adapt their lives to new realities. The quality was low, mainly based on 16 mm cameras and 12-inch discs for sound recording. The Colonial Film Unit was established in 1939, with a branch in Nigeria, partly to mobilize the people in British colonies to support World War II and enlist in the army. In 1955, the Overseas Film and Television Center replaced the Colonial Film Unit, and it produced a variety of unsophisticated movies for Africans. Actors were few, story lines were simple, the pace was slow, Africans were presented as primitive and superstitious, and Britain was valorized at Nigeria's expense. At the same time, commercial films, notably those of stars like Charlie Chaplin, were becoming known.[1]

After independence, the industry grew rather slowly since there was no technical experience or money during the first years. The Colonial Film Unit left behind small laboratories, studios, and many 16 mm cameras. Three government agencies subsequently emerged: the Film Unit, the Nigerian Film Corporation (NFC), and the National Film Distribution Company (NFDC), all under the Ministry of Information. The Film Unit continued with the production of documentaries and the training of filmmakers for the government. The NFC and NFDC were created in the 1970s and were meant to encourage the promotion of a local film industry, forcing cinemas to show at least one local film after ten foreign ones. The NFDC also regulated the importation of films and their distribution within the country. These government agencies have produced many educational films since their inception.

The most active and impressive film production, however, has come from independent filmmakers. A pioneer company, Fedfilms, produced *Son of Africa* in 1970, but its commercial success was limited. A second company, Calpenny Limited, adapted two of Chinua Achebe's novels (*Things Fall Apart* and *No Longer At Ease*) to produce *Bullfrog in the Sun* (1975). The most prolific of the pioneer Nigerian filmmakers is Ola Balogun, who sought the means to create an authentic industry and to collaborate with other countries to produce films. Balogun produced a dozen films between 1972 and 1977. Many of the pioneer films did not enjoy commercial success, but they laid a firm foundation for the industry. Technical expertise gradually improved, and talented actors now abound.

The themes of the early films are dominated by cultural issues, the impact of British rule on Nigerians, and criticisms of the assimilation of Western habits. A few express radicalism and condemn neocolonialism and bad leadership. The 1960s were a period of both hope and disappointment: hope about the newly won independence, but frustration with the lackluster performance of the Nigerians in power. Nigerian filmmakers regard it as their obligation to correct the negative images of Africa and Nigerian customs and culture as presented by outsiders. The better presentation of Nigeria is meant to inspire Nigerians to appreciate their culture and work for its development.

Meanwhile, foreign films continue to grow in popularity and dominate the cinemas in the cities. In the north, Indian films have always been popular. Everywhere, action movies command respect, especially among the youth who enjoy the violent and dramatic episodes.

The massive growth of the local film industry began in the 1980s. The market has become large, movie theaters and hundreds of small video stores and viewing places operate in nearly every city. Each month, many new films are released, usually in a video format that can be bought in small neighborhood stores. The quality of production varies greatly, although some films are excellent, with highly skilled and talented artists. Movies can be filmed in indigenous languages, English, or pidgin. The most successful are in the indigenous languages because they allow the artists a greater expression of their creative talents, unlike those that use English, which requires many to memorize. They may even add to the script during production without damaging the story line. Successful theater actors have moved to films in order to create what the public really loves to watch and discuss. Famous artists, such as Ade Folayan (alias Ade Love), featured in *Ajani Ogun*, Chief Hubert

Ogunde, the guru of Yoruba drama, and Moses Olaiya, the leading comedian, have also become directors and producers of successful films. The popularity of the movies is due to the celebrity of the stars, the emphasis on culture, and the distortion of reality. Local producers, originally using 16 mm and super 8 cameras and now cheap recording equipment, focus less and less on high quality cinematic form and more on an appealing story, good actors, and attractive costumes.

Nigerian films reflect both old and new themes. These include the clash of Nigerian and Western cultures; the alienation of urban dwellers in places such as Lagos; the alienation of Nigerians from traditional cultures; the problems of city life, notably crime, fraud, and prostitution. The use and abuse of power is yet another recurrent theme expressed in films on corruption, the excesses of political and military leaders, the dangers of ethnic conflict, and the inability to solve the problems of poverty. The films reflect economic conditions by celebrating wealth and presenting existing problems of poverty and unemployment. Social conditions are always a rich source of topics, such as aspects of family life and the conditions of women, children, and health services. Irrespective of the theme, aspects of traditional culture are injected: the techniques of indigenous storytelling may be adopted, diviners are involved to cure problems, and the power of witches is exposed.

While the film industry enables the depiction of Nigerian reality and culture, it has also broadened the scope of leisure. As people watch, they reflect on what they see on the screen. Nigerian films are also being exported abroad, mainly to meet the demands of Nigerian migrants.

OLD AND NEW: VILLAGES AND CITIES

Divisions keep emerging between those who are described as traditionalist and rural, and those considered Western and modern. These divisions are presented in both positive and negative terms. Sometimes those who subscribe to traditional cultures regard the followers of the West as aggressive, consumer-oriented, and decadent while they see themselves as simple, humble, and peaceful. To the Westernized, the rural population may be seen as backward, uncivilized, and primitive in contrast to their own liberated minds, sophistication, glamour, and beauty. They will add that a Western education and the ability to travel and speak in different languages benefit both themselves and their country.

Cultural division is reflected in the organization of space, the city in contrast with the village. The big cities such as Lagos and Abuja pride themselves on Western amenities—cinemas, hotels, and restaurants. Villages lack these and often even the basic amenities of electricity and clean water supply. Cities pride themselves on having what is fashionable and appealing.

Urban areas have exploded, as more and more people have been moving to them for over a century. Cities are magnets for jobs and industries, home to the middle class, professionals, and the wealthy. The majority of the people still live in rural areas engaging in agricultural production. But they are still losing people due to migration in the cities. Some migrants leave only temporarily, but for young migrants and wage earners, returning on a permanent basis to the village is out of the question.

Pastoralism, Farming, and Villages

Animal husbandry remains the traditional occupation of the Bororo Fulani and Shuwa Arabs, both in the north. Cattle are moved from one area to another in search of natural grazing and to avoid a dangerous animal disease, trypanosomiasis, caused by the bites of tsetse flies. Thus, cattle breeding necessitates either a seminomadic or a nomadic lifestyle.

The nomadic Bororo Fulani tend goats, sheep, and cattle. They live in camps, a simple life well adapted to quick relocations. Between July and December, the Bororo stay with their cattle in the northern Sudan, which has grass available and is free of tsetse flies. From December to June, they move southwards to the guinea and savanna areas, keeping on the move for about 400 miles. The seminomadic Bororo and Shuwa combine cattle breeding with trade and small-scale farming.

But the lifestyle of the nomads is gradually changing. The state governments are improving water supplies by building boreholes and artesian wells around Lake Chad. The wells open new opportunities for animals to graze. Some groups of nomads are actually settling down around the Mambilla Plateau and Cameroon Highlands because their animals can survive there year-round. However, there are conflicts with farming communities over land. Herders like to burn the bush in the dry season in order to produce a quick regeneration of green grass, but cultivators are offended as they may lose their crops. Various state governments and entrepreneurs are establishing poultry, pig, and dairy farms and cattle ranches; but these have not been cost-effective nor have they marginalized the role of the nomads and semi-nomads. Mobile schools and clinics have been established to move with the nomads as they travel from one area to another.

Farming is a larger-scale industry than animal husbandry and is carried on throughout the country. Nigerian farms produce cereals, roots, and legumes, various cash crops (peanuts, cocoa, rubber), fruits, and vegetables. The farmers specialize in crops that grow well in their ecological zones (for example, cocoa in the southwest and peanuts in the north). The majority of Nigerians are farmers, working on small farms in villages all over the country. They still supply the bulk of the country's food. Farmers engage in limited trading and keep a few animals as sources of protein.

By and large, farming has followed established traditional practices. Farmers use hand tools, such as hoes, machetes, sickles, and knives. While these tools served well in the past, they have become inadequate to produce sufficient food for a large population. The difficulty of using them, compared with mechanized ones, drives young men and women away from farming. Farmers work mainly on the land they inherit from their parents, or as tenant farmers if they work outside their original homelands. Whereas access to land was assured in the past, land acquisition by the government and the rich has tended to reduce the acreage available to small-scale cultivators.

Farmers rely mainly on family members for labor. Where cash crops are grown, it is possible to recruit seasonal laborers, who migrate from lands that are less productive. Where it is possible, farmers form cooperative societies and combine to sell their crops or to save money. The most reliable system is still shifting cultivation—the farmer uses a piece of land for a few years, abandons it for some years to allow it to regenerate, and then returns to it. Where irrigated farming is possible, as in areas close to a river basin, it is possible to cultivate the same land for the entire year and for more years at a time. The farmers now use fertilizers, especially where they know that these will increase their yields.

Other traditional craftsmen and women still make a living from established occupations. Among these are blacksmiths, weavers, barbers, tailors, carvers, and packaged food producers. These are small-scale businesses with an average of one to ten workers. They do repairs, produce new items needed at the local levels, and imitate imported items. Like the farmers, many of them have benefited only indirectly from the oil economy: while they do profit from the spending generated by other groups including the middle class, the government has done little for them by way of improving the tools of their trades, making capital accessible to them to expand their businesses, or helping them in moments of disaster.

The villages are not as unchanging as city-dwellers portray them. Many local government authorities now provide dispensaries, schools, roads, and markets that transform the villages and bring a small elite group to live among them. Changes in material culture are widespread, thanks to trade that takes goods to all the nooks and crannies of the country. Locally manufactured or imported cooking utensils, imported cloth, local textiles sewn and designed in foreign ways, building materials, and farming equipment can be found in the most remote corners of the country.

Agencies of Change

Nigerian society and culture have always experienced changes and will continue to adapt. If a segment of the population thinks scientifically and rationally, another segment will think differently and show a commitment to indigenous philosophy. Various sectors of the economy are being modernized and mechanized, but traditional occupations exist as well. A Japanese car can be parked in a garage, but one can also see goats and chickens roaming freely in villages and along city roads. Changes can be rapid in some sectors (as in the demand for Western education), persistent in most aspects, slow in some, and revolutionary in others, as in the impact of Islam and Christianity.

The agencies of the spread of Western culture include colonial rule, Christianity, increasing contacts with Europe and the United States, and industrialization. Colonialism, Western education, and industrialization will be examined here.

British rule accelerated the pace of social and cultural change. New institutions and ideas (sometimes regarded as strange by Nigerians) were introduced in the first half of the twentieth century, were subsequently accepted, and are now part of the modern culture. Among these changes are a new system of government, a modern police force and army, an import-export economy, the English legal system, and Western education. These changes were originally uneven in their spread. In the first half of the century, a minority elite emerged in opposition to the uneducated majority. The majority was marginalized in the formal sector as the minority acquired great influence. This dichotomy was reproduced in the years following independence. A large majority population lives in poverty and a small minority is prosperous and lives in exclusive areas.

The colonial economy has grown into a modern economy. The colonial economy was based on commerce that rewarded large-scale producers and foreign traders. Nigerian peasants cultivated cash crops (peanuts in the north, cocoa in the west, rubber in the mid-west, and oil palms in the east). The peasants had to sell at prices determined by the government or the market, and only a small percentage grew rich as farmers. Nigerian and foreign businessmen were more successful and many reinvested their profits in acquiring land from the peasants.

The missionaries pioneered Western education and subsequent colonial and Nigerian governments improved upon it. The south took a major lead as early missionary efforts were concentrated there. The country's first university, the University of Ibadan, was established in 1948, and southerners dominated admissions in the early years. After independence, the number of universities increased, reaching close to forty by the end of the century, in addition to a number of polytechnics and colleges of education. Primary schools are located in almost every big village and there are many secondary schools.

Western education is not concerned with such things as initiation ceremonies or other aspects of indigenous socialization. The missionaries saw education as an avenue to conversion. The Nigerians regard education as an avenue to high social status and profitable occupations. In the first half of the twentieth century, the educated group was small and enjoyed a very high status. Western education brings new values and attitudes. Educated people accept changes that "modernize" them and make them competitive. Consumption habits change as well, as people read newspapers, watch television, and visit movie theaters.

After independence, many educated people moved into positions vacated by the British, believing that it was not necessary to work hard to enjoy excellent remuneration. Service in the government is regarded not as an opportunity to serve the people but as an opportunity to engage in business, make money, order ordinary people around, and promote personal interests. To the masses, the government becomes an enemy—the taxman visits to demand tax receipts; the police come to make arrests; the judges throw people in jail; and the clerks speak in a foreign language that ordinary people do not understand.

The formal school system has taken over many of the socialization roles performed by the family, circumcision experts, and elders. The relevance of age and social status may diminish as the possession of higher education becomes both prestigious and necessary. While men still enjoy more prestige than women, prestigious occupations are no longer necessarily restricted to men. While respect for elders is still very important, the knowledge accumulated through formal education is far more relevant to professions than the knowledge the elders store in their memory.

Hospitals and modern doctors exist side by side with traditional healing homes. If an illness is common, such as headaches and malaria, people can take the appropriate pills. However, when the illness is regarded as mysterious, they will consult the local herbalist or diviner.

Changing Economy and Values

Western education has created new occupations and economic lifestyles. The traditional economy is dependent on agriculture, but the role of this sector is declining. Young people are abandoning farming to work in administration, mining, and manufacturing. The modern industrial economy comprises the production of consumer goods and processing. This includes the making of tools and agricultural equipment; the production of cement, tiles, bricks, glass, tubes, and tires; saw-milling and grain-milling. Many consumer goods are produced, ranging from food processing of different kinds to the manufacturing of shoes, cigarettes, plastics, and soap.

Industrialization brings changes to society and culture. Whether in Kano in the north or Lagos in the south, it contributes to urbanization. It requires workers, many of whom may lack sufficient resources to cope with city life. But the well paid among them are able to move up the social ladder. They make a good income, enjoy a better standard of living, and develop an urban culture that contrasts sharply with that of the traditional culture. They may be seen in the morning in shirt and tie driving to work in a car, drink coffee with breakfast, eat in good restaurants, and enjoy their dinner while watching a video.

Industrialization makes new consumer goods available, thereby diversifying consumption patterns. New occupations, such as engineering and computer-related professions, are generated, thus diversifying economic and employment opportunities. The universities have to respond to these needs by creating relevant courses and departments. Technical skills spread in a variety of areas. The informal sector has received a boost as it caters to the needs of industries and the demands generated by new consumer habits. Bicycles and cars have to be repaired; tubes and tires have to be fixed; and plates and cups are needed to cater to the demands of the food industry. The population becomes more mobile as people seek opportunities provided by new occupations and economic changes. As land is required to build factories and millions of new houses, the land tenure system has to adjust to allow for more commercialization and the development of individual property rights. As companies and the government acquire land leases, the traditional opposition to land sale has to give way. Land that is commercially viable becomes an opportunity for litigation.

Accountants, lawyers, doctors, and others perform various services as modern professionals. These men and women form professional associations, such as the Nigerian Medical Association and the Academic Staff Union of Nigerian Universities, to serve as pressure groups to negotiate with the government for better working conditions. Strikes have been organized against employers and governments to ensure that their demands are met.

Modern occupations attract more rewards than traditional ones. A Western-trained doctor enjoys a better income than a local herbalist. This higher income translates into a higher living standard and prestige. Whereas the herbalist lives in a mud house, the doctor lives in the best part of the "new" city; the herbalist walks, the doctor drives a car; and the doctor is well-connected to other members of the elite. Modern occupations provide opportunities to become rich, to migrate out of the country to achieve career goals, to participate in politics, to acquire those material objects that define the life-style of the most successful, as well as great prestige.

Nigerians have come to realize that educational and economic changes will be accompanied by problems. In the cities, they have to cope with the problems of prostitution, crime, theft, adultery, sexual discrimination, and inter-ethnic rivalries. Traditional ethics of hard work may give way to a reckless search for money.

Changing Political Culture

As new institutions of government take root, they affect the power of kings, chiefs, and clan elders. Chieftaincy systems continue to exist, but not with their former power and prestige. In the villages, clan heads and chiefs still occupy important positions. The elders are still trusted to resolve family conflicts and small cases. Customary and Islamic laws enable the traditional and Islamic elite to exercise judicial power. The government calls on the chiefs and kings for support and makes use of them to resolve disputes, collect taxes, and popularize projects.

Elements of indigenous political ideas and values are retained in modern politics. Chiefs and kings are still regarded as legitimate, even when they exercise little political influence. Their legitimacy derives from the power of tradition. These are offices that are justified by history and can only be competed for by a limited number of families with long-standing historical claims to titles. Honorary chieftaincy titles are valued, which is why wealthy Nigerians and politicians acquire them and are known as "chiefs."

Many voluntary associations are formed on the basis of ethnic or town origins and membership in the same clan. Many of these associations exist in cities or among Nigerian migrants in other countries. They may be known as the "Ibibio Descendants Union" to show that members are from the Ibibio area; or the "Okebadan Club" to imply that only people from the city of Ibadan are members. These associations provide support for their members, organize social events that bring them together, donate to charity, pay for projects in their home cities, and serve as sources of political mobilization for politicians looking for constituencies that will support them.

Ethnicity plays a major role in politics. Nigerians belong to different ethnic groups. The existence of groups is not the problem, but ethnicity becomes an issue when these groups compete for power and resources and discriminate on the basis of origin. When people stress the ties to their kinship and ethnic group to obtain an advantage, this becomes an issue that can create political instability and war. The culture of ethnicity created a major civil war in Nigeria in the 1960s.

The British colonial government and Nigerian politicians have turned the multiplicity of groups to selfish advantage. For the British, preventing the leaders of the ethnic groups from forming powerful alliances stabilized their colonial government. For Nigerian politicians, emphasizing their ethnicity will win them votes and attention. When in power, they may use ethnicity to distribute political offices to aggressive supporters. When a politician is in trouble, he can mobilize his ethnic group for support and accuse rivals from other ethnic groups of plotting his downfall. When people identify themselves as Yoruba, Efik, or Jukun, they suggest that their commitment to their groups is more important than their commitment to Nigeria and that the determinant of power may be ethnicity.

There is a political elite as well, operating either as representatives of ethnic groups or as emerging political networks. The political culture favors a tiny political elite and the military, both of whom struggle to gain control of the state and federal governments. The political elite includes educated southerners and members of the traditional elite in the north who took power from the British, and it has acquired some of the authoritarian colonial tendencies of the British. The political elite is not united, it depends on ethnicity to manipulate politics, and it uses power for self-interest, especially to accumulate wealth. The most successful beneficiaries in the political system have been the senior military officers who have governed the country for most of the years since independence. They come to power through coups and are corrupt and greedy. The political and military elite have turned politics into business and corruption into an integral aspect of political culture.[2]

It is the number one passion for Nigerians to talk about Nigeria, usually in a negative manner among themselves but in a protective manner with strangers. The hope for a greater country makes most Nigerians political analysts. The majority are politically aware, understand national and world events, and tend to have very strong opinions. Issues are generally discussed against the background of ethnicity and corruption. There is a national identity crisis, as many do not accept being called Nigerians, but prefer being known as members of a particular ethnic group (such as Nupe or Igala). When the subject changes to culture, they are very proud, and they boast that their own is superior to that of the West.

Notes

1. Jean Rouch, *Films ethnographiques sur l'Afrique noire* (Paris: UNESCO, 1967), 375–408.

2. Toyin Falola and Andrew Clarno, "Patriarchy, Patronage, and Power: Corruption in Nigeria," in John Mukum Mbaku, ed., *Corruption and the Crisis of Institutional Reforms in Africa* (Lewiston, NY: Edwin Mellen, 1998), 167–192.

8

Music and Dance

IN NIGERIA, music and dance very often go together. Sometimes a dance type accompanies a specific music, for example, the music and dance of hunters (traditional music) or the "Synchro System" for the *juju* music of King Sunny Ade (modern music). Although traditional music genres are numerous, they are united in their song content, singing styles, instruments, and functions. Traditional music and its contents is never written down, but transmitted orally and produced from memory.

If Western music focuses on sound, the instruments producing the sound, and the composers of the sound, Nigerian music deals with all of these as well as with the connections between a song and the belief systems and rituals of the community. Music and dance are used to express every type of human emotion and the values of society.

Music from other lands also reaches Nigeria. Whether it is jazz, blues, reggae, pop, or hip-hop, any musician who is popular in the West, Latin America, and the Caribbean will be known in Nigeria. Not only is the music from these various places played on the radio, on television, and in clubs, Nigerian musicians also adapt imported forms to create new innovations. Popular music successfully combines Western and African traditions to create innovative genres such as *juju, fuji*, Afro-beat, and others. Similarly, famous Nigerian musicians play outside the country. In Berlin or New York, one can easily find stores that sell the compact discs of King Sunny Ade, Fela Anikulapo-Kuti, I. K. Dairo, Ebenezer Obey, Warrior, Sikiru Ayinde Barrister, Salawa Abeni, and many others. These musicians have also given successful concerts in major Western cities.

Both in the past and in the modern world, traditional music is a core aspect of social life, celebrations, festivals, and ceremonies. Not only is traditional music still being played, but it has been incorporated into most aspects of modern music.

MUSICAL GENRES

Nigerian music can be classified in various ways: by the age of production (traditional or modern); sources of origin (local or foreign); means of production (instrumental, vocal, or mixed; solo or group); structural forms; repertoires; and the occasions and functions of use. Nigerian music will be discussed on two levels, first considering who listens to the music, and second describing its function and performance.

Traditional music forms may be classified according to the audience, whether targeted or spontaneous. There can be a target audience for a specific kind of music. A musician may play to entertain a king or chief in his court; and a poet may sing in honor of a bride or bridegroom. Although others certainly enjoy the music, it may be directed to certain primary listeners. One may also sing for personal enjoyment. This involves both amateurs and professionals, singing with or without instruments. The reasons may be to attain self-esteem or overcome boredom and loneliness in circumstances where others are not present. The instruments may range from sticks to dry fruits or snail shells. It is not unusual for women to sing as they cook or do other housework, play with their children, or engage in their crafts. Group music is yet another form, where many singers perform for a crowd that listens and dances. Group music and dancing occur during festivals and celebrations such as weddings, in moments of cooperative work, or even when a gathering of children or adults are just playing together. This may involve a professional musician or simply hand clapping. Group music most commonly involves an ensemble of about three drummers or a combo playing drums, flutes, and trumpets along with vocalists.

If traditional music is classified by function and context of performance, there are no less than eight major musical genres.

Court Music

Court music is the music for the king, members of his household, important dignitaries, chiefs, and visitors. It can also be the music associated with the rituals of kingship—the making of a new king, ceremonies to renew the kingship institution, and the funeral of a king. In all the palaces of the

Ritual Music

Singing is involved in the rituals that serve to purify society, that is, to apologize to the gods and expel all the evils of the preceding year. Music is also connected with the rituals of the rites of passage, the essential life history of birth, puberty, marriage, and death. The gods have inspired special instruments and music to appease them. The drums of the Yoruba deity, Obatala, *iya nla, iya agan, afere,* and *keke,* represent its four wives and they must be used in the god's honor. Four drums are also used for Sango, the god of thunder and lightning. An Ibibio woman who feels rejected or thinks that her beauty is waning may pay for an *uta* orchestra to perform a ritual song of regeneration.

There are special orchestras for ritual purposes. One example is the *ekpri akata* of the Ibibio that tries to restore morality and societal values. From time to time, it embarks on moral crusades. Like the Oro among the Yoruba, the *ekpri akata* orchestra comes out at night, around 2 A.M. The members move around the city, warning evildoers, thieves, and witches to stop their activities and voluntarily leave the city. They may mention people's names to embarrass them so that they can run away or mend their ways.

Festival Music

Songs form an essential part of all traditional festivals. They not only provide an opportunity to praise the gods and give thanks, but they also serve to make social commentaries. Songs can affirm the trust in spiritual beings; or when things are bad, they may express grief. They can express fear, or warn that a person is strong, as in the following example:

What a friend?
I praised him, he threatened me
But he cannot overcome me
The burning torch enters water and quenches
The lizard who wages war against the landlord ends in death
The parrot is never caught in a land trap
He who pursues Yemi Owo-Egbeleke, the husband of Sade Itabale, cannot catch him.[1]

Music is a medium of political and social articulation, and the various festivals provide the public with the opportunity to speak their minds. Satire is a major medium, with songs mocking all sorts of people—those who are

prominent kings are quarters where the musicians and drummers stay, som
on a permanent basis. Consequently, the music or drumming professio
often becomes a family occupation as the children are trained in the instru
ments and musical tradition of their parents.

Court music embodies power. In some places, court music is restricted t
royal use. Drums and certain instruments are the monopoly of kings. Th
emedo emighan, music of the Benin court, is not supposed to be playe
elsewhere. In Oyo, the Alaafin (king) enjoys monopoly use of *gbedu*, *kos*
and *ogidigbo* music.

A combination of vocal and instrumental arrangements, court music
elaborate and reflects the range of palace activities. Some music serves as th
facilitator of administration—to wake up the king and members of his hous
hold in the morning; to celebrate the arrival of the king in his office for th
day's work; and to announce various daily events, such as the times whe
guests arrive and leave and when the king is tired or wants to rest for th
evening. Much of the music is meant to praise the king, for his listenin
pleasure and that of his guests. Music is also used to announce disasters, suc
as the outbreak of war or the passing away of a king.

Music for Entertainment

As in most cultures, music provides entertainment for the Nigerian peopl
Even such forms as ritual and ceremonial music have their dimension
entertainment. A number of secret societies, such as the Ekpo among th
Ibibio, organize a "non-secret" branch of their organization, such as the Ndo
Ekpo, whose members perform entertaining comedies for the general publi
Masquerades include dances to entertain as well as recognizing the ritu
significance of performance. Many orchestras combine music with drama t
enhance the pleasure of their audience. Entertaining songs are also include
in ceremonies associated with the various stages of life, from birth to death
They express love, praise, and the joy of celebrations.

Work Songs

Work-synchronizing songs are very common, serving as therapy and minimizing the hardship of work. Farmers sing while hoeing a field; blacksmith
sing as they beat a hot iron rod; and women sing as they make pots. Among
professional associations, such as that of the hunters and smiths, songs serve
to unite the members in celebrations. Among traders, songs are used as advertisements to attract customers.

evil, those who flaunt their wealth, those who have adopted new customs, and those who are morally bankrupt. In small communities, people tend to know their neighbors and their inadequacies. Festivals provide the opportunity to criticize. To cite one example, which lampoons a rich and powerful politician disliked by his own people:

> The false man, Oh terrible man!
> The villain who looks like a beast
> Massive chin, convex back
> Insolent man, man of excess
> His head is like that of an elephant, his cheeks are rotund.

The man is being mocked, described as ugly both in looks and action.

Many songs are colored with political commentary, reflecting contemporary events. In recent times, the songs have captured the evils of military rule, the failure of civilian politicians, and the corruption of power. They can praise popular politicians, as in festival songs among the Yoruba that eulogize the achievements of Chief Obafemi Awolowo. Songs can also interrogate people's habits, government spending, and the sources of the wealth that some people parade. One example is as follows:

> The road is built for million millions of money;
> The road lasted a year.
> How many million millions can build a road?
> Who keeps the change, who pockets our money?

When singers complain or query, they also compose entreaties to appeal for change, calm, peace, and progress. They appeal to the deities to help, to give support, and to smile on the community. To give an example:

> Our gods, the gods of our fathers
> Deliver us from misery.
> We do not want to toil day and night
> Give us money to spend
> Our gods, deliver us from poverty.

Festival songs reveal the musical repertoire of the community and the products of the new creative talents that arise each year. A new song can be a product of hard work in the weeks preceding the festival during which the composer has given careful thought to the words and their effects. Yet, many songs are created fresh, improvised as the occasion demands.

Recreational Music

Game-songs, dance music, wrestling music and folk-tale songs are among the most popular forms of recreational music. These are all rich, creative, and adapted to the needs of various segments of the community. In a folk-tale song, for example, a narrator can tell a long story to children and adults as they sit outside the house during the evening.

Music Drama

Dance-drama and music drama associated with various festivals are forms of theater. Masks and acrobatic displays are combined with music to create impressive events. Examples include the water regatta in coastal areas, burial rites among the Yoruba, and masquerade festivals in various places.

Panegyric Music

Panegyric music—praise singing and praise chanting—is very widespread. The songs cut across other genres. Known as *oriki* among the Yoruba and *kirari* among the Hausa, panegyrics narrate the history of individuals, families, cities, royal dynasties, and even objects. Qualities, achievements, and defining characteristics are emphasized in a praise name. This may take the form of a poem, which combines creative statements with praise. Panegyrics are a source of motivation for individuals: they affirm greatness and establish pride in people and places.

MUSICAL INSTRUMENTS AND SINGING STYLES

Musical instruments vary in their look and sound; they include an array of drums, gongs, bells, flutes, and stringed and keyboard devices. To produce sound, instruments can be blown (as in the trumpet), shaken (as in *sekere*, the rattle made with a gourd and beads), scraped (as in sticks), struck (as in drums or the xylophone) or plucked (all stringed instruments). The most notable Nigerian instrument has been the drum, and it is so important that many assume that it is the only available musical instrument. Whether in solo drumming or ensembles, most music relies on the drum and many dancing styles respond to its rhythm. There are, however, some musical performances without the drum. Monochord fiddles (stringed instruments) used in various parts of the savanna, called the *goje* in many parts of the country, are one such example. Stringed instruments are of various types and sound qualities. Flutes come in different shapes and sizes. Other instruments, including single-note trumpets (made from wood, animal horns, and elephant tusks), bells, rattles, and wooden sticks (claves), are all used to supply rhythm.

The instruments can be divided into four groups. One is the aerophone group, that is, wind instruments. These are made from bamboo, shells, animal horns, gourds, wood, and metal to produce vibrations from their air columns. Notable examples include the *kakaki, alghaita, farai, kaho, ofi, oja, tiyako*, and the *odo*. Next are the instruments that can be described as chordophones, that is, tension strings with sound boxes that serve as resonators. They serve well as solo instruments and examples are the *goje, komo, gormi*, and *nwolima*. Then we have the membranophones, including a variety of drums. Finally, idiophone instruments produce either specific melodies (as in the case of the hand piano and xylophone) or sounds of indefinite pitch (as with rattles and calabash drums). Instruments may also reproduce or imitate the voices of ancestors (as among the Igbo), or the sounds of animals and the environment.

These varied instruments can be used in both solo and group performances. They substitute for the human voice when necessary. The gong and bell can be used to call meetings; the drums can talk; and the trumpet can announce the arrival of a king. They are also used as signals; for instance to declare and end wars, to announce the outbreak of fire, and to announce the beginning of a major ceremony.

Instruments may be invested with cultural meanings. The Yoruba use the *oma* and *apa* trees to carve drums. The belief is that the two trees can hear people talk and are therefore valuable for making the talking drums. Certain drums may be beaten a certain number of times to communicate an intended meaning (for example, the *osima* in Ondo is struck seven times to announce a war). Instruments can also reveal ethnic identities. To those in the forest region, the drum is the primary instrument; in the grassland, the string and wind instruments are the most important. The *gbedu* drum among the Yoruba symbolizes royalty; and the *tambura* stands for kingship authority among the Hausa.

The instruments and the songs they produce may also have special meanings. The elephant-tusk horn is blown only for kings and chiefs among the Igbo and Yoruba. When the *kakaki* is blown among the Hausa or Yoruba, it means that the king is about to appear in public; and in Katsina, the *tambari* drum is struck a dozen times to announce a new king. In Benin, the *emoba* drum is beaten only within the palace by six drummers to indicate the majesty of the king.

Instruments are used essentially to facilitate singing. Instrumental genres may exist but they are not as popular as those combining instruments with singing. A song holds together the various instruments played in an ensemble. Instruments can be used to voice oral expressions. In the case of the talking drums, there are so many pitch variations that the musician can imitate various human sounds and communicate messages. A Yoruba drummer can use the talking drum, by squeezing the cords for effects, to communicate anything, including proverbs, names, and praise poems. The drum can be played at various times to greet, abuse, praise, and express gratitude.

Many musical genres make no distinction between instrumental music and vocal music and utilize a combination of the two. The vocal parts are structured in what is known as a "call and response" approach: the soloist sings and calls and the chorus answers. The calls may be short or long; likewise, the chorus may either be long, short, or two choruses may be alternated. Other songs may be performed as solos or in a group that includes a soloist and a chorus. In either case, the singer thrives on the ability to improvise because the text is often more important than the melody. The chorus may be repetitive, but not necessarily the text. In many cases, it is important to understand the text, which may be a long story, before one can enjoy the music, especially when a simple instrument is used to accompany the narration of a long text.

Songs can take the form of ballads, poems, incantations, and long passages of prose. In the verse form, the song can consist of many stanzas or a single stanza and may combine the lead singer with a chorus. One-stanza songs thrive on repetition and the multi-stanza version on recurrent elements or themes. Songs tap the resources of imagery and diction. Good singers are masters of language: they manipulate metaphor, action words, and hyperbole. In drawing on imagery, they push language use to the limit of its creativity by drawing from the forest, animals, plants, agriculture, war, occupations, and history of people and cities. The singer, like a poet, can take liberties with words and expressions, using them as he or she deems fit. Nigerians are inflectionary and this is reflected in the pitches—the high, low, and medium pitch of vowels. Both men and women sing; soloists demonstrate the power to sing, lead, and extemporize; voice quality can vary from one singer to another and can be open-throated. Musicians can compete as members of different bands at community events. Among the Tiv, rivalries may develop among singers as they compete for attention or as they criticize one political group in order to praise another.

DANCE

Whether traditional or modern, most musical genres are accompanied by dance, although there are occasions to sing without dancing, as in the songs to mourn the dead or to organize a procession. In general, music is not treated as an activity on its own but stimulates a physical response from the listener. As an aspect of performing art, dance is as old as the earliest Nigerian. It reflects people's behavior and attitudes to life, leisure, and tragedy. Dance may reflect the daily reality of life as moods change. As an integral part of festivals and celebrations, dance captures people's morality, codes of conduct, and sanctions. Dance brings people together, old and young, male and female, rich and poor, as they are all joined in celebration, even as onlookers. There is, however, a minority opinion found, for example, among some members of the Hausa-Fulani Islamic aristocracy, who regard dancing as the preserve of members of the lower class.

Dance is interpreted as a harmonious, patterned, or rhythmic movement of the body, or any part of the body. Men and women can dance together, not necessarily as couples but as part of a crowd. There are also occasions when they dance separately. Group dancing in choreographed steps is common. Among the Hausa, the dancer moves slowly, reacting to gentle melodies. Where people react to rhythmic beats, as among the Igbo, Edo, and Itsekiri, the dance tends to be more vigorous.

There are four major dance patterns: the leap dance, the stride dance, the close dance, and the stamp dance. In the leap dance, performed by the *atilogwu* among the Igbo, the *bata* among the Yoruba, and masquerade dancers among the Edo, the dancer lifts the feet off the ground, as if preparing for an acrobatic display. In a stride dance, the dancer moves gracefully in a rather slow movement, taking one step at a time. Yoruba chiefs and elders dance this way, as well as the Hausa and Fulani. The maidens of Afikpo and such groups as the Ijo and Ibibio do the close dance, in which only the waist moves while the other parts of the body stay still. The Tiv are best known for the stamp dance, a combination of the leap and stride.

Whether traditional or modern, there are different dances, each with its own name and character. Among some groups, there is a distinction between male and female dancing, or dances associated with various occupations. For instance, the hunters' guild among the Yoruba has the *ijala*, a male dancing tradition, while the Tiv have the *telegh ishol*, a female dancing pattern.[2]

Professionals perform certain dance categories. One example is the pantomimic dance, which is similar to the masquerade. The pantomimic dancer can imitate animals and well-known individuals, or dramatize sexual acts through dance. The *agbegijo* among the Yoruba move from one part of the city to another to dance for a living. Such dancers will imitate crocodiles or perform love dances. One popular dance imitates the white man. Wearing a colobus monkey skin, the dancer adds fake hair and a long nose and performs a ballroom dance meant to ridicule. The puppet dancer among the Tiv does similar things, using dance to create satire.

Professional dance involves elements of competition and organization. As they need to satisfy the public in order to survive, dancers pay attention to their appearance, costumes, and instruments. The majority operate within urban settings and thus draw on issues that interest city-dwellers. Sexual symbols are manipulated to attract both women and men. Dancers can enter into ethnic politics as members of one culture lampoon those of another.

Dance is associated with most religious and ritual performances. Masquerades dance in many cases to take the spirits to the world of the living. Some ritual dances such as those of Oro among the Yoruba and the Ekpo and Ekpe among the Ibibio manifest power. In these examples, powerful members of the association involved may dance before implementing an important decision.

A good performance is usually one in which music leads to spontaneous dancing. The musician may invite people to dance and change the music to respond to their steps. Many dances require no special costumes, but dancers may use flywhisks, masks, leather fans, and handkerchiefs to enhance their movements. People may dance erect, bend at the waist, make various body turns, stamp their feet, and use their hands in gestures.

Just as all kinds of foreign music reaches Nigeria, so, too, does the dance. If a new dance is popular in New York, it will get to Nigeria within the month!

The Functions of Dance

Certain aspects of dance carry meaning or can be interpreted symbolically. For example, rites of passage are marked by dance. There is the "baby's dance" to calm, lull to sleep, and appease the baby when angry. Among the Yoruba, where twin babies are common, a traditional custom is for their mothers to do a weekly dance in their honor. As a child grows up, he or she gets to dance with a group of children. Part of socialization is to introduce children to community music and dance and their rewards. As songs communicate social commentaries and reflect on events, the children also begin to pick up important ideas and information about their society. Where dance groups exist, children are drawn into them as members. The youth are also known for composing protest songs about the elders and their bad leadership. Dance culture is reinforced with graduation to adulthood and marriage. This may include an initiation dance, a wedding dance, and membership and leadership in professional singing clubs. Elders become dance critics, as well as "gentle dancers" when occasions demand. When elders pass away, dance is part of the funeral ceremony. Funeral songs are numerous, as are the dances that go with them.

A second function of dance is to serve as an avenue for social criticism. Both directly and indirectly, dance can criticize the social order. The masquerade among the Tiv can turn a dance into a direct physical assault on allegedly wicked people. Agile youth can do a sex dance to demonstrate their prowess, as a way of telling the elders that they are incompetent. Permissive and erotic dances can be performed to annoy the prudish and to celebrate liberal culture. Dance is a creative way to make political statements. Among the Tiv, dance is used for political mobilization and campaigns. Politicians recruit dancers in their support and to criticize their opponents.

Third, dance serves as an agent of emotional and physical release. Funeral dances help to deal with the emotion of loss. Dance may be fast-paced and serve as a form of exercise, as in the *diga* and *kuza* dances among the Tiv or the *bata* dance among the Yoruba.

Fourth, dance is connected with religion and rituals. It may be used to contact spiritual beings. When trance and magic are involved, dance can aid the skills of hypnotism. Ritual dances are associated with many gods and also with masquerades. Finally, dance is a transmitter of history and culture. Through mimetic gestures and songs, dance makes statements about the past. Such events as the civil war, major political transitions, and events that shape the conscience of the community are captured in dance.

It is important to emphasize that most of the traditional music genres, instruments, and dances described above are very much alive. Thanks to technology, many have been recorded on audiotapes, videotapes, and compact discs, thus ensuring their preservation and survival. A number of "traditional musicians" have become famous among their people. Many plays and music dramas have profited a great deal by the repackaging of traditional songs and drama. Legends, histories, and stories are replayed in creative ways. Thus, Duro Ladipo performed *Oba Koso*, a play full of songs about Sango. However, the attractions of urban life, Western instruments, and all sorts of foreign music now draw many people away from traditional music and dance to the modern forms.

MODERN MUSIC

Many aspects of traditional music continue to impact the modern. The functions of modern music are often much the same as those of traditional music. However, there is more focus on entertainment than on anything else. Musicians can sing solo or in groups to advertise products or conduct campaigns for government projects. Whenever a major program is launched, it is certain that one musician or another will popularize it through songs. In some cases, they may be commissioned, as in songs in support of family planning, paid for by the United Nations. Most often, musicians create songs on their own. Thus, many songs have been composed to announce and support government decisions to change the currency, control rents, fight against indiscipline, go to war, and conduct elections and censuses. Nigerian musicians have joined in the crusade for social and political change. They comment on contemporary politics, criticize political leadership, and demand justice.

Modern musicians are also great commentators on culture and customs. They reinforce society's values on marriage, divorce, children, education, and ceremonies. They praise the traditions of old, and they support positive current changes. Many of them sing the praise of the wealthy and successful, caring less how these people acquire their wealth and more how they display generosity.

As in traditional music, rhythm is important. If Western music thrives on harmony, modern Africa uses rhythm as its base. The most successful musician is the one most able to create and master the complexity of rhythm while not ignoring melody, harmony, and text.

Christian Music

Christian music is firmly established as an aspect of modern music. The number of new releases each year is high, as every religious organization produces cassettes and compact discs. Like African American Spirituals, Christian songs are meant to energize worshipers (who clap their hands, sing intensely, shout, and dance) and to recruit new converts.

The "emotionless" worship of the early Christian missions has given way to an intense mode that has acquired most of the characteristics of indigenous ceremonies and festivals. But the relationship between Christian music and Nigerian culture and customs has passed through several stages. In the early period of the introduction of Christianity during the nineteenth century, the leading missions (the Roman Catholic, Anglican, and Methodist Churches) were hostile to indigenous religions and the music and instruments associated with them. Early converts were asked to burn their instruments and stop performing ritual songs, as if these contained the power to stop the converts from becoming true worshipers. As Nigerians began to establish their own churches, they drew freely from their heritage to enhance the quality of worship. Even adherents of the first three missionary churches began to complain that worship was un-interesting and monotonous. Converts want to reach God by clapping, praying loudly, dancing, and singing.

Christian hymns have been translated into Nigerian languages. In the early years, this was done according to the liturgy of the established churches. The hymns enable worshipers to use their own languages to sing and pray. The major difference in the hymns is that the Nigerian vowel sounds differ from those in English. While the hymns have not been dropped, a revolutionary music tradition has been initiated and incorporated by the churches created by Nigerians, and it is now common in all churches. Nigerian musical instruments are used, as well as local songs and traditional dance. Thus, one can attend a church service where the members of the congregation dance as if they are celebrating a naming ceremony. The church becomes energized in moments when traditional songs and dance are introduced. The worshipers may take over from the priests and organized choirs and spontaneously introduce a popular song, thus turning the church into a big dancing hall.

Neoclassical

Through the impact of the church and Western education, a tiny elite appreciates neoclassical composition. The pioneer in such composition is Fela Sowande, who acquired national prominence in 1956 when he entertained the Queen of England during her visit to Nigeria. Sowande composed the *African Suite*, a European orchestral arrangement that drew on Nigerian themes. Many were influenced by Sowande to develop neoclassical music in his style and others. Sam E. Akpabot, Akin Euba, Ayo Bankole, and Adam Fiberisima are the heroes of the neoclassical tradition. They studied music in Western schools.

The neoclassicists do not use local nightclubs to showcase their music, but elite arenas such as universities, five-star hotels, and major music festivals. In 1963, the American Wind Symphony Orchestra of Pittsburgh organized the Nigerian Music Festival, which enabled Euba, Bankole, Akpabot, and Wilberforce Echezona to write and present original music. All of them emphasized indigenous traditions and tunes. Three years later, the Commonwealth Arts Festival in London featured Echezona as a composer and educator; and Akpabot performed *Scenes from Nigeria* with the BBC Welsh Orchestra. All of them continue to be featured in Europe, the United States, and Moscow.

These musicians also began to serve as teachers when music was included in degree programs in Nigerian universities and high schools.[3] Their compositions are well known in educated circles, less so among the public for whom popular music is the preferred choice. Yet, none of them has abandoned Nigerian traditional music—they draw from indigenous legends, folk tunes, and idioms. Nevertheless, the neoclassicists still have a long way to go in making their music acceptable to the majority of the Nigerian population.

Highlife

Highlife music came to Nigeria from Ghana in the 1930s. A Ghanaian band, the Sugar Babies, visited the country and was very successful in popularizing its music. Highlife developed during the colonial period based on a variety of instruments: the bugle, other military brass instruments, accordion, guitar, harmonica, two-finger guitar, and local gongs. It is an urban music whose special appeal to the educated and successful probably gave it the name of "highlife" to reflect its association with high culture. However, it also became a popular music since it adopted local tunes and used traditional instruments, notably the drum, in addition to foreign ones. Calypso and other local forms were also added to the emerging style of highlife.

Perhaps the greatest influence on Nigerian musicians was E. T. Mensah of Ghana, the celebrated "King of Highlife," a master of the trumpet, saxophone, and lyric writing. Mensah's themes of love, politics, philosophy, and social commentary also dominate this influential musical genre. Mensah visited Nigeria in the 1940s and immediately transformed the music scene. A number of Nigerian musicians began to play like him as the instruments and resources, already used for church- and school-oriented performances, were available.

Many new groups emerged in the 1950s, leading to the emergence of such talents as Victor Olaiya, Bala Miller, Eddie Okonta, Jofabro Aces, Roy Chicago, Eric Onuga, Stephen Amechi, Chris Ajilo, Billy Friday, Charles Iwegbue, E. C. Arinze, and Erasmus Januwari. The giant among them is Victor Olaiya who recorded one successful hit after another. Olaiya added some Yoruba rhythms as well as Nigerian-cum-Western pop elements in order to satisfy the youth. Rex Jim Lawson is next in fame, but his career was cut short when he died in 1970. Generally, a highlife band includes between eight and twenty members, with two playing the trumpet, another two the saxophone, one member each for an upright brass, electric guitar, and trombone, and others contributing percussion and vocals.

Innovations define highlife music, as the various musicians compete. One of the most enduring names in the industry is Bobby Benson who died in 1983. Having been a sailor in the British navy in the 1940s, he returned to

Nigeria in 1947 to begin a long and productive career, starting with the formation of the Bobby Jam Session Orchestra. He introduced various acts aided by his wife, Cassandra. Benson was a great innovator and pioneer so much so that many now call him the "Father of Nigerian Music." Benson had no formal training or apprenticeship. He learned his craft as a sailor, but he was so talented that he could play many instruments, notably the piano, guitar, drums, string bass, saxophone, and electric guitar, which he introduced to the country. He was also a singer and comedian. He played highlife and jazz, and introduced calypso. He carried jazz to a popular audience and built a club, the Hotel Bobby, which entertained a diverse audience in Lagos.

Juju Music

Juju music, represented by the international figure, King Sunny Ade, dates back to the colonial period as one of the emergent popular music forms. *Juju* includes both the percussive section of highlife and a guitar band style combined with rich Yoruba drums. *Juju* started as a less popular genre than highlife, but achieved its own prominence from the 1960s onward, thanks to the successful career of I. K. Dairo.

Many of the early *juju* bands began in palmwine bars that were visited by urban dwellers during evenings and weekends. With a few instruments, notably box guitars, beer bottles, and sticks, new musical genres emerged. These instruments were combined with Yoruba drums to invent *sakara*, a Yoruba music type that produced a famous star, Olatunji Yusuf. From the 1940s onward, *juju* (and *sakara*) began to migrate to the public, notably to social ceremonies where musicians play to entertain. The texts of the music are rich with long words and social commentary. Singing in praise of famous men and women and their clients is a prominent aspect of the music in addition to its entertainment value.

Some musicians were itinerant, including early pioneers of *juju* music—Ojoge Daniel, Irewole Denge, and Kokoro, "the blind minstrel." All three sang in Yoruba about love, money, conflicts, and urban decadence. Others were able to form bands with drummers, singers and guitarists. The band includes the leader who plays the guitar and leads the vocals and a number of drummers who also form the chorus line. These are the groups that turned *juju* into a famous, popular music. Notable among the bandleaders are J. Oyeshiku, Tunde Nightingale, and Ayinde Bakare. All three distinguished themselves, and Bakare was able to carry *juju* music to England.

Apala music, a genre distinct from highlife and *juju*, was also developing about the same time. This was a genre popularized by Haruna Ishola and later by Ayinla Omowura. Haruna Isola did not adopt the guitar, but focused instead on the use of Yoruba drums. As the Igbo returned to the east between 1967 and 1970, the music scene was monopolized by Yoruba musicians, and *juju* displaced highlife in popularity.

Innovations to *juju* came from Julius Araba who added an electric guitar to his instruments. I. K. Dairo carried *juju* to recognition as a music that the rich and poor alike could enjoy. A master of the accordion and drums, Dairo covered a variety of themes, and he incorporated Yoruba values into his song texts, as well as familiar traditional lyrics and harmonies. Innovations were extended in the 1960s by Chief Commander Ebenezer Obey and King Sunny Ade. Obey formed his band in 1964 and later became a star and one of the richest men in the country. Sunny Ade began his own band soon afterward, and the popularity of his 1968 song in praise of a soccer club, Stationery Store, led to a gold album. Known as the "master-guitarist," he can play for long hours, and his band entertains the audience with dance and jokes.

Both Obey and Ade added many guitars, the hourglass drum, the double bass, the steel guitar, the vibraphone, and the Western drum set. They also borrowed from other musical genres, notably highlife, to carry *juju* music to its peak. Obey and Ade kept extending the size of their bands and adding new instruments. The competition between the two of them encouraged great innovations and they dominated the music scene for over two decades.

Obey has changed from *juju* to gospel music, even turning his nightclub into a church and his band into a choral group. Sunny Ade remains committed to *juju* and continues to innovate. In 1983, following the death of reggae superstar Bob Marley, Island Records in the United States saw Sunny Ade as a successor. Concerts were arranged for him in New York and other places with great publicity. His albums, however, did not make as much money as expected, and his tours did not attain the stadium-level audience that his promoters expected. While he remains an international star, the dream of turning him into a legend as big as Marley has not been realized. However, Sunny Ade continues to consolidate his music in Nigeria and remains successful.

In the 1980s and 1990s, Sunny Ade continually sought to innovate with new instruments and fast-paced rhythms. Competition came from other musical genres and another generation of *juju* musicians including Admiral Dele Abiodun, Prince Segun Adewale, and Sir Shina Peters. It is not uncommon for these musicians to draw heavily from other musical traditions such as jazz, Afro-beat, reggae, and highlife in order to create their own distinctive styles. For instance, Dele Abiodun is a master of the steel pedal guitar; Adewale plays a fast-paced combination of *juju* and pop; while Sir Shina plays even faster rhythms in order to appeal to a younger generation.

Juju music borrows heavily from Yoruba proverbs, myths, and worldview to address ethics and dominant values, and to draw on an established culture of praise songs to celebrate the rich. Indeed, *juju* musicians rely on wealthy patrons, whose praises they sing, for money lavished on them in private parties. At such parties, which may last all night, groups of people dance in turn and people give money to one another, with most money going to the musician who remains calm and is careful not to forget to praise all donors and important guests. The need to praise partly explains why *juju* music is less confrontational and political than many other musical styles.

Other Hybrids

Other hybrid musical genres have grown from *juju*, highlife, and traditional music. Currently, the most prominent is *fuji*, which combines an Islamic singing tradition with aspects of *juju* and the use of Western instruments and drums. The stars of *fuji* are Sikiru Ayinde Barrister and General Kollington Ayinla, both of whom are national figures and have entertained different communities in Europe and the United States. *Fuji* relies less on electric instruments and more on percussion. Ayinla added the double-headed *bata* drum and later the piano, while a generation of younger *fuji* players also use the steel guitar. The themes are no different from *juju* and the two types of music share the same audience.

Igbo highlife has continued to grow, even after this genre declined elsewhere in the 1970s. The stars of this style include Joe Nez, Osita Osadebe, Chief Ngozita and His Ngozi Brothers, Charles Iwegbue and His Hino Sound, Oliver de Coque and His Expo 76, and the Oriental Brothers International. The best-selling record is *Sweet Mother* (1976), produced by Prince Nico Mbanga (originally from Ghana), who successfully fused highlife with Congolese jazz. These groups entertain at all occasions for which they are contracted, they play in nightclubs, and they record music for sale. They use Igbo, English, and pidgin to communicate their messages.

Sir Victor Uwaifo of Benin developed what he calls *akwete*, a highlife style, and his *Joromi* is one of the best-selling albums. Uwaifo became a member of Olaiya's band in 1959, and there he mastered the techniques of highlife. He became a skilled guitarist and in 1965 he formed his own band, the Melody Maestros. He added the electric bass, the rhythm of the Edo, and rock and roll music. From the same area comes another household name,

Sonny Okosun, who calls his own music *ozzidi*; this is a blend of highlife, reggae, rock, and African rhythm. Okosun's original influence came from Elvis Presley, and he played Beatles' songs very early in his career. He later changed course after a period with Victor Uwaifo. He established his own band in 1974, and he became so successful that nine of his fifteen albums have made huge sales. Okosun is superb on the guitar and trumpet; he preaches a message of unity for Africans, and his antiapartheid, anti-imperialist song, "Soweto," was a major hit. Sunny Okosun still sings, but he has moved to gospel music which he has brilliantly radicalized with reggae rhythms.

A number of female singers have come to the limelight, the majority of whom have used their talents in spiritual and gospel music. The Lijadu sisters, twins who commanded attention for a while in the 1980s, were in the pop tradition, but their music brought together pop, Afro-beat, and reggae. On-yeka Onwenu, Christie Essien Igbokwe, and Dora Infudu are others in the pop tradition. Salawa Abeni, starting her career as a teenager, has become the most important singer of *waka*, a type of Yoruba song that is neither *juju* nor *fuji*.

Afro-Beat: Fela Anikulapo-Kuti

Afro-beat began as an attempt to play pop music and use European instruments. Orlando Julius and Fela Anikulapo-Kuti are the best representatives of this genre. Afro-beat is a creative combination of European dance band instruments with new rhythms and traditional Nigerian instruments, notably the drum. Styles and rhythms from jazz are incorporated as well. Orlando Julius faded out rather quickly and the scene was then dominated by Fela until his death in 1997. Fela's son, Femi Kuti, continues to play in his father's style.

Fela is the undisputed king of Afro-beat, the best-known Nigerian musician, and one of the country's heroes during the twentieth century. Fela was an eclectic musician who reinvented his style many times. He began his musical career playing with Victor Olaiya, the great master of highlife music. Fela and J. K. Braimah, a friend who had introduced him to Olaiya, were later to reconnect in Britain in the late 1950s. Fela was in college, studying classical music, but he and Braimah, a law student, formed the Koola Lobitos.

Fela returned to Nigeria in 1963 and continued with the Koola Lobitos, playing what he called highlife jazz. He wrote all the songs and played his favorite instruments, trumpet and saxophone. He transformed his music within the decade. Influences came from two sources—one musical, the other political—and Fela's genius fused both of them to develop a very distinctive style. The first influence came from the music of Geraldo Pino of Sierra Leone, who performed like James Brown. Fela saw Pino in action in Nigeria and Ghana and marveled at his style, instruments, arrangements, and lifestyle. Without copying Pino, Fela changed his music, now labeled Afro-beat, and founded a club known as the Afro-Spot. He received great publicity. The second influence came from the United States where, after playing at a function organized by the NAACP, he met Sandra Smith, a member of the Black Panthers, who introduced him to the civil rights movement as well as to the writings of Malcolm X and other great African-American leaders. He became more politically conscious. One success followed another and he became Africa's music legend of the twentieth century.

Fela's fame derives from two sources: the quality of his music and his confrontational politics. To start with his music, his ability to coordinate musicians in a "jam session" was a feat in itself. Fela's band was usually large, with many guitarists, trumpeters, saxophonists, drummers, and female singers. Many instruments and singers were combined to produce a combination of highlife, jazz, and blues, in an exceptionally distinct and original music. He was quick to detect an error, and as he suffered no fool, he would show his anger almost immediately. His concerts were also opportunities for teaching. He would stop singing to talk about his vision of society and to make social commentaries that were echoed in his lyrics. Fela abandoned the use of "pure English" in preference for pidgin, which most members of the public can understand. Virtually all his records are smash hits, including *London Scene* (1971), *Zombie (1977), Lady* (1984), and *Army Arrangement* (1985).

Politically, he started as a cultural nationalist. His early songs defended patriarchy, indigenous customs, the unity of Nigeria, and black culture. In the 1960s, when he was laying the foundation of his career, the politics that made him famous in later years did not feature prominently in his music. But political culture runs in his family. His mother, Funmilayo Ransome-Kuti, was a leading revolutionary who had taken her son to political meetings.[4] But it was contact with the Black Panthers that had a transformational influence on his politics.

Many of Fela's songs deal with development issues in Nigeria. Always looking at the big picture, he makes fun of social and political chaos and he condemns those who undermine Nigeria—the big plunderers, the leaders without vision. He regards the unity of Nigerians and Africans as essential to their development. His music is anticorruption, antimilitary, and anti-imperialist. *Zombie*, his antimilitary, antiauthoritarian album, is one of the classics of African political music. In *I.T.T.: International Thief Thief*, he sings against the power of transnational companies.

He was a Pan-Africanist, a nationalist, and a radical. He admired Kwame Nkrumah, Ghana's first leader, and African-American civil rights leaders such as Malcolm X. He infused his music with aspirations of development, nationalism, Pan-Africanism, and the liberation of Africa from imperialism.

His lifestyle, not without some contradictions, reflected his politics. As his music became successful, in the 1970s, attention and money followed. He spent his money as the leader of a movement, catering to hundreds of people. He built a compound called "Kalakuta Republic" in Lagos, named after the prison cell in which he was incarcerated in 1974. The compound attracted hundreds of followers and became a haven for restless youth, marginalized urban dwellers, and music lovers. The more conservative segment of the population was unhappy about what appeared to them to be an anarchist movement.

His music brought him into trouble with the military, which tried to destroy him. He had many brushes with the law, sometimes over the use of marijuana, at other times over his political statements. There were even clashes between soldiers and his followers over traffic control near the Kalakuta Republic. In 1977, the government attacked the Kalakuta Republic with force: the residents were beaten, Fela's mother was thrown out of a window and later died of her injuries, and the compound was destroyed by fire. Fela relocated to Ghana for a while and then returned to Lagos to resume his glorious career. But one persecution followed another, as he was beaten, detained, imprisoned, and prevented from fulfilling his contracts to play in other countries. All this took a heavy toll on him. His new nightclub was not as successful as his first, some of his best musicians left, and his resources dwindled in the 1990s. He died an optimistic man, however, leaving behind a proud legacy of solid accomplishments in creativity and in building the power of music in a developing country.

Music from Other Lands

The Caribbean is a great exporter of music to Nigeria. Virtually all the great Caribbean traditions appeal to Nigerian youth. Either they play and dance to such Caribbean superstar artists as Bob Marley or to Nigerian musicians who adopt Caribbean styles. Afro-Cuban, Haitian meringue, Trinidadian calypso, and Jamaican reggae are the most popular Caribbean styles in Nigeria. Reggae is probably the best known, thanks to the idolization of

Bob Marley and Jimmy Cliff. From the United States and Europe have spread contemporary blues, jazz, spirituals, gospel, pop music, and hip-hop. Many of their instruments and rhythms have been adopted by Nigerian musicians.

When foreign musical genres are imitated, the main audience tends to be the urban youth who are already familiar with those forms. When Western instruments or foreign rhythms are incorporated into such national traditions as *juju* or highlife, the local artist may in fact be given the credit for their invention. Israel Njemanze, an ex-serviceman, was one of the earliest to combine Nigerian music with exported traditions. Leading a band known as The Three Wizards, Njemanze played a brand of West Indian calypso with the themes of women, love, and the problems of city life.

Attempts have also been made to adapt European music. Christianity and colonial rule brought with them such European dances as the waltz, Argentinian tango, quickstep and foxtrot. Not only did many Nigerians accept them, but a number of orchestras grew to provide local opportunities of performing. In addition to imitating European artists, these orchestras were creative in adding Nigerian folk tunes and instruments, notably the drum. They created a ballroom setting, used Western instruments, but also composed unique rhythms for their Nigerian audience. Among the pioneers were the Bosocal Orchestra, the Chocolate Dandies Orchestra, and the Lagos Rascals. These attracted high-school students and a number of prominent church organists, and they appealed to educated people. Various innovations were made by these early orchestras. Some musicians branched into local highlife and more popular artists such as I. K. Dairo came on the scene to make a major impact. The adaptation of foreign music to local culture is a continuous process. The never-ending creative ingenuity of Nigerian musicians creates new musical genres and modifies older ones to satisfy a discriminating audience.

NOTES

1. Except where otherwise stated, all songs quoted in this chapter were translated by the author.

2. On Tiv dance, see Iyorwuese H. Hager, "The Role of Dance in Tiv Culture," *Nigeria Magazine*, 55:1 (January–March, 1987), 26–38.

3. Music education teaches all the genres described in this chapter.

4. For her life story, see Cheryl Johnson-Odim and Nina Emma Mba, *For Women and the Nation: Funmilayo Ransome-Kuti of Nigeria* (Urbana: University of Illinois Press, 1997).

Glossary

abeti-aja. cap

afere. drum of the Yoruba god, Obatala

Afin. Yoruba palace

Afro-beat. musical genre popularized by Fela Anikulapo-Kuti

agbada. flowing gown

agbegijo. dramatist

agbo-ile. rectangular compound

aje. god of wealth

akwete. "highlife" music style developed by Sir Victor Uwaifo

alaafin. king of Oyo

aladura. group of indigenous Christian churches

Alhaja. title for Muslim women who have performed the pilgrimage to
Saudi Arabia

Alhaji. title for Muslim men who have performed the pilgrimage to Saudi
Arabia

amala. starchy food made from yam

apala. modernized traditional music

ayo. game carved from wood, played by two people

babalawo. Ifa priest and diviner

boubou. poncho sewn at the sides

buka. restaurant

chinchin. made from wheat flour and served as snacks

Chukwu. Igbo's name for the Supreme God

diga and kuza. fast-paced dances among the Tiv

dundu. fried yam

efo elegusi. vegetable soup with melon seed

ekpo. secret society among the Ibibio

emedo emighan. music of the Benin court

emoba. drum beaten only within the Benin palace

esu. god of energy and crossroads among the Yoruba

fufu. carbohydrate food

gari. cassava powder

gari. Hausa nucleated villages

gbedu, koso, and **ogidigbo.** exclusive drums and music for the Alaafin (king) of Oyo

gurudi. coconut biscuits

Ifa. divination system

iya nla, iya agan, afere, and **keke.** drums of the Yoruba deity, Obatala

iyan. carbohydrate food made from yam

jihad. Holy War

juju. popular music

kakaki. flute blown among the Hausa or Yoruba to announce the presence of the king

kanye. Hausa dispersed compounds

khasa. handwoven, embroidered cloth

kirari. to entertain kings and guests at weddings and other important ceremonies among the Hausa

kulikuli. peanut cake

maboube. Fulani word for a group of makers of wool blankets

Mahdi. last prophet who will appear one day to "clean" society of all of its problems

mosa. corn fritter

odu. body of religious, social, and philosophical knowledge

odun egungun. celebration of ancestors among the Yoruba, with masquerades appearing in public

ofi. handwoven textile

ofor. symbol of oath making

ogun. god of iron

oje. material world among the Kalabari

ojebe. poems among the Igbo that praise noble title holders

omolangidi. toy

ori. destiny, as symbolized by the head

oro. cult of a secret society

orunmila. god of wisdom.

osima. drum beaten in Ondo to announce a war

owo. money

owo. Urhobo soup

oya. river goddess

ozzidi. musical blend of highlife, reggae, rock, and African rhythm played by Sunny Okosun

poncho. variety of traditional dresses such as the buba and babban rigga

purdah. married women isolated from public view

Ramadan. thirty-day fasting period among Muslims

Sabon Gari. also known as "Hausa Quarters," it is a community of migrants who live in separate neighborhoods

sakara. Yoruba music type

sango. god of thunder and lightening

sanyan. silk cloth among the Yoruba

suya. roasted beef or chicken with a combination of savanna spices served on skewers

tambari. drum is struck a dozen times to announce a new king in Katsina

telegh ishol. female dancing pattern among the Tiv

teme. layers of spiritual forces among the Kalabari

tsamiya. silk cloth among the Hausa

tunga. Kanuri hamlet that farmers reside in while exploring fertile farm-lands

ulama. communities of learned Islamic men

unguwa. number of compounds located outside of a walled village among the Hausa

uta. Ibibio orchestra that performs ritual songs of regeneration

waka. type of Yoruba song that is neither juju nor fuji

zakat. almsgiving to the poor and the needy by Muslims

zoure. reception room for guests among the Hausa

Bibliographic Essay

MANY BOOKS and essays on the subjects discussed in this book have been published in Nigeria; because they are not always accessible to the readers in the United States, I have included only a few of the most important ones and those that I have consulted as sources.

GENERAL

On culture and customs in Africa in general and Nigeria in particular, see Simi Afonja and Tola Olu Pearce, eds., *Social Change in Nigeria* (London: Longman, 1984); Z. S. Ali, ed., *African Unity: The Cultural Foundations* (Lagos: Centre for Black and African Arts and Civilization, 1988); Bassey W. Andah, A. Ikechukwu Okpoko, and C. A. Folorunso, eds., *Some Nigerian Peoples* (Ibadan: Rex Charles, 1993); Molefi Kete Asante and Kariamu Welsh Asante, eds., *African Culture: The Rhythms of Unity* (Westport, CT: Greenwood, 1985); William R. Bascom and J. Herskovits, eds., *Continuity and Change in African Cultures* (Chicago: University of Chicago Press, 1959); Peter P. Ekeh and Garba Ashiwaju, eds., *Nigeria Since Independence: The First 25 Years, Vol. VII, Culture* (Ibadan: Heinemann, 1989); Toyin Falola and A. Adediran, eds., *A New History of Nigeria for Colleges, Book One: Peoples, States and Culture before 1800* (Lagos: John West, 1986); T. O. Odetola, O. Oloruntimehin, and D. A. Aweda, *Man and Society in Africa: An Introduction to Sociology* (London: Longman, 1983); Marcellina U. Okehie-Offoha and Matthew N. O. Sadiku, eds., *Ethnic and Cultural Diversity in Nigeria* (Trenton, NJ: Africa World Press, 1996); and Kwesi Wiredu, *Philosophy and an African Culture* (Cambridge: Cambridge University Press, 1980). Documents relating to cultural policy can be found in Garba Ashiwaju, ed., *Africacult: Intergovernmental Conference on Cultural Policies in Africa* (Lagos: Cultural Division, Federal Ministry of Information, 1979).

INTRODUCTION

For the history of Nigeria and other important facts on the country, see the following: Toyin Falola, *The History of Nigeria* (Westport, CT: Greenwood, 1999); Toyin Falola et al., *The Military Factor in Nigeria* (Lewiston, NY: Edwin Mellen, 1994); Tom G. Forrest, *Politics and Economic Development in Nigeria* (Boulder, CO: Westview, 1993; rev. ed., 1995); A. Kirk-Greene and D. Rimmer, *Nigeria Since 1970: A Political and Economic Outline* (London: Hodder and Stoughton, 1981); Eghosa E. Osaghae, *Nigeria Since Independence: Crippled Giant* (London: Hurst and Company, 1998); and Stephen Wright, *Nigeria: Struggle for Stability and Status* (Boulder, CO: Westview, 1998). For development during the colonial period, see J. F. Ade Ajayi, "The Continuity of African Institutions under Colonialism," in T. Ranger, ed., *Emerging Themes of African History* (Nairobi: East African Publishing House, 1968), 190–199; and James S. Coleman, *Nigeria: Background to Nationalism* (Berkeley: University of California Press, 1971). Dated in parts, but still reliable for information on geography is K. Michael Barbour, Julius S. Oguntoyinbo, J. O. Onyemelukwe, and James C. Nwafor, *Nigeria in Maps* (London: Hodder and Stoughton, 1982). For a very useful bibliographical work, but one that is also dated in parts, see Jean-Pascal Daloz, *Le Nigeria: Société et politique (Bibliographie annotée, réflexions sur l'état d'avancement des connaissances)* (Paris: Institut D'Etudes Politiques, Université de Bordeaux 1, 1992). On the oil industry, see Peter O. Olayiwola, *Petroleum and Structural Change in a Developing Country: The Case of Nigeria* (New York: Praeger, 1987).

RELIGION AND WORLDVIEW

On indigenous religions and worldview, the following are useful: Wande Abimbola, *Ifa Divination Poetry* (New York: Nok Publishers, 1977); F. A. Arinze, *Sacrifice in Igbo Religion* (Ibadan: Day Star Press, 1970); Karin Barber, "How Man Makes God in West Africa: Yoruba Attitudes towards the Orisa," *Africa* 51 (1981), 724–745; Sandra T. Barnes, ed., *Africa's Ogun: Old World and New* (Bloomington: Indiana University Press, 1997); E. Bolaji Idowu, *African Traditional Religion: A Definition* (New York: Anchor Books, 1973); M. D. W. Jeffreys, "Witchcraft in the Calabar Province," *African Studies* (Johannesburg) 25:2 (1966), 95–100; A.J.H. Latham, "Witchcraft Accusations and Economic Tensions in Pre-Colonial Old Calabar," *Journal of African History*, 13:2 (1972), 249–260; John Mbiti, *Introduction to African Religion* (London: Heinemann Educational Books, 1979); John Mbiti, *African Religions and Philosophy* (Garden City, NY: Anchor Books, 1970); J. C. Messenger, "Ancestor Belief among the Anang: Belief Systems and Cults" in S. Ottenberg, ed., *African Religious Groups and Beliefs* (Meernt, India: Archana Publications for Folklore Institute, 1982); M. E. Noah, "African Religion in Old Calabar," *Journal of African Studies* 5:1 (1978), 3–8; G. I. Nwaka, "Secret Societies and Colonial Change: A Nigerian Example," *Cahiers d'Etudes Africaines*, 18:1–2 (1978), 187–200; Victor C. Uchendu, *The Igbo of Southeast Nigeria* (New York: Holt, Rinehart and Winston, 1965); and G. M. Umezurike et al., eds., *The Igbo Socio-Political System: Papers Presented at the 1985 Ahijoku Lecture Colloquium* (Owerri: Ministry of Information, 1986). On ethics, see E. Amadi, *Ethics in Nigerian Culture* (Ibadan: Heinemann Educational Books, 1982). Islam has received extensive treatment from different perspectives and disciplines. Notable works include the following: Peter B. Clarke, *West Africa and Islam: A Study of Religious Development from the 8th to the 20th Century* (London: Edward Arnold, 1982); Lamin Sanneh, *The Crown and the Turban: Muslims and West African Pluralism* (Boulder, CO: Westview, 1997); and J. Spencer, *A History of Islam in West Africa* (Oxford: Oxford University Press, 1970). Studies of Christianity have grown both in quantity and quality since the 1950s. Among others, see J. F. Ade Ajayi, *Christian Missions in Nigeria, 1841–1891* (London: Longman, 1965); E. A. Ayandele, *The Missionary Impact on Modern Nigeria, 1842–1914* (London: Longman, 1966); Felix K. Ekechi, *Missionary Enterprise and Rivalry in Igboland, 1857–1914* (London: Frank Cass, 1972); C. P. Groves, *The Planting of Christianity in Africa, 4 vols.* (London: Lutterworth Press, 1954); A. J. H. Latham, "Scottish Missionaries and Imperialism at Calabar," *Nigeria Magazine*, 132–133 (1980), 47–55; O. U. Kalu, *Divided People of God: Church Union Movement in Nigeria, 1875–1966* (New York: Nok Publishers, 1978); O. U. Kalu, ed., *The History of Christianity in West Africa* (London: Longman, 1980); O. U. Kalu, *Christianity in West Africa: The Nigerian Story* (Ibadan: Day Star Press, 1978); and J. B. Grimley and G. E. Robinson, *Church Growth in Central and Southern Nigeria* (Grand Rapids, MI: William B. Eerdmans, 1966). On indigenous adaptation of Christianity, see Rosalind I. J. Hackett, *Religion in Calabar: The Religious Life and History of a Nigerian Town* (Berlin: Mouton De Gruyter, 1989); J. C. Messenger, "Reinterpretation of Christian and Indigenous Belief in a Nigerian Nativist Church," *American Anthropologist*, 62:2 (1960), 268–278; J. D. Y. Peel, *Aladura: A Religious Movement among the Yoruba* (London: Oxford University Press, 1968); J. B. Webster, *The African Churches Among the Yoruba, 1888–1922* (Oxford: Clarendon Press, 1964). Short summaries of the historical developments of Islam and Christianity include: Toyin Falola and Biodun Adediran, *Islam and Christianity in West Africa* (Ile-Ife: University of Ife Press, 1983); and N. S. S. Iwe, *Christianity and Culture in Africa* (Onitsha: University Publishing Co., 1975). On new religious movements, see Rosalind I. J. Hackett, ed., *New Religious Movements in Nigeria* (Lewiston, NY: Edwin Mellen, 1987). Recent developments in religious activities and conflicts are discussed in the following works: I. M. Enwerem, *A Dangerous Awakening: The Politicization of Religion in Nigeria* (Ibadan: IFRA, 1995); Toyin Falola, *Religious Violence in Nigeria: The Crisis of Religious Politics and Secular Ideologies* (Rochester, NY: University of Rochester Press, 1998); Jibrin Ibrahim, "Religion and Political Turbulence in Nigeria," *Journal of Modern African Studies*, 29:1 (1991), 115–137; Simeon O. Ilesanmi, *Religious Pluralism and the Nigerian State* (Athens: Ohio University Press, 1997); Matthew Hassan Kukah, *Religion, Politics and Power in Northern Nigeria* (Ibadan: Spectrum, 1996); Mathews Hassan Kukah and Toyin Falola, *Religious Militancy and Self-Assertion: Islam and Politics in Nigeria* (London: Avebury, 1996); and Pat Williams and Toyin Falola, *Religious Impact on the Nation State: The Nigerian Predicament* (London: Avebury, 1995).

LITERATURE AND MEDIA

Materials on indigenous literature and folklore are many and varied. Among others, see Uchegbulam N. Abalogu et al., eds., *Oral Poetry in Nigeria* (Lagos: Nigeria Magazine, 1981); Ulli Beier, ed., *African Poetry: An Anthology of Traditional Poems* (Cambridge: Cambridge University Press, 1966); J. P. Clark, *The Ozidi Saga* (Ibadan: Ibadan University Press, 1977); Ruth Finnegan, *Oral Literature in Africa* (Oxford: Oxford University Press, 1970); Graham Furniss, *Poetry, Prose, and Popular Culture in Hausa* (Washington, DC: Smithsonian Institution Press, 1996); H.A.S. Johnston, *A Selection of Hausa Stories* (Oxford: Oxford University Press, 1966); Bernth Lindfors, *Folklore in Nigerian Literature* (New York: Africana Publishing Company, 1973); Oyekan Owomoyela, *Yoruba Trickster Tales* (Lincoln: University of Nebraska Press, 1997); and Wole Soyinka, *Myth, Literature and the African World* (Cambridge: Cambridge University Press, 1976). Extensive information on the print media can be found in Dayo Duyile, *Makers of Nigerian Press* (Lagos: Gong Publications, 1987); Festus Eribo and William Jong-Ebot, *Press Freedom and Communication in Africa* (Trenton, NJ: Africa World Press, 1997); Onuora E. Nwuneli, *Mass Communication in Nigeria: A Book of Readings* (Enugu: Fourth Dimension, 1985); Chris W. Ogbondah, *Military Regimes and the Press in Nigeria, 1966–1993* (Baltimore, MD: United Press of America, 1994); and Edyinka Orimalade, ed., *Mass Media and Nigeria's Development* (Kuri, Nigeria: National Institute for Policy and Strategic Studies, 1987). On the history of the television in Nigeria, see Obaro Ikime, ed., *20th Anniversary History of the WNTV* (Ibadan: Heinemann, 1979); V. I. Maduka, "The Development of Nigerian Television (1959–1985)," in Peter P. Ekeh and Garba Ashiwaju, eds., *Nigeria since Independence: The First 25 years, Vol. VII, Culture* (Ibadan: Hienemann, 1989), 107–138; and Adeyinka Orimalade, ed., *Mass Media and Nigeria's Development* (Jos: National Institute for Policy and Strategic Studies, 1987). Information on drama and theater can be obtained from the following sources: Ebun Clark, *Hubert Ogunde: The Making of Nigerian Theatre* (Oxford: Oxford University Press, 1979); Ernest Ekom, "The Development of Theatre in Nigeria, 1960–1967," *Journal of the New African Literature and the Arts*, 11–12 (1971), 36–49; Michael Etherton, *The Development of African Drama* (London: Hutchinson, 1982); Yemi Ogunbiyi, ed., *Drama and Theatre in Nigeria: A Critical Source Book* (Lagos: Nigeria Magazine, 1981); Bakary Traore, *The Black African Theatre and Its Social Functions* (Ibadan: Ibadan University Press, 1972); and Biodun Jeyifo, *The Yoruba Popular Travelling Theater of Nigeria* (Lagos: Nigeria Magazine Publications, 1984). Works of and on literature are rich, but space does not allow a listing of the creative works. Among the works that analyze creative writings, see the following: Chidi Amuta, *The Theory of African Literature: Implications for Practical Criticism* (London: Zed, 1989); J. Booth, *Writers and Politics in Nigeria* (London: Hodder and Stoughton, 1981); Chinweizu et al., *Toward the Decolonization of African Literature* (Enugu: Fourth Dimension, 1980); Chinweizu, *Invocations and Admonition* (Lagos: Pero Press, 1986); Katherine Fishburn, *Reading Buchi Emecheta: Cross-Cultural Conversations* (Westport, CT: Greenwood, 1995); James Gibbs, *Wole Soyinka* (Westport, CT: Greenwood, 1988); George M. Gugelberger, ed., *Marxism and African Literature* (London: James Currey, 1985); Eldred Durosimi Jones, *The Writing of Wole Soyinka* (London: Heinemann, 1983); Bernth Lindfors, *Popular Literatures in Africa* (Trenton, NJ: Africa World Press, 1991); Bernth Lindfors, *Early Nigerian Literature* (New York: Africana, 1982); Bernth Lindfors, ed., *Conversations with Chinua Achebe* (Jackson: University Press of Mississippi, 1997); Bruce King, ed., *Introduction to Nigerian Literature* (Lagos: University of Lagos Press, 1971); Obi Maduakor, *Wole Soyinka: An Introduction to His Writing* (New York: Garland, 1987); Adewale Maja-Pearce, *A Mask Dancing: Nigerian Novelists of the Eighties* (London: Hans Zell, 1992); Adewale Maja-Pearce, ed., *Wole Soyinka: An Appraisal* (Oxford: Heinemann, 1994); Craig W. McLuckie, *Nigerian Civil War Literature* (Lewiston, NY: Edwin Mellen, 1990); Benedict Chiaka Njoku, *The Four Novels of Chinua Achebe* (New York: Peter Lang, 1984); Donatus Ibe Nwoga, ed., *Critical Perspectives on Christopher Okigbo* (Washington, DC: Three Continents Press, 1984); Chikwenye Okonjo Ogunyemi, *Africa Wo/man Palava: The Nigerian Novel by Women* (Chicago: University of Chicago Press, 1996); Raisa Simola, *World Views in Chinua Achebe's Works* (New York: Peter Lang, 1995); and W. H. Whiteley, *A Selection of African Prose, 2 vols.* (Oxford: Oxford University Press, 1964); For a useful summary, see Yemi Ogunbiyi, ed., *Perspectives on Nigerian Literature, 2 vols.* (Lagos: Guardian Publishers, 1988).

ART AND ARCHITECTURE/HOUSING

Various aspects of Nigerian art have received scholarly attention. See, for example, Rowland Abiodun, Henry J. Drewal, and John Pemberton, *The Yoruba Artist: New Theoretical Perspectives on African Arts* (Washington, DC: Smithsonian Institution Press, 1994); C. O. Adepegba, *Yoruba Metal Sculpture* (Ibadan: Ibadan University Press, 1991); C. O. Adepegba, *Nigerian Art: Its Tradition and Modern Tendencies* (Ibadan: Jodad, 1995); Paula Girshick Ben-Amos, *The Art of Benin* (Washington, DC: Smithsonian Institution Press, 1995); Philip J. C. Dark, *An Introduction to Benin Art and Technology* (London: Oxford University Press, 1973); Simon Ottenberg, *New Traditions from Nigeria: Seven Artists of the Nsukka Group* (Washington, DC: Smithsonian Institution Press, 1997); Thurstan Shaw, *Nigeria: Its Archaeology and Early History* (London: Thames and Hudson, 1978); Frank Willett, *African Art* (New York: Thames and Hudson, 1993); and Kate Ezra, *Royal Art of Benin* (New

York: Harry Abrams, 1967). On the impact of religion on art, see J. A. Adedeji, "The Church and the Emergence of the Nigerian Theatre, 1866–1914," Part 1, *Journal of the Historical Society of Nigeria*, 6:1 (December, 1971), 25–46; Part 2, 6:4, (June, 1973), 387–396. On housing types, see J. W. Leiber, *Efik and Ibibio Villages* (Ibadan: Institute of Education, University of Ibadan, Occasional Publication, 13, 1971). On architecture, see Claude Daniel Ardouin, *Museums and Archaeology in West Africa* (Washington, DC: Smithsonian Institution Press, 1997); and Labelle Prussin, *African Nomadic Architecture: Space, Place, and Gender* (Washington, DC: Smithsonian Institution Press, 1997).

CUISINE AND TRADITIONAL DRESS

Among accessible books are: Nancy Braganti and Elizabeth Devine, *Travelers' Guide to African Customs and Manners* (New York: St. Martin's Griffin, 1995); Heidi Cusick, *Soul and Spice: African Cooking in the Americas* (San Francisco: Chronicle Books, 1995); Dorinda Hafner, *A Taste of Africa* (San Francisco: Ten Speed Press, 1993); and Bertha Montgomery and Constance Nabwire, *Cooking the African Way* (New York: Lerner Publishing, 1988). The most simplified book is by Dokpe Ogunsanya, *My Cooking: West African Cookbook* (Austin, TX: Duspy Enterprises, 1998). On the chemistry and nutritive values of food and crops, see V. A. Oyenuga, *Nigeria's Foods and Feeding-Stuffs* (Ibadan: Ibadan University Press, 1968). On the history of crops and changing food habits, see Eno Blankson Ikpe, *Food and Society in Nigeria: A History of Food Customs, Food Economy and Cultural Change, 1900–1960* (Stuttgart: Steiner, 1994). Information on dress, textiles and body adornments is available in Susan B. Aradeon, *Traditional African Dress and Textiles* (Catalogue of the Exhibition of West African Dress and Textiles, at The Museum of African Art, Washington DC, April–September, 1975); Eve de Negri, *Nigerian Body Adornment* (Lagos: Nigeria Magazine, 1976); and T. A. Ogunwale, "Traditional Hairdressing in Nigeria," *African Arts*, 3 (Spring, 1972) 44–45.

GENDER ROLES, MARRIAGE, AND FAMILY

On women and politics, three valuable studies are by J.A.A. Ayoade, Elone J. Nwabuzor, and Adesina Sambo, eds., *Women and Politics in Nigeria* (Lagos: Malthouse, 1992); E. Nina Mba, *Nigerian Women Mobilized* (Berkeley: Institute of International Studies, University of California, 1982); and *Women in Nigeria* (WIN), *Women in Nigeria Today* (London: Zed, 1985). The impact of education and urbanization on women is discussed in K. Little, *African Women in Towns* (Cambridge: Cambridge University Press, 1973). On marriage types in different cultures, see, for example: Josephine N. C. Agbamuche, *Customary Marriage in Akwukwu-Igbo* (Lagos: Unicom Enterprises, 1981); J. C. Cotton, "The Calabar Marriage Law and Custom," *Journal of the Royal Anthropological Society*, 4: 15–16 (1905), 302–306;

Jerry Nickson, *The Nigerian Family* (New York: Hanville, 1985); and Vincent B. Khapoya, *The African Experience: An Introduction* (Englewood Cliffs, NJ: Prentice-Hall, 1994). On kinship, family, and marriage see, among others, B. J. Callaway, *Muslim Hausa Women in Nigeria: Tradition and Change* (Syracuse, NY: Syracuse University Press, 1987); C. Cole and B. Mack, eds., *Hausa Women in the Twentieth Century* (Madison: University of Wisconsin Press, 1991); Mary Douglas and Phyllis M. Kaberry, eds., *Man in Africa* (New York: Anchor Books, 1971); James L. Gibbs Jr., ed., *Peoples of Africa* (New York: Holt, Rinehart and Winston, 1965); Diane Kayongo-Male and Philista Onyango, *The Sociology of the African Family* (New York: Longman, 1984); Jacques Maquet, *Africanity: The Cultural Unity of Black Africa* (New York: Oxford University Press, 1972); and A. R. Radcliffe-Brown and Daryll Forde, eds., *African Systems of Kinship and Marriage* (New York: Oxford University Press, 1965). For church-oriented materials on bridewealth and suggestions for modern living, see S. T. Akande, *Marriage and Home Making in Nigerian Society* (Ibadan: Day Star Press, 1971); F. A. Arinze, *The Christian and Chastity in Living in Our Faith* (Onitsha: Tabaisi Press, 1983); B. Kisembo, L. Magesa, and A. Shorter, *African Christian Marriage* (New York: Macmillan, 1977); and John Osom, *Moral Implication of High Bride-Price in Nigeria: Annang Case Survey* (Rome: Pontificia Universitas Lateranensis, 1989). On other issues pertaining to gender, see Nancy J. Hafkin and Edna Bay, eds., *Women in Africa* (Stanford, CA: Stanford University Press, 1976); and Onaiwu W. Ogbomo, *When Men and Women Mattered: A History of Gender Relations among the Owan of Nigeria* (Rochester, NY: University of Rochester Press, 1997).

SOCIAL CUSTOMS AND LIFESTYLE

See Ramatu Abdullahi, *Self-Concept and Cultural Change among the Hausa* (Ibadan: Ibadan University Press, 1986); Angela Fisher, *Africa Adorned* (London: Collins, 1984); and Julian H. Steward, ed., *Contemporary Change in Traditional Societies* (Urbana: University of Illinois Press, 1967). Valuable works on the growth of cinema include: Manthia Diawara, *African Cinema: Politics and Culture* (Indianapolis: Indiana University Press, 1992); Hyginus Ekwuasi, *Film in Nigeria* (Ibadan: Moonlight, 1987); Francoise Ptaff, *Twenty-Five Black African Filmmakers* (Wesport, CT: Greenwood, 1988); David Robinson, *The History of World Cinema* (New York: Stein and Day Publishers, 1981); Dina Sherzer, *Cinema, Colonialism, Postcolonialism* (Austin: University of Texas Press, 1996); and Kristin Thompson and David Bordwell, *Film History: An Introduction* (New York: McGraw-Hill, 1994). On urbanization, industrialization, and changing economies, see, for instance, Godwin Ukandi Damachi, *Nigerian Modernization* (New York: The Third Press, 1972); Poju Onibokun, *Urban Housing in Nigeria* (Ibadan: Nigerian Institute of Social and Economic Research, 1990); Margaret Peil, *Lagos: The City Is the People* (Boston: G. K. Hall, 1991); and David R. Smock, *Cultural and Political Aspects of Rural Transformation* (New York: Praeger, 1972).

MUSIC AND DANCE

For a quick introduction to modern African music and dance, see Wolfgang Bender, *Sweet Mother: Modern African Music* (Chicago: University of Chicago Press, 1991); Billy Bergman, *Goodtime: Emerging African Pop* (New York: Quill, 1985); John Mill Chernoff, *African Rhythm and African Sensibility* (Chicago: Chicago University Press, 1979); John Collins, *African Pop Roots* (London: Foulshams Publications, 1985); Ronnie Graham, *Stern's Guide to Contemporary African Music* (London: Off the Record Press, 1965); A. M. Jones, *Studies in African Music* (Oxford: Oxford University Press, 1959); and John Storm Roberts, *Black Music of Two Worlds* (New York: William Morrow, 1974). References to published materials can be found in L. J. P. Gaskin, *Selected Bibliography of Music in Africa* (London: African Bibliographical Series B, 1965). On *juju* music, see Christopher Alan Waterman, *Juju: A Social History and Ethnography of an African Popular Music* (Chicago: University of Chicago Press, 1990). On Fela, see Carlos Moore, *Fela Fela: This Bitch of a Life* (London: Allison and Busby, 1982). Other important materials include Roger D. Abrahams, *African Folktales* (New York: Pantheon Books, 1983); S. Akpabot, *Ibibio Music in Nigerian Culture* (East Lansing: Michigan State University Press, 1975); E. J. Alagoa, "Ijo Drum Lore," *African Notes*, 6:26 (1971), 63–71; S. Bedford, *Yoruba Girl Dancing* (London: Heinemann, 1974); R. E. Egudu, "Igodo and Ozo Festival Songs and Poems," *Conch*, 3:2 (1971), 76–78; A. Euba, "An Introduction to Music in Nigeria," *Nigeria Music Review*, 1 (1977), 1–38; Charles Kell, *Tiv Song* (Chicago: University of Chicago Press, 1970); P. Klaus Wachsman, *Music and History in Africa* (Evanston, IL: Northwestern University Press, 1971); Roderic Knight and Kenneth Bilby, "Music in Africa and the Caribbean," in Mario Azevedo, ed., *Africana Studies: A Survey of Africa and the African Diaspora* (Durham, NC: Carolina Academic Press, 1993), 243–276; M. Laurence, *Long Drums and Cannons: Nigerian Dramatists and Novelists, 1952–1966* (London: Macmillan, 1968); and Oyin Ogunba, "The Poetic Content and Form of Yoruba Occasional Festival Songs," *African Notes: Bulletin of the Institute of African Studies* (Ibadan), 6:2 (1971), 10–30.

Index

About the Author

TOYIN FALOLA is the Frances Higginbothom Nalle Centennial Professor in History at the University of Texas at Austin. He has written many works on Nigeria, including *The History of Nigeria* (Greenwood 1999).